# For Us,
# the Living

# For Us, the Living

Myrlie B. Evers

*With William Peters*

With an introduction by
*Willie Morris*

*Banner Books*
University Press of Mississippi / Jackson

First published in 1967 by Doubleday & Company, Inc.

Copyright © 1967 by Myrlie B. Evers and William Peters

Introduction copyright © 1996 by Willie Morris

Manufactured in the United States of America

Print-on-Demand Edition

The paper in this book meets the guidelines for permanence and durability of the Committee on Production Guidelines for Book Longevity of the Council on Library Resources.

*Library of Congress Cataloging-in-Publication Data*

Evers, Myrlie B.

    For us, the living / by Myrlie B. Evers, with William Peters; with an introduction by Willie Morris.
        p.      cm. — (Banner books)
    Originally published: Garden City, N.Y. : Doubleday, 1967.
    ISBN 0-87805-840-0 (cloth). —ISBN 0-87805-841-9 (paper)
    1. Evers, Medgar Wiley, 1925-1963. 2. Afro-Americans—Mississippi—Jackson—Biography. 3. Civil rights workers—Mississippi—Jackson—Biography. 4. Jackson (Miss.)—Biography. 5. Civil rights movements—Mississippi—History—20th century. 6. Afro-Americans—Civil rights—Mississippi. 7. Mississippi—Race relations. I. Peters, William, 1921-  . II. Title. III. Series: Banner books (Jackson, Miss.)
F349.J13E94 1996
323'.092—dc20                           95-43705
                                            CIP

British Library Cataloging-in-Publication data available

For Darrell, Rena, and Van

Medgar Evers believed in his country;
it now remains to be seen whether
his country believes in him.

*Roy Wilkins*
June 19, 1963
Arlington, Virginia


... It is for us, the living, rather, to be dedicated here to
the unfinished work which they who fought here have
thus far so nobly advanced. It is rather for us to be here
dedicated to the great task remaining before us—that from
these honored dead we take increased devotion to that
cause for which they gave the last full measure of devotion;
that we here highly resolve that these dead shall not have
died in vain; that this nation, under God, shall have a new
birth of freedom; and that government of the people, by
the people, for the people, shall not perish from the earth.

*Abraham Lincoln*
November 19, 1863
Gettysburg, Pennsylvania

# INTRODUCTION

When Myrlie Evers's *For Us, the Living*, written with William Peters, whose books and television documentaries had distinguished him as an influential interpreter of the South, was originally published by Doubleday in 1967, her husband Medgar had been dead more than four years. She and her children had moved from Mississippi to California. She was thirty-four years old. We were approaching the crest of the tumultuous sixties, when the very fabric of American society seemed ripped asunder by elemental forces beyond its control. The assassination of Medgar Evers would be followed by John F. Kennedy's, then Martin Luther King's, then Robert Kennedy's. The Vietnam quagmire was worsening.

As vividly as yesterday I remember first reading *For Us, the Living* in an apartment across the street from my magazine offices in Manhattan. The power of its writing, its poignance and passion and candor and beauty, deeply affected me. Not long ago, during the re-trial of Medgar Evers's murderer Byron de la Beckwith in Jackson, Mississippi, I returned to *For Us, the Living* with a certain trepidation, the trepidation of re-reading after the passage of almost thirty years a work I so admired, as if time itself might have diminished its strength and significance. My worries were unfounded. The book endures. I consider it one of the finest of our American memoirs.

Medgar Evers was a native Mississippian, a veteran of World War II in Europe, and after the war a running back for the Alcorn A & M Braves. Later, as Mississippi field secretary for the NAACP in the fifties and early sixties, he was the most prominent and visible advocate in the state for equal justice for blacks, for fair employment, school integration, access to public accommodations, and the vote. Blacks by many extralegal devices were largely excluded from the ballot, and schools and public facilities were assiduously segregated. Whites addressed black adults as "boy" or "girl." Such day-by-day meannesses ranged from the mundane to the ritualized. Proper white kids such as myself were dutifully instructed on all sides in what was called "the Mississippi Way of Life." For various reasons there was no real freedom of expression. Race was the thread that ran through everything. The noted historian James Silver, driven from Ole Miss for his views, called his subsequent book *Mississippi: The Closed Society.*

These were the years of racial murders, threats, bombings, and methodized hostility from official state agencies. All this was by no means confined to anxious, marginal individuals like the members of the Klan. In town after town in this state the respected and lofty and established men of the White Citizens Council—bankers, lawyers, preachers, planters, merchants, dentists, doctors—organized and accomplished economic boycotts and reprisals against blacks who espoused school integration and the franchise; they tacitly encouraged physical intimidation. These respectable men knew of this intimidation and silently condoned it. They allowed the Byron de la Beckwiths their way with the Negro. Many of these men who supported Beckwith then with their quiescent encouragement, indeed some who raised money for his legal fees in his two trials in the sixties, are today as influential as ever. An institution called the State Sovereignty Commission, a sort of boondocks Gestapo, drew state funds to spy on civil rights activists, integrationists, intellectuals, and just about anyone else who was considered "different."

As attractive, college-educated, family-oriented black Mississippians, Myrlie and Medgar Evers could easily have closed their eyes to these things and let others lead the struggle: Or they could have joined the continuing exodus of Southern blacks to the north and the west—some three million after 1960 alone. Yet they loved Mississippi and felt its promise. They chose to stay and to lead the fight. By innumerable accounts of those who knew him well, Medgar Evers was a fine, decent, efficient, highly likeable man with rather conservative personal traits, who could not ignore the compulsions of his heart. "It may sound funny," he once told a reporter from *Ebony*, "but I love the South. I don't choose to live anywhere else. There's land here, where a man can raise cattle, and I'm going to do that someday. There are lakes where a man can sink a hook and fight bass. There is room here for my children to play, and grow, and become good citizens—if the white man will let them." When the NAACP offered to send him to California, he said: "I belong here."

In *For Us, the Living*, Mrs. Evers movingly recounts how her husband was constantly torn between love and anguish for Mississippi. His first job after college was selling insurance to black sharecroppers in the Delta, who lived in virtual peonage to the planters, while his wife supplemented the family income as a typist. She writes of how Medgar would return home at night "bursting with stories"

of adults with nothing to eat; of sanitary conditions no self-respecting farmer would permit in his pigpen. He painted word pictures of shacks without windows or doors, with roofs that leaked and floors rotting underfoot. For a while he had ignored the worst of these shacks, sure that no one could live in them. But then he was sent to one and began to visit them all. "They are all of them full, Myrlie!" he would exclaim as he drove me by a cluster of the worst of them on a Sunday afternoon. "Every one of them! People live in there. Human beings. People like you and me."

In his initial bitterness and rage, she describes how he flirted briefly with radical approaches, then decided to work for reform within the democratic system. When he moved to Jackson in 1955 to become the NAACP field secretary, frightened and dispossessed people called on him about everything, and he comforted them "with a furious sort of desperation." He travelled the dark roads of the Delta in the nighttimes investigating killings and other transgressions, often in the disguise of a sharecropper.

Soon his name was prominent on "the death lists" in circulars and advertisements. By the spring of 1963 both he and Myrlie knew the end was near. They also knew that his murderer, whoever it was to be, would never be convicted. He was destined to become a singular American martyr not because he died in his prime, more than that: because he learned to live and work with the mounting inevitability of being killed and refused to turn away. He and his wife taught their children how to fling themselves onto the floor of their house on Guynes Street in Jackson (now Margaret Walker Alexander Drive) with the sound of a strange noise, to train their ears to the sound of a passing car or the bark of their dog. "To three-year-old Van, it was all a game," Mrs. Evers writes, "and he dropped to the floor with complete abandon. Darrell, eleven, and Rena, ten, were serious about it; they listened carefully and practiced conscientiously. In the midst of the lesson, Darrell asked what they should do if Van forgot to fall. Medgar told him to pull Van down with him." *For Us, the Living* is dedicated to the three children.

When he had told his wife for the first time of the real fear of something happening to him, they talked about it, and he said that if anything should happen to him, she must promise to take good care of the children.

> I pretended to take offense and reminded him that I, too, had played some part in their being here, that they were my children, too. And then I noticed tears in his eyes, and I said, "Oh, Medgar!" and we both broke down and cried together.

We clung to each other as though it were our only hope, and in my heart I felt that time was running out. There was no anger, no bitterness, not even a sense of having been robbed of what other people took for granted. There was just a bottomless depth of hopelessness, of hurt, of despair.

"The story of young Medgar Evers—a young David determined to do open battle with the Goliath of evil, injustice, and discrimination," Ralph McGill wrote in a review of *For Us, the Living* in 1967, "is one of the most heroic stories of our time."

On June 12, 1963, President Kennedy delivered on national television the strongest civil rights speech he ever gave. Medgar and some of his colleagues watched it in their office in Jackson and then worked late that night. He drove home shortly after midnight and turned his Oldsmobile into his driveway. He got out of the car. He was carrying a number of sweatshirts saying: "Jim Crow Must Go." Beckwith was crouching in honeysuckle vines in a vacant lot across the street. Medgar was struck from behind by his bullet. As the blood streamed down the driveway, his wife and three children rushed to him from inside the house. "Daddy, what's happened to you?" one of the children cried. He was buried four days after in Arlington National Cemetery.

Why should this book be read three decades after its original publication? Its importance lies in its human dimensions, its everlasting themes: courage, sacrifice, grief, loyalty, and love, Old Testament in their intensity. These are what give *For Us, the Living* its force and beauty. Reviewing it in November 1967 in *The New York Times Book Review*, North Carolinian Fred Powledge wrote:

> Mrs. Evers... could have presented an emotional, slick history of the life and death of her husband, and she would have been congratulated, but, like her husband, she chose to do a thorough job.... For Mrs.

Evers shows us a normal human being who gets tired and lonely, who sometimes wants to take a vacation from the struggle and devote full time to ironing and cooking and raising a family, but who learns, through being married to someone like Medgar Evers, to transcend herself.

More than anything, *For Us, the Living* is a love story: a tale of love between a man and a woman. In describing their courtship in college, she writes: "I was an accepting person, willing to deal within the framework of the small world I know, never really questioning that framework. Medgar was a rebel, ready to put his beliefs to any test." Among her memoir's finest passages are her very personal depictions of her marriage, especially in its early years. She was the product of a protective middle-class black family in Vicksburg, and she loved music and the piano. The man she married was eight years older, the son of a poor but prideful farmer in Decatur. At first she was baffled and alarmed by her husband's perilous, exhausting work. She craved more privacy and security for her family, but with time she grew to believe profoundly in his unwavering dedication; they would become in every sense collaborators.

Along the way there is humor. When they opened the NAACP office in Jackson, the staff consisted of the two of them. He insisted that if they were to work together they must conduct themselves in the office strictly as employer and employee, not only because of the appropriate forms but to avoid any charge that he was taking more money out of the organization for his wife. This behavior included never discussing personal problems in the office and addressing each other as Mr. and Mrs. Evers.

I must admit I found it hard to adjust to this kind of formality for eight hours each day. Once or twice, when there was no one around and the work was caught up, I went into his office and sat on his lap. He was abrupt and businesslike.

"No, Myrlie. Not here."

"Oh, Medgar," I said. "Who's going to know? Even if someone walked in, it isn't important. We *are* married."

But he would firmly push me off his lap and explain all over again that the association was paying us to work and run a dignified office, and that was what we were going to do.

Her keen regard for detail helps shape a graphic mosaic of daily life in Mississippi in that era. A clerk in a shop on Capitol Street will not allow her to try on hats unless she puts Kleenex inside them. Whites address her by only her first name. When the Everses buy a house in 1957, black neighbors threaten a petition to keep them out because of her husband's work. To avoid letting his colleagues know that he has black patients, her dentist, a member of the White Citizens Council, schedules appointments to allow twenty minutes between patients, and insists that you arrive and leave on time. In all her visits to him, she never once sees another patient.

In the sorrowful days after his death, she stood at the bedroom window watching her son Darrell playing baseball with some other boys:

> He hit the ball as it was pitched to him, and a boy ran to catch it, and Darrell stood there a moment and then threw the bat on the ground. His whole body shook and he broke into sobs and he ran from the street around the house to the back yard and the plum tree. I ran to meet him, and he cried as though his heart would break standing there under the tree that Medgar had planted. It was the first time he had cried.

"Somewhere in Mississippi," *For Us, the Living* begins, "lives the man who murdered my husband. Sometimes at night when my new house in Claremont, California, is quiet and the children are in bed I think about him and wonder how he feels.... He cannot escape it completely."

In California Mrs. Evers got a degree in sociology at Pomona

College and became development director at Claremont College. For five years she served as a commissioner on the Los Angeles Board of Public Works, the first black woman to have done so. She married Walter Williams, a longshoreman and union organizer with a distinguished record as a civil rights activist. As the years passed, she kept her contacts in Mississippi. In February 1994, at the third and final trial of Byron de la Beckwith in Jackson, she and two of her children came from California to be there every day. Once more she would testify, just as she had at the trials of '64 and '65 before all-white, all-male panels that had ended in hung juries.

There is no statute of limitations on murder. Beginning in 1990, an intrepid young white Assistant District Attorney named Bobby DeLaughter had come forward with evidence of jury tampering by members of a state agency in the '65 trial. His exhaustive research had led to new evidence, including Beckwith's own statements to individuals and audiences over the years that he had murdered Medgar Evers.

It was one of the most dramatic events I have ever witnessed as a writer, fraught with passion and consequence. The third trial of the seventy-three-year-old Beckwith in every measure brought the contorted history of the contemporary South full-circle. In the closing days of that uncommon reckoning Jackson was seized by old serpentine emotion, by strange and painful memories, by the dark ambivalent shadows of the past. The trial in February 1994 and the arduous investigative digging that led to it constituted one of the most unusual episodes of criminal prosecution in American history. Beckwith's conviction by a Mississippi jury and his sentencing to life in prison could possibly open a new era in which unresolved racial murders of a generation ago will come to justice.

Observing the former fertilizer salesman in all his squalid arrogance as he sat in the defendant's chair, restless and wiry and of singularly average countenance, a Confederate flag pin in the lapel of his cardinal-red sports coat, ostentatiously taking off his hearing aid when the testimony was not to his satisfaction, grinning occasionally at the spectators, I was overcome with my own memories from a Mississippi boyhood. The trial was a warp of old time, a *déjà vu* of stunning dimensions, the sixties sprung full-born again in the nineties, aging witnesses from the earlier trials, a tableau unto itself of the passing of eras in the South and America, moving ineluctably from past to present and back again. And through it all the compelling presence of Myrlie Evers.

In the earlier trials the principal query for jury selection, as asked by the prosecutor, was "Do you believe it a crime to kill a nigger in Mississippi?" Beckwith had the support of the state's most powerful political organization, the White Citizens Council, and Governor Ross Barnett came to the trial to socialize with him. The sheriff shook his hand when the hung juries were announced. When Beckwith returned to his hometown, Greenwood, he was greeted with "Welcome Home" signs.

Now, in the final summations of the third trial, the Assistant DA, holding the murder weapon and facing the jury, declared "for the sake of a civilized society, that justice in this case is what you ladies and gentlemen say it is. You twelve are Mississippi. What is Mississippi justice for the defendant's hate-inspired assassination, assassination of a man who just desired to be free and equal?... Is it ever too late to do the right thing?" And the District Attorney Ed Peters: "All we are asking you people to give the Evers family, to give the state of Mississippi, is some justice. We want a murderer who has been walking around for thirty years bragging about back-shooting to be stripped of that badge of honor and have a murder conviction hung around his neck. Just justice."

In a press conference after the verdict Mrs. Evers, flanked by her son and daughter, fought tears. She raised her hand and shouted, "Yea, Medgar!" Then, ruefully: "My God. I don't have to say accused assassin anymore. Now I can say *convicted* assassin. Medgar's life was not in vain and perhaps he did more in death than he could have in life. Somehow I think he is still among us."

In February 1995, in New York City, at age sixty-two, the author of *For Us, the Living* was elected president of the NAACP.

To understand the world, William Faulkner once said, you have to understand a place like Mississippi. There has always been what the historian David Sansing cites as "the *other* Mississippi," the Mississippi not of illiteracy but of literary tradition, not of ignominy but of nobility, not of nihilism and injustice but of charity and humanity. Mrs. Evers embodies the best of that indwelling vein. Surely it is appropriate that it is the University Press of Mississippi that is reissuing her book. Whites and blacks, conservatives and liberals of this latter day will be touched by its honesty and dignity, and I think our children will be too.

Myrlie Evers will continue to be an eloquent and salutary presence in America for many years to come. *For Us, the Living* will itself live forever in its own words and pages and in the extraordinary remembrance of this brave and beautiful woman.

*Willie Morris*
Jackson, Mississippi
September 1995

# For Us,
# the Living

## I

Somewhere in Mississippi lives the man who murdered my husband. Sometimes at night when my new house in Claremont, California, is quiet and the children are in bed I think about him and wonder how he feels. I have never seriously admitted the possibility that he has forgotten what I can never forget, though I suppose that hours and even days may go by without his thinking of it. Still, it must be there, the memory of it, like a giant stain in one part of his mind, ready to spring to life whenever he sees a Negro, whenever his hate rises like a bitterness in the throat. He cannot escape it completely.

And when that memory returns to him, I wonder if he is proud of what he did. Or if, sometimes, he feels at least a part of the enormous guilt he bears. For it is not just that he murdered a man. He murdered a very special man—special to him, special to many others, not just special to me as any man is to his wife. And he killed him in a special way. He is not just a murderer. He is an assassin.

He lived in a different world from the one Medgar and I shared for eleven and a half years, though all three of us must have spent most of our lives within a few miles of each other. And those different worlds we inhabited had been there, side by side in Mississippi, all along. When they collided, finally, my husband lay dying outside the door of our home, his key clutched tightly in his hand, a trail of his blood bearing witness to his struggle to reach safety inside. And as his life's blood poured out of him, his assassin dropped his weapon and slunk away through the underbrush of a vacant lot, hidden by the darkness of night. What were his feelings then? Joy? Fear? Triumph?

What are his feelings now?

I wonder if he has told others of his act that night, if, perhaps, he brags about it. And if he does, I wonder how those awful boasts are received. Do the other white men who hear his confession congratulate him? Do they laugh and slap him on the shoulder as though to share in his deed? Or do some, at least, stir uneasily at his tale? Do they, perhaps, even turn their backs on him, blotting him out, unwilling or unable to be a part of his murder even after it is done?

Much of the recent history of Mississippi could be told in the lives of these two men, my husband and his killer, the murdered and the murderer—one dead but free, the other alive and at large but never really free: imprisoned by the hate and fear that imprison so many white Mississippians and make so many Negro Mississippians still their slaves. Medgar and his assassin shared not only a state but a time; they grew up and lived in the same years, subject to the same influences. They breathed the same air, may have even brushed shoulders on the street or in a store.

Surely they heard the same speeches about the question that was central to both of their lives and yet moved them in such profoundly different directions. And that, too, is a strange thought: that there were times when both men sat by radios or television sets hearing the same news, the same words spoken about the racial crisis in Mississippi. But, oh, what different thoughts they must have had!

Medgar used to astonish Northern reporters who asked why he stayed in Mississippi by answering simply that he loved Mississippi. He did. He loved it as a man loves his home, as a farmer loves the soil. It was part of him. He loved to hunt and fish, to roam the fields and woods. He loved the feeling that here there was space for him and his family to grow and breathe. He had visited many other places. He had served in the Army in England and France; he had worked summers in Chicago during his college years; but always he came back to Mississippi as a man coming home.

Chicago held no appeal for him; he called life there a "rat race," and he was puzzled and a little resentful that all the Negroes from his part of Mississippi seemed to live in the same area of Chicago's South Side—the same block, almost; often the same buildings. He would say with disgust that Negroes who left his home town of Decatur, Mississippi, for the North all ended in the same neighborhoods of either Chicago or Flint, Michigan. He didn't like the dependence that implied, and he didn't like the Negro ghettos either. Both offended his sense of freedom. Chicago to him was a place to work, a place where you could earn better wages. Mississippi, with all its faults, was a place to live.

Medgar, of all people, was not blind to Mississippi's flaws, but he seemed convinced they could be corrected. He loved his state with hope and only rarely with despair. It was his hope that sustained him. It never left him. Despair came infrequently, and a day of hunting or fishing dispelled it. The love remained.

I suppose the man who killed Medgar loved Mississippi, too, in his twisted, tortured way. He must have loved the Mississippi that divides whites from Negroes, that by definition made him better than any Negro simply because he was white. In a way, I suppose, he was a jealous suitor, seeking by his murder to eliminate a rival, for he loved the Mississippi Medgar sought to change. What Medgar loved with hope, his assassin loved with fear. And he killed, I suspect, largely out of that fear.

But knowing this, thinking about it, wondering at it in the stillness of the night these many months after that act of horror cannot change the emptiness of life without my husband. There are times when I pause in a busy day and realize with surprise that I survive, that I am continuing, that my life goes on. For a long time after that shot rang out in the darkness and put an end to my life with Medgar, it seemed impossible to go on. And yet I do; the children eat and sleep and go to school, their lives almost complete; day follows night; and emptiness is, if not filled, at least ignored a little more each day than the day before.

But there are moments when it all comes back, when the warmth of those years with Medgar floods in on me, when I live again those shattering moments after the crack of the rifle. And then I wonder about the man who saw my husband's back in the sights of a high-powered rifle and coldly squeezed the trigger. What kind of man could that be? What kind of life brought him to that clump of bushes where he hid and waited? What can he be thinking now that the act is committed and he has escaped its legal consequences?

They are all questions I cannot answer in any sure or final sense. I can only speculate out of an intuitive knowledge of what hate can do to the human soul. For I, too, have been tempted to hate. It has been difficult, living in Mississippi, not to. Hate is one of the rare commodities whites and Negroes are permitted to share equally in that state. It is one of the few things in more than adequate supply for all.

But if I cannot know what brought my husband's murderer to that awful, final moment, I can at least hope to understand what brought my husband there. It may even be that the answer to both questions is the same, for Medgar, too, grew up in Mississippi, the same Mississippi that produced enough hate in one man to bring him to kill in the night. Medgar, too, was subject to the same forces that drove his assassin toward that desperate, fanatical moment. They affected Medgar differently, of course, for he lived at the other end of those forces, even as he died at the other end of that rifle.

But surely there must be in Medgar's life and mine at least a mirrored reflection of the life that produced his killer. Surely what Mississippi made of us should provide a clue to what it made of him. It is not so strange, when you think of it, to hope to learn something about a killer by an examination of his carefully chosen victim. And of one thing I am sure: Medgar was carefully chosen. No other victim would have served at that moment in time. Medgar was killed specifically because of what he represented, of what he had become, of the hope that his presence gave to Mississippi Negroes and the fear it aroused in Mississippi whites.

In many ways, the act of murder that deprived me of a husband was an official act, for Medgar's energies were all directed against the official state of things in Mississippi: against official positions of the state, official proclamations, official regulations relegating Negroes to an official status of inferiority. It is almost as though the assassin had been appointed by the state to carry out the execution of an

5

enemy of the state, an execution that the state could not, in all good public relations, openly carry out itself.

And yet, as time goes by, I think that official view will change. There will, I believe, be a day when Medgar Evers will be remembered, in Mississippi as elsewhere, as a true friend of his state. Surely the day must come when his assassin and people like him will be remembered in Mississippi as the state's real enemies.

## II

I was seventeen and had never been away from home
when I went off from Vicksburg to Alcorn A & M College
in Lorman, Mississippi. It was just a forty-six mile drive in
a friend's car, but I saw it as the beginning of a new life.
Squeezed in the back seat between my grandmother and
Aunt Myrlie, the two people who had raised me and surrounded my childhood with adoration, protection, and tower-
ing hopes, I tried hard to conceal the pride, the nervousness,
the joy and the fear that fought for possession of me.

My pride was of two sorts; first, in the certainty that by
going off to college I was fulfilling ambitions both of these
strong and loving women had held for me almost since I was
born. Both, being teachers, were strong believers in higher
education, and both had sacrificed to achieve at least part of
a college education for themselves. In a way, I suppose, I
represented their hopes and ambitions for themselves, and
in any case I was carrying on an important tradition.

But there was a more personal kind of pride as well, and
I confess to a certain vanity in the picture I had of myself
that day: grown up, mature, a college coed dressed in a
bright, new cotton print and my first pair of really high

7

heels. A snapshot reveals today what an exaggeration this was, and I can see what others must have seen: a tall, very thin young Negro girl, wide-eyed and innocent-looking, with long hair worn page-boy style. But though I wobbled awkwardly on my new high heels, my uncertain steps were that day transformed in my mind into stately strides, and I remember seeing myself as an arresting figure that soon would be strolling under giant oaks along the campus paths that led from one exciting class to the next.

My sense of nervousness was that of any girl going off to college for the first time, but it was magnified in my case by a childhood well laced with often-expressed fears of what the outside world might do to me once I left the shelter of my aunt's and grandmother's protectiveness. I had always rejected these fears of theirs, mostly in annoyance at the restrictions they placed on me; yet now, suddenly, so near to being on my own, I began to doubt my complacency. I had been warned all my life about the dangers particular to whatever I was doing, and going off to college was no exception. This time, I had been told, the major menace was involvement with an older, wise and worldly veteran, for the year was 1950, and Alcorn was coeducational, and it was known that there were young men returned from the debauching experiences of the Army stalking the campus in search of innocent young girls from Vicksburg.

I don't know what I expected, but as mile followed mile and we finally reached the point at which we turned off the main highway to drive the last seven miles through piny woods and scattered cotton fields, I scanned each turn of the road for the sight that would tell me I had arrived at the place where I would be tested. In the end, there was sheer joy, for Alcorn was beautiful, set back in the woods with enormous old trees studding the sprawling campus. The out-

8

standing building was the chapel, built entirely without nails by slaves more than a hundred years earlier. For Alcorn, like virtually everything else in Mississippi that had been set aside for Negroes, was a hand-me-down. It had been built originally as a white military school.

Parting with my aunt and grandmother an hour later heightened both my fears and my excitement, but it was quickly done with appropriately renewed warnings of the dangers of the big new world of the college campus. Then they were gone, and I was on my own. Two hours later, gathered in front of the college president's house with a group of other freshman girls, I met the older, wise and worldly veteran my aunt and grandmother had warned me about. His name was Medgar Wiley Evers.

Looking back now, I can see that it was indeed the beginning of a new life. What I saw then was a well-built, self-assured young man, a junior, an athlete back on the college campus early for football practice. We met—the football team and the freshman girls—in what seemed a casual way. I am sure now that it was carefully planned by both groups. We spent most of that first afternoon looking each other over, fencing, probing, pairing off and then regrouping. I was intrigued by what I saw. Although for a week I thought his name was Edgar Evans, there was to me something special about Medgar almost immediately. It was not until later that I learned he was, indeed, a veteran, that he was a football star, the president of the junior class, a campus leader. All I really knew at the time was that he was different from the boys I had known. There was something in the way he spoke, the way he carried himself, in his politeness, that made him stand out even from the others I met that day.

Though I had mistaken his name, he remembered mine, and he spoke each time we met. The more I saw of him, the more interested I became. He had a certain refinement, the air of a gentleman, and I learned that unlike many of the younger men he neither smoked nor drank. He was known on the campus as a hard worker, not only in his studies and athletics but in the many part-time jobs he held. He had a reputation for being stingy with money for dates and, paradoxically, for being something of a Don Juan. I was told by girls who knew him that he never went out with the same girl for more than a month.

The other college men knew him as an intellectual because he read a good deal and was serious about his studies. They said he never let his hair down, rarely clowned, and yet it was obvious just from knowing him slightly that he had a quiet sense of humor. The more I heard, the more fascinated I became. The more I saw him, the more I wanted to know him better.

I was accustomed to boys my own age, a happy-go-lucky crowd interested mostly in having fun, and the freshman boys at Alcorn were much like those I had known in high school in Vicksburg. Medgar, being a veteran, was older than most of the juniors, but it was maturity more than age, his air of having a goal and knowing precisely how to reach it that made him stand out. It was well known that he had refused to join a fraternity because he thought them somewhat childish, and this did not make him popular with some of the more typically carefree college men; yet even they respected him for his leadership in college activities.

I saw Medgar several times in those first few days at college. I used to go with a group of freshman girls to watch the football team practice, and my eyes were always drawn to him. As the rest of the student body arrived and classes began, I saw him around the campus, and we always spoke in passing. For a while, that was all.

Then, late in the fall, two months after I had first met him, Medgar took to walking past the music studio when I was practicing piano. At first I would notice him passing by, stopping, looking in at me, and I would nod and go on playing. Then, more and more, he would stop by the open window and wait, and we would exchange a few words when I had finished. Once he explained that he enjoyed hearing me play, and it was only much later when I learned that he really didn't think much of classical music that I realized this had simply been an excuse to explain his presence. More and more, I found myself bumping into him, and eventually I knew he was searching me out deliberately.

We began having lunch together, and sometimes we'd see each other after dinner. Several nights a week he would walk me back to the dormitory after our choir practice, where I played the piano to earn money for school expenses. We talked mostly about school, though he seemed amazingly up-to-date on current events, and I found myself reading newspapers more carefully in order to keep up with him. Eventually he asked me for a date. We went to the Saturday-night movie. I didn't tell him I had seen it a year before in Vicksburg.

But even after we began to have dates, Medgar remained slightly aloof. I knew that he liked me, though he was never one for saying so. He didn't go in for holding hands or other demonstrations of affection; he didn't even try to kiss me until we had been out together a number of times. He was friendly, but he kept his distance, and after all the talk of his being a Romeo, I was puzzled. Eventually I asked if he really liked me at all, and his reply was typical. He said he thought his actions ought to tell me, that I shouldn't have to ask. I was hurt, though I tried not to show it. I couldn't understand how anyone could be so businesslike about his emotions.

Toward the end of the year, it was generally assumed on campus that Medgar and I were getting serious about each other. I guess he and I assumed it, too, though it could hardly have been proved by anything he had said to me. He had still not said he loved me, though he had told me he would never say that to anyone unless he really meant it. Somehow, that both disturbed and reassured me. And, meanwhile, we had developed a crazy pattern of arguments that threatened to put an end to everything once each week.

Medgar liked to argue with me anyhow. He was forever telling me I was too timid, that I'd been too sheltered, that I should stand up and fight for what I believed. I knew in my heart it was true, but I conceded nothing. We were usually friendly all week, and then on Friday night we would almost always find something to disagree about. Saturday night would come, and with it the weekly campus movie, the only social event of the college. Medgar would either go alone or take another girl. I would accept a date with another boy and then try to make sure Medgar saw us together. Then, on Sunday afternoons, we always managed to find each other and make up. That, at least, was great fun.

I had been warned by a number of upperclassmen to watch my step with Medgar because he was known to change girls frequently. People said I should beware of falling in love with him because he always dropped the girls that did. I knew by this time that I had certain advantages over at least some of these former girl friends. Medgar liked girls with long hair, and I wore mine long. He used to say he liked girls who could do something more than just grin up in his face, and I had managed to make the honor roll at every grading period. I had even achieved a modest celebrity on the campus by winning second place in a state-wide oratorical contest sponsored by the Negro Masons, the prize a scholarship of $650 toward my college expenses.

He had clear-cut ideas about the girls he took out, and he made no secret of them. Even before our first date, he had told me he expected his girl friend not to go out with other boys. Since he made no such rule for himself, I thought it quite unfair and said so. And after we started dating, I made it a point to continue going out with other boys whenever he took out another girl. I think he both resented and respected it.

He had a sharp picture of the girl he wanted to marry, and he spoke about it openly. She must be well educated, friendly, neat and clean, he said, and she must love children. He hoped to have four. And the woman who would someday become Mrs. Medgar Evers, he said, would be completely devoted to him. There could be no question about that.

At the end of my first year at Alcorn, Medgar finally told me he loved me. It was a glorious moment, though we were both still hiding how deeply we felt about each other. There was still something tentative, something indefinite, something withheld. I wonder now how I managed to do so well in my studies when my emotions were in so constant a state of turmoil. Medgar was so intelligent and kind, so irritating and confusing and lovable all at the same time, that I think back on those first months of knowing him today with some of the same jumbled emotions I felt then.

In a way, I think we were attracted to each other largely because of our differences. He was right in saying I had been sheltered. And he had been raised with a certain independence. He was eight years older, had served with the Army in England and France during the war. I had never been anywhere. He came from a large family, with brothers and sisters. I was an only child, raised by a grandmother and an aunt. He grew up in the country on a farm. I was a city girl.

But the greatest difference between us, I think, was in our attitudes toward life itself. I was an accepting person, willing to deal with problems within the framework of the small world I knew, never really questioning that framework. Medgar was a rebel, ready to put his beliefs to any test. He saw a much larger world than the one that, for the moment, confined him. And he saw a place in that larger world for himself.

There was nothing on the surface in Medgar's childhood and family to account for the sort of man he was when I met him. But the explanations were there, and slowly, over the years, I found them. His father, James Evers, did not seem an unusual man. Quiet, stern, hardworking, he was a Baptist, a deacon of his church, a man who believed in work almost as an end in itself.

The family lived in a frame house on the edge of town in a Negro section of Decatur, Mississippi. They had enough land to farm, and James Evers kept cows, pigs, chickens, and a pair of mules for plowing. He grew vegetables for the table and cotton for cash. But, like most Mississippi Negroes, he could not survive on what he made from one job. He worked at times in a sawmill and at others for the railroad. Over the years he built two small houses on his property to rent out. Even before that, his wife, Jessie, rented a room in the main house to teachers to bring in additional income.

Jessie Evers did not share her husband's Baptist religion. She was a member of the Church of God in Christ. But she shared with him a belief in hard work, and besides running the house and caring for her children, she did housework for a white family and took in ironing. The children, from the time they were old enough, worked around the house and farm. As the girls reached an appropriate age, they too worked out in white homes. The boys did odd jobs for white families in town.

They were a poor family in spite of all the work, but they were never destitute, and they managed to take care of themselves without help from anyone. They took pride in that and in the respect in which they were held by the community generally, both white and Negro. Jessie Evers was a deeply religious woman, a leader of her church, a woman who kept an almost fanatically neat house and raised her children to be well mannered and clean.

She was proud of her mixed heritage. One grandmother had been an Indian; her father had been half-white. But it was the Negro half of her father's ancestry that she spoke of with fire and flashing eyes. As a mulatto, he had spent most of his adult life getting into and out of scrapes having to do with race. Once he had shot two white men and left town in the dead of night. It was a story that was told in later years to explain that the Evers fighting spirit had origins on her side of the family as well as her husband's. For there was never any question about James.

James Evers was paid on Saturdays, and with his money he did the week's shopping for staples in Decatur on Saturday night. It was a ritual on these trips for him to buy a big, round peppermint stick to be broken up at home and divided among the children. Medgar loved these trips to town with his father, but the candy was only a secondary reason. It was the obvious respect of the townspeople for his father and the way his father accepted this respect as his due that made those weekly trips really memorable. It was more than a custom, it was unwritten law that Negroes leave the sidewalks of Decatur for approaching whites. James Evers was one of the few Negroes that refused to do it. On the contrary, he behaved as though he had never heard of such a custom. "He stood up and was a man," was the way Medgar put it years later.

There was a frightening incident of his father's refusal to bow before the white man and his customs, and on one of those trips to town Medgar and his older brother, Charles, were witnesses to it. The arrangement with the stores was for credit all week with a final cash settlement on Saturday. One Saturday there was a dispute in a store. The argument over James Evers' account led to insults, and Medgar heard his father called "nigger" by two white men. When they advanced on him with the obvious intent of beating him, James Evers picked up a bottle, smashed the end of it over the counter, and held it in front of him as a weapon.

He told the boys to leave, to go home without him, and at their hestitation he made it an order. As they scampered out of the store, their last sight of their father was of a calm, grim man retreating slowly toward the door, holding the advancing white men at bay with the jagged glass of the broken bottle. He arrived home soon after the boys, unhurt, the bottle still in his hand.

But there were limits to what any Negro could do and get away with. It hurt Medgar to hear his father called "boy" by white men, and as he grew older, he began himself to experience racial incidents. For years he went with his mother on occasional days to the home of the white family where she worked. He played with white children both there and on the white fringes of the neighborhood where he lived. As he grew older, the white boys played less and less with him, and in the end there was a day of racial insults and the rupture of all friendly childhood relationships.

Race was a constant fact of Medgar's life; it was not something he had to ask his parents about. The only things to learn were the boundaries within which your race restricted you, and you learned these early and well from watching those around you.

It may have been the example their father set that led Medgar and his brother, Charles, constantly to test these boundaries, to push against them, to attempt to widen them, for there is evidence that they both did. There was the time that Mississippi Senator Theodore Bilbo, perhaps the most vicious racist of modern times to serve in the United States Senate, spoke in Decatur. Medgar and Charles went to hear him. The speech was given in the town square, and the two boys, sitting on the grass at one side, were the only Negroes in sight.

In the course of his usual racist speech, Bilbo warned the local whites of the dangers of educating Negroes, of associating with them, of letting down even slightly the bars of complete segregation. As he warmed to his theme, he pointed to Medgar and Charles at the edge of the crowd. "If we fail to hold high the wall of separation between the races," he shouted, "we will live to see the day when those two nigger boys right there will be asking for everything that is ours by right." The crowd turned to stare at Medgar and Charles. The two boys stared right back. They remained at the edge of the crowd until the end of the speech.

But the rules of racism were not just learned from speeches. Medgar must have been about twelve when a Negro man, accused of leering at a white woman, was snatched by a mob and dragged through town and out the road that led past the Evers' house. In a near-by field he was tied to a tree and shot dead. It was an event that Medgar recalled with horror, but his special revulsion was reserved for the Negro men who slunk from the sight of the mob without lifting a hand. The sickness he felt returned again and again in the months that followed, for when the lynching was over, the white mob stripped the Negro and left his bloody clothes at the foot of the tree. Medgar would pass the spot while hunting, drawn against his will to see the rotting clothes with their blood stains turning slowly to rust.

Within the larger world dominated by an obsession with race, though, was the smaller world of Medgar's family, and here was a world of warmth and closeness, of discipline and family pride. Jessie Evers had been married once before, and her older children, two sons and a daughter, were part of Medgar's family. The oldest, a son, died, but there was a daughter, Eva Lee, and a second son, Gene. Medgar was the third of James and Jessie Evers' four children. The oldest, Charles, was three years Medgar's senior. Then came Elizabeth, a year older than Medgar. Medgar was born on July 2, 1925. Two years later, the fourth child, Mary Ruth was born.

In a family that large, with both mother and father often working out of the home, there was inevitable delegation of authority to the older children. Medgar writhed under the demands of his older sisters, frequently setting out deliberately to irritate them. The arguments that followed were invariably reported to their mother. Punishment for serious breaches of the rules consisted of a number of strokes across the legs and thighs with a peach tree switch administered by his mother, and no one who has not felt the sting of a supple peach tree switch can guess at the effectiveness of such a penalty. Once Medgar's mother started after him with one of these switches, and he ran under the house. His father took over, pulling him from his sanctuary and spanking him with a leather belt. It was a spanking he never forgot, and it was the last time he ever ran from his mother.

Jessie Evers often entertained. She was an active church worker and her door was open to anyone that came by. It was a tradition for ministers to take their Sunday meals with members of their churches, and there were always church meetings that required the feeding of guests. People were constantly dropping in, and it was nothing for Jessie to get up in the middle of the night—or anytime, really—and prepare a meal. Jessie Evers' meals were famous, not only with her family but throughout the Negro community of Decatur. She was a marvelous cook, and the taste she left with Medgar for large and excellent meals was to make the early years of our marriage something of a trial for both of us. The only food that was a rarity in the Evers house was candy. Candy had to be bought for cash.

If the Everses ate well, they all worked hard enough to account for their appetites. Three times a year, a truckload of wood was delivered at the house, and Medgar and Charles had the job of cutting it into sticks of a size for the wood stove on which their mother cooked her magnificent meals. From an early age, it was Medgar's job to bring in firewood for the fireplaces and start fires before the rest of the family arose in the cold mornings. He mended fences, milked the cows and drove them home from the pasture at night. And in the fall it became a specialty of his to range the neighborhood killing pigs at hog-killing time. It was a thing he had to force himself to learn, for at first it had seemed a cruel and bloody occupation, and Medgar shrank from cruelty. But he learned the necessity for hog-killing in his family's smoke house, where he helped smoke hams and bacon, and at the table, where he helped to eat them.

Medgar and Charles were especially close, and they spent

much of their youth together. They built scooters from skate wheels and boards, hunted squirrels and rabbits and possum and coons, went fishing in the many creeks and streams near the Evers' farm. Medgar learned to swim when Charles pushed him into a swimming hole far over his head.

The Evers children went to a one-room school heated by an old-fashioned potbellied stove, and here, too, it became Medgar's job to cut wood and make fires. Charles had a way of promoting fights between his younger brother and other boys, and for years the two brothers would range the countryside for miles around to carry out one of these arrangements by Charles. Medgar must have had a distinctive gait as they moved along the roadside, for he picked up the nickname "Lope," and it stuck.

It was a busy childhood, what with school and work, yet somehow Medgar left with his mother an impression of a boy who played often by himself. After he started school, he spent hours reading. Medgar himself later recalled a frequent solitary pastime that gives a picture of him as a quiet, reflective child. When something bothered him, he would leave the house, taking an empty tin can from the kitchen, and start off down the road kicking it ahead of him. Miles later, he would leave the road for the woods to find a place to sit and think. His thinking done, he would kick the can all the way home again.

When he was old enough for high school, Medgar left the one-room elementary school and began walking twelve miles each way to the Negro high school in Newton. James and Jessie Evers were both strong believers in education, and while many of the Negro children of Decatur never went beyond the small grade school, the Everses pushed their children to stay in school as long as possible. In the end, Elizabeth had some high school before she married, Mary

Ruth finished high school, and both Charles and Medgar finished college. It was an unusual record for Negro children in Decatur.

The long walk to Newton was something Medgar resented, knowing as he did that the white children of Decatur had their own high school right in town. There was, of course, nothing he could do about that, but by working summers at cutting lawns and painting for white families, Medgar saved the money for a bicycle that made the long trip easier. He was an average student with no special interest in any subject, but he knew that getting an education was the only way he would get a better job than his father had at the sawmill. Both he and his father wanted that.

There was little in the way of entertainment to amuse a Negro boy growing up in Decatur, and what there was cost money. There was a small motion-picture house with a balcony known as the "buzzard's roost" reserved for Negroes. Occasionally Medgar saw a matinee on Saturday. But the big social events nearly all had something to do with church.

There was, each August, something called a tractor meeting, and after we were married, Medgar took me to one. It was held on a Sunday at the picnic grounds of a church far out in the country, and from just after dawn families would begin to arrive from all over that part if the state. It seemed to me that all of the families were huge and that somehow all were related, for nearly everyone you met was introduced as a cousin. Each family brought with it what seemed a ridiculous amount of food, and what developed was a sort of all-day picnic, with preaching and singing groups from different churches competing with one another.

A family would set itself up at a picnic table and spread out its food: three or four different kinds of cake, meats, vegetables, everything imaginable. During the day, whole families or groups of two or three would drift from table to table, from family to family, carrying baskets of food, sampling the delicacies of others and leaving something in return to be sampled. I never quite understood how it worked, for in spite of the enormous quantities of food consumed on the spot, everyone seemed to take home more food than he brought.

The primary reason for the success of the affair was that it served as a sort of reunion. This was where you found relatives and friends seen only once a year. It was where you learned who had married whom, who had died, who had graduated, and who had had another child. It was where the men discussed their crops and their jobs and the price of cotton and the impossibility of making a living cropping shares. It was where the women compared recipes and children and the white families they worked for and, I suppose, their husbands. It was where the ministers looked over one another's congregations and choirs and preaching techniques, and where the teachers talked about their schools and their students. Above all, it was where the genealogists in each family spent a happy day untangling the exact relationships of sixth cousins four times removed.

In a way these tractor meetings were both a time of renewal of bonds and a release from the drudgery of a year of hard work. They were the only real means of communication among the Negro families in that part of Mississippi. They represented the only large social gathering of the year, and there was a special sadness in going home when they were over.

In a smaller way, the various churches in each community filled many of the same needs throughout the year. Medgar's mother never missed a Sunday, and there were services all day long. With the older children, she would set off for Sunday school, which ran from nine to eleven, stay for church from eleven until two, and then break for two hours to visit and eat until four, when the young people's meeting would begin. At six o'clock the young people's meeting would end, and after supper, at seven, the evening service would begin. For years Medgar went to all of these, and it was only when he was old enough to assert himself that he managed to convince his mother that one, or at most two services each Sunday would satisfy the Lord.

Jessie Evers carried her devotion to God into her home with family prayers involving each member of the family on Sunday mornings. No meal was begun without the saying of grace, and a longer than usual blessing was said at one meal each day. Medgar's mother would tolerate no alcohol or tobacco in her home, and wearing of make-up by the girls was forbidden. She prayed on rising and before bed, and she sang hymns as she worked around the house. She was an indefatigable woman, a warm and loving mother.

Like many Southern Negro men, Medgar's father was sometimes out of work. His mother saw the family through these times, and the children never lacked for food or clothing and a warm house. She made sure that they stayed in school throughout the entire term, rather than quit during the harvest season as so many Negro children did. But, in spite of the occasional periods when James Evers could find no work, when the cash income came solely from his wife's earnings, Medgar's father was seen by all of his family as its indisputable head.

Medgar was sixteen and a sophomore at Newton High School when the United States entered World War II. Within a year he had quit school and followed his brother, Charles, into the Army. Eventually he wound up in a segregated port battalion that saw service in England and, after the Normandy invasion, at Le Havre, Liège, Antwerp, and Cherbourg. It was a rugged unit and a rough bunch of men, most of them considerably older than the seventeen-year-old lad from Decatur, Mississippi. Though Medgar neither smoked nor drank, his language was strongly influenced by the men around him. Obscenity must have seemed incongruous in one so young, and one day a white lieutenant took him aside.

"You're too intelligent to talk that way," the lieutenant said. "You have a good vocabulary. You can say what you want without swearing every other word. Some of these men can't. They don't know any better. You do. You can go a long way if you use the intelligence you've got."

There were other talks after that, and Medgar slowly realized that the lieutenant was right. As the war ended, the same lieutenant urged him to go back to school, to improve his mind, to finish his education, to make something of himself. He proved an important influence in Medgar's life.

Medgar had had no close friends among whites since his childhood, and I have no doubt that at first he regarded the lieutenant's interest in him with suspicion. But the whole experience of the Army was a new one, a broadening one, and it opened up new worlds to a young Negro boy from rural Mississippi. The fact that his unit was segregated, that its officers were white, would not have seemed strange to Medgar. That was the way his world had always been. But the trip by troop ship across the Atlantic was straight from a storybook, and though Medgar was seasick most of the way, the body's misery could not dampen the spirit's sense of adventure. In such an atmosphere, even a deeply ingrained suspicion of white men had to be questioned.

In France he found a whole people—all of them white— who apparently saw no difference in a man simply because of his skin color, and this was perhaps the greatest revelation of all. In time, he came to know a French family near where he was stationed, and they accepted him as one of them. A romance with a daughter developed, and nobody flinched. Before it could amount to much, the battalion was moved.

And yet even here, in France, where the French accepted both white and Negro American troops simply as American soldiers, the long arm of racism intruded. For white American soldiers brought their prejudices with them and imposed them wherever possible on the French. The white troops whispered stories about the colored troops, and more than once Medgar was asked by a naïve French girl if it were true that Negroes were some kind of monkey whose tails came out at night. There was embarrassment and shock when the lies were exposed, and there remained, for the French, wonder at what lay beneath the lies. Why should Americans hate each other? Why should they separate their troops according to color? There had to be reasons.

And so, in the end, even the openness and friendliness of the French were tainted by the presence of American racism. There was apparently no escape from it. And even the pleasant memory of Medgar's romance with the young French girl was later spoiled when, after the war, his mother pleaded with him to end his correspondence with her for fear that whites in Decatur would find out and take offense. Negroes have been lynched in Mississippi for less.

The war was liberating to Medgar in several ways. Both he and his brother, Charles, saved money from their army pay and sent it home to their parents. With some of it, Jessie and James Evers modernized their house, replacing the wood stove and bringing plumbing inside. Four rooms were added, and by the time the two boys came home, the family's living conditions were much improved.

There were many times during Medgar's army service when he felt how impossible it would be to return to Mississippi and settle down to the life he had known before the war. For if Mississippi hadn't changed, he had. He had a whole new vision of what life could be like, of the way it was lived in other places by other people. The simple fact that he had helped earn money that had done so much to improve his parent's home was an indication of the possibilities of life outside his native state.

And yet, when the war was over, back to Mississippi he went, along with Charles. Charles, who had finished high school, enrolled at Alcorn Agricultural and Mechanical College on the G.I. Bill of Rights. Medgar took a job while he decided what to do. But the changes wrought in both young men by their years outside Mississippi were not long in asserting themselves. In the summer of 1946, Medgar turned twenty-one. He and Charles rounded up four other young Negroes and went to the county clerk's office to register to vote. It was not such an innocent venture as it might seem. All of them knew that of the 900-odd voters on the rolls in Decatur none were Negroes. And all of them knew why.

A small crowd of whites gathered when the word went out that Negroes were registering. For the moment, that was all. "I never found out until later," Medgar said afterward, "that they visited my parents nightly after that. First, it was the whites, and then their Negro message-bearers. And the word was always the same: 'Tell your sons to take their names off the books. Don't show up at the courthouse voting day.' Then, the night before the election, Bilbo came to town and harangued the crowd in the square. 'The best way to keep a nigger from the polls on election day,' he told them, 'is to visit him the night before.' And they visited us.

My brother came from Alcorn College to vote that next day. I laid off from work. The six of us gathered at my house and we walked to the polls. I'll never forget it. Not a Negro was on the streets, and when we got to the courthouse, the clerk said he wanted to talk with us. When we got into his office, some fifteen or twenty armed white men surged in behind us, men I had grown up with, had played with. We split up and went home without voting. Around town, Negroes said we had been whipped, beaten up, and run out of town. Well, in a way we were whipped, I guess, but I made up my mind then that it would not be like that again—at least not for me."

It may have been this incident, along with the memory of that white army lieutenant, that helped Medgar decide to return to school. Alcorn, where Charles was already enrolled, had a laboratory high school as part of its education department, and Medgar enrolled there as a high school junior in the fall of 1946. He was years older than most of the high school students, though there were other veterans completing high school, too. It did not bother him at all. For suddenly he had purpose and direction, even if it was nothing more than completing his education, and he plunged into it as he was to plunge into nearly everything he did from that time on. It was during that first year at Alcorn's laboratory high school that Medgar really began enjoying learning for its own sake.

There was an English teacher, Mrs. John H. Jackson, who gave Medgar his first real knowledge of how to study. Under her guidance, he began to develop a tremendous vocabulary, one that in later years often sent me to the dictionary to look up a word he had used. But while Medgar liked Mrs. Jackson and admired her, he had no desire himself to become a teacher. He regarded the teaching profession for Negroes as something close to an insult, because it was the one profession Negroes were encouraged by whites to aspire to. While most Mississippi Negroes reacted too little to the deprivation of segregation and racism, Medgar had a tendency during those years to over-react. Were the whites for it? Then he was against it. Did the whites approve? Then it was suspect.

This was, I think, the basis for his refusal even to consider a teaching career. He did not yet know what he wanted to do, but he was sure he would never teach. Looking back today, there is a certain irony in this, for Medgar undoubtedly turned out to be one of the more important teachers his people have ever had in Mississippi. But I suppose Medgar could say, with justice, that he taught in a way that Mississippi whites certainly did not approve.

If Medgar came alive as a student at Alcorn, he also found himself as an athlete. He had always loved sports and participated in them where he could, but Newton High School had had no organized teams. Now he made the first team in football and went out for track as well. These were interests he was to continue all through college.

With the G.I. Bill behind him, there was no real doubt that Medgar could finish high school and go on to college, but he was never one to waste either time or money—or the time to make money. Beginning that first summer after his junior year in high school, he and Charles began going to Chicago for summer jobs. Their half-sister, Eva Lee, had moved to Chicago's South Side, and each spring as soon as school was out, the two brothers would go home to Decatur, pick up some friends, and set off for Chicago in a rattle-trap car that always threatened to break down along the way but somehow never did. Medgar held a number of different jobs over those summers, usually doing manual labor on some construction job.

There was little about Chicago that Medgar liked except the higher wages. He always said he'd hate to live there. I think this was a reaction mostly to the ugly Negro ghetto on the South Side where first one sister and then eventually all three moved. It annoyed Medgar that the three of them— Eva Lee, Elizabeth, and finally Mary Ruth, toward whom Medgar had always felt particularly close and protective— all settled in the same neighborhood of that vast slum, the same neighborhood in which one could find hundreds of other Negroes from Decatur. He was constantly urging them to move, to spread out, to try something different and new, but they, like their friends and neighbors from Decatur, found it easier, friendlier, and perhaps even safer to stay together.

Many white people had pointed to this tendency of Southern Negroes to cluster together in Northern cities as proof that Negroes prefer segregation—that they really want to live among themselves. I think it was his knowledge of this charge, as much as anything, that disturbed Medgar about what he saw in his sisters' neighborhood in Chicago. In fact, of course, there is nothing about Negroes from the same places in the South living together in small neighborhoods in Chicago that differs very much from the clusters of European immigrants that for generations settled in small sections of our Eastern cities on their arrival in the United States. And the reasons are much the same. New arrivals in any strange place tend to seek out friends and relatives, to settle near them and depend on their experience for help in getting started. The only real difference is that, for Negroes, the opportunity to escape these ghettos once this original purpose has been served has always been much more difficult. It remains that way today.

But if Medgar disliked Chicago, he nonetheless took advantage of some of the things it offered that were new and different. He swam at the lakefront beaches, visited museums and libraries, and luxuriated in the sense of freedom it gave him to enter such places with no thought to race or color. Strangely, his reaction to all of this was not that of many Southern Negroes: a desire to remain in the North. Instead, he would begin to talk about what a wonderful place Mississippi would be if it could only rid itself of racism, how much better, really, than Chicago.

Medgar knew, of course, that there was racism to be found in Chicago, too, but at least there were no desperate problems in Negroes and whites mixing freely at beaches, in school, on buses and trains, in the libraries and museums and restaurants and shops and movies and at work. All of this he took as proof of how easy it really ought to be to convince white Mississippians of the error of their traditional views, if only they could see how it all worked. Rather than incline him toward staying in the North, Medgar's enjoyment of the North's extra freedoms always seemed to send him hurrying back to the South with new hopes of changing it.

One of Medgar's greatest pleasures during those summers in Chicago was the chance to explore the suburbs. Whenever he could, he would borrow a car and drive out of the city to wander up one street and down another looking at houses. He had a dream of the sort of house he hoped someday to live in, the kind of street and neighborhood and town where he might raise a family, and the white suburbs of Chicago seemed to him right out of that dream. He would spend whole days just driving slowly through the suburbs of

Chicago's North Shore, looking at the beautiful houses and wishing. Years later, when we were in Chicago together, he took me on these drives, and by that time he had picked out specific houses that came closest to the dream.

One of them was in Evanston, a two-story house with tall shade trees and shrubbery neatly placed throughout the green yard. It was an older house with a settled look about it, and as we sat in the car across the street, Medgar began to dream out loud.

"Listen," he said suddenly, and I did. "Do you hear how quiet it is? This is the kind of neighborhood to raise children in. Look at that lawn, like a carpet almost. And those big old trees. Wouldn't you like to just lie down under one of them?"

I suppose that Medgar's dreams of what America might be were derived, as many of our dreams are, from what he had seen in the movies. No one who saw the Andy Hardy pictures in the 1930s and '40s and drank in the warmth of that small town and its life could help identifying with it. No one, that is, except a Negro who knew that there was no place for him in that America. And that, in a sense, is what has been wrong with American movies: that white Americans could sit through them week after week, year after year, and never realize how distorted they were. For if Andy Hardy's town was anything like Evanston, Illinois, in the years that Medgar used to park on its streets and admire its houses, then fifteen per cent of its population was Negro, and they lived in a segregated ghetto that was never seen on the screen. If Andy Hardy's town was like Evanston, it had both a white and Negro YMCA; its public high school had no swimming pool because that would mean whites and Negroes swam together; and its hospital did not admit Negroes as patients. I don't know that Medgar knew these facts; I myself learned them only recently, and some of them have changed in the years since then; but Medgar would not have had to know specific facts about Evanston—or any other white suburb—to know the truth. The truth is concealed from whites, not from Negroes.

It was this kind of knowledge, I think, that drove Medgar to try to change his world and his place in it. It is the same drive that moves millions of Negroes today to demand at least a chance at some of the good things in life. Nearly any movie, almost any page of *Life* magazine, the advertising on the billboards and in the newspapers, most of what we see each day on television—all of these constitute a kind of torture to many Negroes. For they know that this, or something like it, is what awaits the American who is willing to work for it—unless he is a Negro. American advertising is responsible for much of the Negro's current demand that he, too, be allowed to participate in the fulfillment of the American dream.

In the fall of 1948 Medgar entered Alcorn College as a freshman majoring in business administration. It was a compromise, I think, between his refusal to become a teacher and his determination to go to college. He used to talk vaguely about someday having a business of his own, though he never indicated just what kind of business it would be. I know that the idea of being his own boss appealed strongly to him, and he had, of course, seen Negroes in white collar jobs during his summers in Chicago. He may even have met some Chicago Negroes who owned their own businesses, though I never heard him mention it. But certainly Medgar, whatever he knew to be possible in Chicago, was enough of a realist to know that few Negroes in Mississippi owned their own businesses, and he never spoke seriously of leaving Mississippi.

Medgar was not a student at Alcorn College long before he had made a name for himself on the campus. He was a member of the debate team, the college choir, and the football and track teams. For two years he was the editor of the campus newspaper, and in 1951 he edited the yearbook. As a business major, he joined the business club on campus, and through his activity in the campus YMCA he had an opportunity to travel to Millsaps College, a white school in Jackson, where every month campus "Y" groups from the two schools met together for panel discussions on world affairs. By the time Medgar was a senior, his leadership on the Alcorn campus was such that he had been chosen for listing in the annual publication of *Who's Who in American Colleges,* quite an honor for a rural Mississippi Negro at a segregated Mississippi college.

## III

It was years before I pieced together enough of Medgar's childhood and youth to begin to see him as a logical result of all that had happened to him. There are still great gaps that have never been filled. For Medgar was never one to dwell on the past, his own or anyone else's. It was the future that intrigued him, that tantalized him, that drew him, and by the end of his junior year at Alcorn he had begun to include me in his thoughts and dreams of the future.

It was a future, as it turned out, for which my own life had done little to prepare me, a future that, if I could have forseen it, would have struck terror in my heart. For Medgar was right when he charged that I had been overprotected. In particular, I had been protected from knowing even the basic facts about racism in Mississippi.

Vicksburg, where I was born on St. Patrick's Day in 1933, had always had a reputation in Mississippi for good relations between the races. It is hard for me to say today on what this reputation was based. But it was there, bragged about, referred to on special occasions, believed in proudly by the whites and hopefully by the Negroes. It was like a mist that obscured one of the basic realities during all the years of my childhood and youth.

Built on a deep bend in the Mississippi River, steeped in Civil War history, Vicksburg is a city of hills. High on one of them in a frame house on a dirt road in the Negro section of town, my mother, then sixteen, gave birth to me. My father, James Van Dyke Beasley, who drove a delivery truck for a local hardware store, was twenty-eight. The house belonged to my mother's mother, my grandmother Washington.

Before I was a year old, my mother and father had separated. Soon after that, my mother, Mildred Washington Beasley, decided to leave Vicksburg. There must have been family consultations about my fate, but in the end it was my father's mother, my grandmother Beasley, who took me into her home, just across Magnolia Street from where I had been born. It would have been impossible for Grandmother Washington to care for me; she worked for a well-to-do white family and was away all day. My mother apparently agreed that she was too young to take me with her.

Grandmother Beasley, whom I called "Mama" from the moment I began to talk, was a retired schoolteacher, one of the first Negro teachers of her generation to have had college training. She had attended Virginia's Hampton Institute, though she had not been able to finish. Long since divorced from my grandfather, she could devote full time to me while keeping house for my father.

There is nothing in my memory to suggest that I suffered from this early breakup in my family. I can recall only warmth and love and protectiveness from all of the people around me. Nor did it seem strange to me as I grew up that my mother did not live with me. I had an identity as Mrs. Beasley's granddaughter and Mrs. Polk's niece, and the fact that both of them were teachers gave me more than a little status in the Negro community.

Mama's house, where I spent my childhood, sat on top of a steep embankment, many steps above the narrow dusty street of dirt and crushed rock that had been scraped straight up the side of one of Vicksburg's steepest hills. It was a frame house, whitewashed outside, neat and clean within, and as a child it seemed to me enormous. There were two large bedrooms, one for my father, one I shared with Mama, with huge beds with carved headboards and feather mattresses into which I all but disappeared at night. A dresser with a heavy marble top held a pitcher and washbowl.

The living room was also large and, in addition to a big overstuffed sofa and other furniture, it had a bed where Mama's own grandmother—my great-great-grandmother—slept. The dining-room table was round and on the same massive scale as everything else; I remember playing house under its generous roof.

Behind the house there was a privy, a lawn with chinaberry and magnolia trees, and behind the lawn a section fenced off for chickens and a garden. Mama and I spent our evenings pulling weeds and hoeing in the garden, keeping the small patch clean around the cabbages, carrots, lettuce, peas, and okra.

I remember the neighborhood as one of neat houses, many with tin roofs on which rain fell melodiously. It was a neighborhood in which people passed the time of day with each other, in which, each Friday, the fishman would appear with his truck dripping with melting ice to shout, "Fresh fish! Catfish and gasper-goo!" and screen doors would slam and women would come running from all the houses to pick out their supper and have it weighed on the scales.

Mama's grandmother, whom I called Grandma, was a big

woman who had been blind for some years when I first knew her. She could see the glow of our heater, an old-fashioned potbellied stove, but little else, and she spent most of the day in a large rocking chair which became a haven from punishment for me when I had been naughty. I would run to her, and she would gather me into her arms, saying to Mama, "You ain't going to hit this child today." It was a declaration from which there was no appeal.

Grandma had been a slave, and she wore a diamond ring her "Massa" had given her, a ring still being passed down in my family. I never knew her exact age, but she must have been nearly 100 when she died in 1940. Both she and Mama sang their way through most days, and when Grandma was not in her rocker, Mama would often take me in her arms and rock me back and forth singing gospel songs. Her favorite was "Pass Me Not, Oh Gentle Savior," and the sound of that song today is still mixed up for me with the creak of that old rocker and a feeling of warmth and security.

Mama was as white as most white people, with the straight hair we called "poor white folk's hair." The explanation was a common one: a white overseer named McCain had fathered Grandma's son when she was still a slave. The son, who could have passed for white, was Mama's father.

School began for me at the age of five in what was called pre-primer grade at Magnolia High School. The school had all the grades through high school and was called "the crackerbox" because it sat high on one of Vicksburg's hills and looked as though it might topple from its perch at any moment. It was fifteen blocks from home, and I walked from the first day, carrying my lunch in a paper bag up and down the steep hills. On rainy days when the unpaved streets of the Negro section ran with muddy water and the torrents formed ruts so deep that cars couldn't make it up

37

the hills, it was great fun to splash along to school in my galoshes.

At the same time that I began school I started taking piano lessons once a week from my aunt Myrlie Polk. Those trips to her house were like journeys to a different world. She and Uncle John lived in a white frame house in a racially mixed neighborhood "on the right side of the tracks." Uncle John was a graduate of Tougaloo Southern Christian College and was the Negro County Agent of the United States Department of Agriculture for Warren County. Aunt Myrlie was still teaching, and the two of them by virtue of their education and jobs were in the upper bracket of Negro professionals, highly respected by Vicksburg's Negroes and whites alike.

The houses in Aunt Myrlie's neighborhood were all painted and well kept, with landscaped lawns and neat sidewalks, curbs, and paved streets in front. Whites lived on one side of her block and Negroes on the other, and just a block away there were apartment houses where some of the wealthy white families of Vicksburg lived.

Aunt Myrlie's house was impressive inside: a real wool carpet in the living room, very good furniture, a study, two bedrooms, a modern bathroom, a nice kitchen and a garage for Uncle John's black Ford. At the back of the property they had built a small house which they rented, one of the few ways a successful Negro like my uncle could invest his money and get a return.

Uncle John, together with my father, provided a male influence in my young life, and I remember how delightful and irritating Uncle John could be at one and the same time. He sometimes called me "Toad" because of my restless hopping around, and that I didn't like. But every Saturday afternoon he took me downtown with him on his trip to buy groceries, and he never failed to buy me paper dolls and a peanut candy bar. That I liked very much.

My mother's mother, Grandmother Washington, whom I called "Big Mama," worked for a white family named Robinson for as long as I can remember, and the Robinson household was the original source of many of my childhood treasures. Big Mama's day off was Thursday, and each Thursday I would cross the street to visit her. She saved the Robinsons' newspapers every week, and on Thursdays I would read the previous Sunday's funny papers. The Robinsons often gave her food to bring home, and Big Mama and I would have a feast over the comic strips, and sometimes she would bring out a dress that was too small for the Robinsons' daughter, Roseann, and try it on me.

Every Christmas I was invited to the Robinsons' house to play the piano, and this and similar special occasions were always the signal for extensive preparations. I could count at such times on a new dress, bag, shoes, and a new hairdo, which meant a trip to the beauty shop. Beauty shops for Negroes in Vicksburg were quite informal. You sat on a wooden chair in someone's kitchen while the hairdresser parted your hair into small sections. Then, with a metal comb heating on the gas flame of the stove, she put oil on your hair, and finally ran the hot comb through each section. When the curl had succumbed to the heated oil, the hair would be braided into pigtails, and the hairdresser's part of the job was done.

At home Mama and I would cut strips from a brown paper bag, twist them, and set them aside while we took out the pigtails and combed out my hair. Then we'd roll up sections of hair on the strips of paper and tie the strips in a knot. I can remember sleeping on my nose all night to keep from mashing my newly rolled hair.

In the morning it would all be worth-while. I'd take out the paper strips, let the hair fall, and after a combing I would have lovely Shirley Temple curls. No one ever said it, of course—no one would have thought of saying it—but everyone knew we were trying to look like little white girls.

With all of the preparations completed, I was ready for my annual Christmas visit to the Robinsons' house. My grandmother Beasley would help me dress and then, as a special touch, tie an enormous bow in my newly curled hair. Then, my head filled with warnings about keeping clean and behaving properly, I would set out. The hardest part of the journey was the first part; I had to walk carefully in the dusty streets of the Negro section to keep my shoes and my long white stockings clean. Finally, when I reached the paved streets and sidewalks of the white section, I could relax and think about the pleasures to come. I loved walking to the Robinsons', because I felt a perfect lady strolling through the wide, quiet streets of their neighborhood. The homes were large, two-story houses with wide, beautiful lawns and big shade trees. It was like walking through a little girl's dream of the world as it should be.

Big Mama was very fond of the Robinsons, and I guess the feeling was reciprocated, because I can remember Mrs. Robinson saying, "Alice is just like a member of the family." Still, there was one moment of those Christmas visits that I came to resent. Dressed as I was and in that lovely neighborhood on Christmas Day, I hated having to enter the house by the back door. But Big Mama would be there to let me into the kitchen, and, the bad moment over, she would inspect me carefully to make sure I was presentable. Then, at the proper moment, Mrs. Robinson would come into the kitchen and take me into the living room. There were always guests, and she would introduce me to them as Alice's granddaughter.

Then, turning to me and using my grandmother's name for me, she would ask, "Little sister, what are you going to play for us?"

This was my moment, and I made the most of it. I would name the piece and its composer and then give a little history surrounding it, all very solemnly. Finally I would turn to the spinet and play. There was always applause when I finished, and usually there were polite questions about how I was doing in school. Then Mrs. Robinson would lead me to the big Christmas tree and give me a present and a bag of gumdrops. I would thank everyone, excuse myself, and go back to the kitchen where, after a few minutes with Big Mama, I'd say goodbye and hurry home to open my gift.

Except for an insurance man who came every week to collect fifty cents from Mama, the Robinsons were about the only white people I knew as a child. The insurance man, Mr. Caldenhead, was a tall, heavy, balding man who would greet me each week with the same question: "Hello, little girl, have you had your orange juice today?" He would come to the door and shout, "Annie!" to my grandmother, and she would come and pay him for her burial insurance.

I knew, of course, that we were different from whites, the obvious differences being skin color and hair texture. But the differences that mattered were those of privilege. The whites had parks, a library, a swimming pool, a YMCA, and the choice seats at the movies and on the buses. On the buses the seating was most annoying, for each bus had only four short seats and one long one behind the sign that read "Colored." All of the seats ahead of the sign were reserved for whites, whether there were any whites on the bus or not. Often the seats in the Negro section would be fillled and we would be jammed together standing in the aisle behind the sign, while the front of the bus would be all but deserted. Later, when I was in high school and rode the bus to school on rainy days, the driver would pack us in and shout at us to move back, though the front of the bus was empty. One driver in particular seemed to take delight in jamming us all toward the rear of the bus and then slamming on the brakes at each stop to make us fall forward.

But for all the imposed differences, for all the indignities, for all the blatant discrimination designed to point up our differences from whites, there was no one among the Negro community who protested openly. In my home the subject was never discussed. There were not only no complaints; there seemed complete acceptance. And if there were resentment of the sort that I, myself, occasionally felt, it was generally unspoken, as was my own, and almost always directed against an individual, like the bus driver, instead of the system. No one seemed even aware that it was the whole system of segregation that made the acts of people like the bus driver possible.

In 1943, when I was ten, my uncle John died. Being a veteran of World War I, he was entitled to a plot in the National Cemetery in Vicksburg, and Aunt Myrlie made sure his wish to be buried there was carried out. She and Uncle John had never had children, and since my great-great-grandmother, Grandma, had died three years earlier, Mama and I moved in with Aunt Myrlie.

She must have been about forty then, a vigorous, intelligent woman still actively teaching and still going back to college in the summertime to complete her work toward a Bachelor's degree. She was the organist at the Mount Heroden Baptist Church and an active clubwoman. She had a good head for business, and after Uncle John died and Mama and I went there to live, she took over the management of everything from household budgets to the rental of the small house at the back of the property.

From the moment we moved in with her, Aunt Myrlie took over as a sort of second mother to me. There was apparently never any question of her marrying again. She grieved actively for Uncle John, whom she called "Hon," for years and was forever saying she'd never find another like him.

Aunt Myrlie and Mama took me everywhere with them. Between them, they soon had me appearing on all sorts of programs. If I wasn't speaking or reciting poetry or singing, I was playing piano solos, either at school, church, or some local club. At each performance they were always there, sitting proudly and stiffly until my turn came and then, invariably, wiping their eyes and sniffling when it was over. At home they were both happy people, and the three of us had great fun at mealtimes. Often we would end a meal laughing until we cried, and it would only be with great effort that we composed ourselves enough to clear away the dishes.

As for boys, Aunt Myrlie and Mama were more lenient with me than the parents of most of my girl friends. At thirteen, I was permitted to have a boy come by to see me. We could sit together on the steps of the front porch for as much as half an hour before Mama would appear with the news that I had something important to do inside. If that didn't work, she would ask without much subtlety if the boy didn't think it was time for him to leave.

The Friday-night dances at the high school were another story. Not until I was sixteen was I even permitted to go. The few boy friends I had before that were always football players, and when there was a football banquet at the end of the season or a big prom or something really special, Aunt

Myrlie and Mama would sometimes let me go with an escort. They would put the two of us into a taxi and send us off to the school. Ten minutes later, Aunt Myrlie would follow in a second taxi. I had no sooner arrived at the high school and said hello to my friends than she would be there, making sure I had arrived safely and then settling down with other watchful parents for the entire evening. When the affair was over, Aunt Myrlie would sometimes save the extra taxi fare by riding home with my escort and me.

The year that I was thirteen the Negro community of Vicksburg was shaken up by the arrival at our church of a new minister, the Reverend Kelly Miller Smith, and his lovely young wife, Mamye, both graduates of Howard University in Washington, D.C. Aunt Myrlie had by this time built a second small house on her property and the Smiths rented it.

Reverend Smith's most radical innovation was a series of joint meetings of our church's Baptist Young People's Union with the youth group of a local white church. How he arranged it I never knew, but once a month we would meet together for religious training and discussion, first in their church and then in ours. We would sit wherever there were seats with no conscious attempt at segregation. Those were the first inter-racial meetings I ever attended, and there was a certain excitement in that alone. I can remember sensing some self-consciousness on both sides, and unfortunately we never really got to know each other, for the meetings continued only a couple of months. I never learned what happened, but I recall rumblings of concern among some of the Negro church members. I suspect there were more than rumblings at the white church. Vicksburg, with all its pride in its good relations between the races, was clearly not ready for so radical an experiment.

I had always been a good student, but it was in high

school that I first began to take real pleasure in my studies. It was also about that time that I began to read avidly. When Aunt Myrlie bought me *The Book of Knowledge*, I read the entire set of volumes during one summer's vacation.

At sixteen I was at last permitted dates without a chaperone. It was a long-awaited emancipation. Now Eugene Broome, the six-foot-two-inch high school football star who was then my boy friend, could walk me to the soda fountain where we entered through the door marked "Colored" to sit on the "Colored" side drinking our sodas and watching the white kids across from us drink theirs. Or we would go with our friends on a hayride or picnic in the national park, or to the movies, where again there was a special door for Negroes and a special section—the upper balcony. Sometimes there was a school dance. Whatever we did, unless it was a very special occasion, I had to be home by ten o'clock. Mama waited up for me, and she waited in the kitchen where she could look straight through the glass pane of the front door. If there was to be a goodnight kiss after one of these dates, it had to be consummated before we turned the corner coming home.

Graduation from high school meant for most of my seventy-five classmates the end of formal education. For some, there must have been a feeling of deprivation and loss. But for most, probably, it was an end long foreseen and long accepted. Higher education for Negroes in Mississippi was, and still is, the rare exception, and for the fortunate few to whom it was even a possibility, it meant, generally, an attempt at a teaching career.

With few exceptions—the ministry, medicine, dentistry, the law—teaching was the only profession really open to Negroes, the only career for which college could prepare you. The idea of going to college simply to become better educated was a fantasy few Mississippi Negroes could afford to indulge.

Graduation was both an end and a beginning for me. I can still feel the excitement and anticipation of that Sunday in May 1950 as we marched in our maroon caps and gowns at the baccalaureate service. The next evening brought formal graduation, and again I was second in my class. I fought down a nervous fluttering in my stomach as I played the piano solo, "*Valse Brilliante*," by Mona Zaka, and Mama and Aunt Myrlie cried on schedule. It was an emotional evening for everyone; even our school superintendent, Mr. Cooper, the only white person present, looked inordinately proud of "his Negroes" as he handed out the diplomas.

I didn't know it then, of course, because I had no basis of comparison, but the speeches given at our graduation were quite different from those of the usual American high school commencement. There was no talk of good citizenship, no suggestion that on our shoulders might rest the future of our community, our state, and our nation. There were no exhortations to continue our educations, whether in college or on our own. No one hinted that in our graduating class there might be a future President of the United States, a future senator, a future governor. And no one said that our achievements would be limited only by our desires and our willingness to work for what we wanted. No one could. For all of us understood, in our bones if not in our minds, that we were Negroes and that this was Mississippi.

—— IV ——

It is one of the ironies of my life that I would probably
never have met Medgar but for the way Mississippi cheats its
Negroes. I had planned for years to major in music in college.
Encouraged by two of my four piano teachers, spurred by
years of applause at recitals, driven by a deep love of music,
it was a goal toward which my whole life had long been
pointed.

Two of my teachers had been graduates of Fisk University's excellent school of music in Nashville, and while
I knew that Aunt Myrlie's modest income would not permit
sending me to a private school like Fisk without some help,
I also knew of Mississippi's system of state aid for Negroes
seeking an education not provided within the state. On paper,
it was simplicity itself: if you wanted to be a doctor or a
lawyer and the state provided no such courses for Negroes,
they would pay your way to an out-of-state school. The
idea, of course, was to prevent Negroes from applying to
Mississippi's white colleges where these courses were offered,
while at the same time seeming to comply with the Supreme
Court's "separate but equal" decision on public education.
And there were conditions: that you agreed to return to

Mississippi to work and that you pay back at least part of the money.

I knew that neither of Mississippi's state colleges for Negroes—Alcorn and Jackson State—offered a major in music, and this, it seemed to me, made me clearly eligible. It was with full confidence in its acceptance that I submitted my application to the state's Board of Higher Learning. At the same time I wrote to both of the Negro colleges asking for confirmation of my understanding that they did not offer a music major, a necessary formality.

It was not to be. I did receive a copy of a letter from Alcorn reporting to the state board that they offered only a minor in music. Then came a letter from the Negro president of Jackson State. He wrote that he thought his college offered enough music for what I would want and need. Soon after that came a denial from the state board of my application for aid.

Aunt Myrlie and Mama accepted this rejection without complaint. I seethed with resentment as at a betrayal. For the president of a Negro college, knowing as a Negro the problems of getting a decent education in Mississippi, to decide without even meeting me what I might want and need in the way of education—for such a man to rule, in effect, that I could have no more than what his school offered—seemed to me outrageous.

I must have known that as a Negro employee of the white Board of Higher Learning he undoubtedly took orders from his white superiors. I could have guessed, had I been more sophisticated in such matters, that he bent over backward to cater to their wishes. And I should certainly have known that the state of Mississippi wished to grant as few requests for state aid from Negroes as possible. But in my anger and hurt I could see no farther than the Negro college president. It did not occur to me that the ultimate cause of my problem was the complete segregation of Mississippi's schools.

School segregation was simply a fact of life. I had never heard it seriously challenged by anyone. And as I slowly recovered from my rage, I swallowed my disappointment and chose, reluctantly, to go to Alcorn, where I would major in education and take a minor in music. I met Medgar my first day on the campus.

I tried, during that first year at Alcorn, to keep my growing involvement with my "wise and worldly" veteran as much as possible a secret from Aunt Myrlie and Mama. Medgar himself was the first to spoil my plans. Away from school with the football team that fall, he found himself near Vicksburg and, on the spur of the moment, telephoned my home. My grandmother answered the phone. After identifying himself as Medgar Evers, which meant nothing to Mama, he proceeded to tell her he was my boy friend. The shock wave soon reached me at school with demands for an explanation. It was impossible to explain Medgar's call, and I didn't try. I don't think I could explain it today. But I filled in as few gaps as possible and attempted to quiet things down. Meanwhile, though, Aunt Myrlie was making quiet inquiries among her many friends on the campus, and inevitably she learned that Medgar was a veteran. That required more explanations. Both Mama and Aunt Myrlie characterized Medgar, whom they had not yet met, as bold and brash, and after his telephone call I found it difficult to disagree.

It was during Easter vacation that Medgar sprang his second surprise. We had both gone home to our families with no plans to see each other, and then, one day, Medgar telephoned along the road from Decatur to Vicksburg. He was hitchhiking down to see me, he said, and he wanted to meet my family. When he arrived in Vicksburg, he took a room at the Negro YMCA and then came over. About all I can remember of that visit is a sense of nervous expectation that with each word Medgar spoke some kind of explosion was bound to occur. The explosion never came, but after he left, Aunt Myrlie and Mama delivered their expected verdict. While they were obviously impressed with Medgar and didn't deny his many good qualities, they declared emphatically that he was much too mature, much too worldly, much too experienced—in short, too old for me. I was advised to find someone closer to my own age, someone who, as Mama mysteriously put it, wouldn't take advantage of me.

Once again I felt forced into secrecy, and by late spring I was busily plotting some way to spend the summer in Chicago, where I knew Medgar would be. I knew I could justify a trip North as a means of earning money for school and that there were two possible places I might go. My father had left Vicksburg during the war, had spent more than a year in India with the Army, and had settled in Detroit when he got out of the service. I had not seen him in almost five years. I knew I could easily arrange to stay with him. The other, and far more interesting possibility lay in the fact that my mother's half-sister, Aunt Frances, lived in Chicago with her husband, Uncle Tommy Cage. I decided I would rather stay with them, and began writing appropriate letters to Aunt Frances.

The last week of school arrived with nothing settled, and I was in a panic. The idea of the entire summer going by without seeing Medgar was not only sad but a little frightening. I could not forget the warnings I had had about Medgar's fickle nature. And Chicago, whatever Medgar said about it, sounded glamorous and exciting and wicked to me.

The day before his last exam Medgar had a telephone call from one of his sisters in Chicago. Mary Ruth, the youngest and Medgar's favorite, was in the hospital with a brain tumor. The doctor would operate the next day. Medgar went through his last exam in a daze. When it was over, he packed and loaded the car for the trip to Chicago. We were saying goodbye at the dormitory when the second call came through. Mary Ruth had died after the operation, and the last person she had asked for was Medgar.

Medgar turned from the telephone a stricken man. He told me the news in a strangled voice, then broke down completely. It was the first time I had seen him cry, and suddenly, with my arms around him, consoling him, I knew with complete and utter finality that Aunt Myrlie and Mama were wrong. Medgar was not too old or mature for me. If he were, how could I now feel so much the older of us? How could I feel so protective about him? For a few minutes, before he got into the car and drove off, I experienced for the first time with Medgar a genuine sense of being needed. It was enough to convince me that somehow or other I had to follow him to Chicago.

I had been home only a day or two when Aunt Frances wrote, enclosing my train fare to Chicago. In the same mail was a letter from Medgar. When Mama saw the postmark on Medgar's letter, her mind began clicking like an adding machine. Within minutes she had arrived at an answer: to come with me. All my plans had been based on going alone, and I had mixed feelings about this abrupt decision, but I kept them to myself out of fear that the whole trip might be canceled.

A day or so later, friends drove the two of us to Jackson and dropped us at Union Station, where in a dirty segregated waiting room we waited several hours for the Illinois Central train to Chicago. The room was crowded with Negroes headed North, their belongings carried in battered suitcases tied with rope and pasteboard boxes held together with twine. They looked like refugees, most of them, carrying their lunches in greasy brown paper bags and shoe boxes. When the train finally came, we all crowded to the platform where conductors and porters hustled us to the Jim Crow cars in the rear of the train with shouts of "Colored folks to the rear!" We rode the crowded, stuffy coach all the way to Chicago, eating the food we had brought along with us.

Uncle Tommy met Mama and me at the Illinois Central Station at two o'clock the next morning. I had read and heard about Chicago all my life, and I was both eager to see it and a little frightened at some of the things I had heard. As Uncle Tommy drove us to his apartment in the 2900 block of South Wabash Avenue, I peered from the window at a world of bright lights and grimy apartment buildings while Mama chattered away about relatives.

Aunt Frances and Uncle Tommy lived just two blocks from 31st Street and South Wabash, known in the neighborhood as "the bucket of blood" for the number of Negroes who had been killed and injured there in Saturday-night brawls. It was a rough, dirty neighborhood, and I disliked it immediately. Later, when I saw it in the daylight, I was revolted. I have never seen such dirty dirt.

Mama and I stayed with Aunt Frances and Uncle Tommy for a week, and Aunt Frances took time off from her job to help me find work. Eventually I found a job with an automobile sales and service company on South Michigan Avenue, four blocks from the apartment. I worked there all summer, typing and doing clerical work. Meanwhile, Aunt Frances had found me a room in the apartment of the woman who lived just above her, and, with these details settled, Mama seemed willing to leave me in Aunt Frances' care. She took the train to Detroit to stay with my father. If I had had any illusions about a summer free of restraints, they were soon gone, for Aunt Frances proved as watchful and cautious about me as Mama and Aunt Mrylie had ever been.

With Mama on her way to Detroit, I wrote Medgar a postcard, telling him where I was. He telephoned a few days later. We were both working, and we talked on the telephone more than we saw each other, but at least once a week for the rest of the summer we spent a day together, usually Saturday or Sunday. The first time Medgar came for me, I introduced him to Aunt Frances. She was clearly impressed with him, I thought, but she didn't let that interfere with the familiar lecture about taking good care of me and getting me home on time.

I met Medgar's sisters, Elizabeth and Eva, that summer. At my request, Medgar took me to outdoor concerts in beautiful Grant Park. At his, I went to see my first stock-car race. We visited the Art Institute and went to the movies, sitting on the main floor instead of the balcony. One day we went to the beach.

I had never learned to swim, there being no pools for Negroes in Vicksburg, and it took some persuading for Medgar to get me to go into the water at all. Once he had, he coaxed me out farther and farther, promising to stay by my side. He assured me he could easily teach me to swim, and with more doubt than faith, I finally allowed him to hold me in a swimming position while he lectured me on what I was to do. Then, just as I had begun to believe I could trust him, he ended the lecture, said, "Go ahead," and let go.

I sank immediately. Terrified, I did all the wrong things. My arms thrashed, my legs struck out trying to find solid ground, and my eyes snapped shut. I was sure I was drowning until, suddenly, I felt sand under one foot. An instant later I was standing up coughing and sputtering furiously at Medgar. He was calmly lecturing me on the mistakes I had made.

Later that afternoon we dressed and walked to a near-by park. Medgar continued to apologize for having frightened me, and eventually I realized I had not really been in much danger of drowning. The incident provided both of us with an opportunity to kiss and make up, and we did that always with great relish.

But if there were happy and tranquil moments with Medgar that summer, there was always a solid week of work between them, and during those long weeks I came to dislike Chicago intensely. I hated to walk to work through the terrible section of the South Side where Aunt Francis lived. There were drunks to be stepped over every morning, and in the evening on the way home there were men who leered and muttered obscene remarks. The mere size of Chicago frightened me, and I realized on those short walks to and from work that in a city like Chicago you were always alone. You were alone from the moment you left your house until you got home, alone wherever you were unless you were with friends. The strangers that surrounded you were not only strangers, they were also indifferent. Strangers in a small town care about you, either because you belong there too, or because you don't. In either case, they are not indifferent. But in Chicago everyone was indifferent, I think, because no one belonged. Millions of people lived in Chicago, it seemed to me, but it was no one's home town.

By the first week in August, Medgar and I had begun talking of marriage. I knew that Mama and Aunt Myrlie would object, so we discussed being married secretly in

Chicago. When that seemed to both of us too abrupt, we talked of being married during the next Christmas vacation from school or after Medgar graduated. We never decided anything definite, but we both knew that the decision had been made and that only a date remained to be fixed.

Money was a prime consideration. Medgar's G.I. Bill and football scholarship at Alcorn were running out, and he needed his savings to see him through the final year. If we married before returning to school, the football scholarship would end immediately. I wondered what would happen to my own scholarship. We both knew our parents couldn't support us in school, and we never questioned our determination to finish college. So the discussion went on and on, whenever we were together, never ending in a decision.

For me, it was a happy discussion, free of any nagging doubts. My grandmother had always told me to go to God in prayer before I made an important decision, and she had said many times that if I asked God for help in choosing a husband, I wouldn't go wrong. She admitted this was something she herself had not done, and I think she felt that this was why her marriage had not worked out.

I had prayed for months about Medgar and me, and by this time I was sure that we were right for each other. I had no illusions about the way Mama and Aunt Myrlie would react to my marrying at the age of eighteen, but I knew that, in some ways at least, they were prepared for it. They knew that I was serious about Medgar; I couldn't have hidden it from them if I had tried. In any case, I had made up my mind to marry Medgar. I had always been an obedient child, but I knew in my heart that this was one time that, if necessary, I would disobey.

And then one day Medgar telephoned, and I knew from

his voice that something was wrong. "I have to see you, Myrlie. I want to talk to you."

I had just washed my hair, and Medgar was the last person I wanted to have see me in the next few hours. "What's the matter?" I asked, afraid, almost, to hear his answer.

With the water from my hair dripping on the floor, I stood and listened, little waves of shock going through me as he spoke. "I want to talk to you," he said somberly. "I've been thinking about us. I think we should bring this thing to an end. May I come over?"

By the time he had finished I was shattered. I saw my whole life disappearing, all of my plans destroyed, my future meaningless. Somehow I managed to tell him he could come. When I put the phone down, I felt exhausted, as drained of energy as if my life's blood had dripped to the floor with the water from my hair.

Forcing myself to move, I tied a towel around my head and put on some make-up. Then I waited, pacing the floor of my tiny room. It was almost an hour before Medgar arrived, and in that hour my heart broke a hundred times. I couldn't imagine what had happened, what I had done or said, what had caused him to make such a decision. But I couldn't fool myself either. I knew Medgar, and he wasn't kidding. Everything—everything was over.

When he finally arrived, I let him into the living room of the apartment, my heart still skipping beats. I asked him all the questions I had asked myself, waiting for him. He was very serious, and that nearly destroyed me. He asked me to sit down, and I collapsed in a chair.

"Myrlie," he said solemnly, and my heart ached just hearing him pronounce my name, "I've been thinking. I don't want to make a mistake about this. I don't know if you're ready to get married. You know you're too young, really. I think it would probably be best if you started dating other people and saw more of the world before you settled down. I want to release you from any agreement we may have."

I sat there motionless, feeling that if I moved I would surely die. His words alone were like a sentence and the formality with which he spoke gave them a sort of finality beyond argument. He was silent a long time before I could speak.

"Is there someone else?"

He shook his head. "No. There's no one else. I've been thinking about you. It's for your benefit."

That made me angry, and I found words to fit my anger. "How kind of you to think of me! Have you thought of me enough to wonder how I feel about all this? Have you even thought of asking me? Why don't you ask me if I feel ready to settle down? Why don't you ask me if I want to date other men?"

My anger sparked nothing in him. "All right," he asked quietly, "do you?"

I spoke then as though I were delivering a speech long since prepared and practiced. In a way, I suppose, I was, for it was much the same speech I would have made for Mama and Aunt Myrlie had they opposed my marriage to Medgar. I went into some detail about what I wanted in a husband, and I said I had found these things in him. I said I had no desire to look elsewhere for anything, because I had found what I wanted. And I insisted that he could not make decisions for me but only for himself, that if he were concealing a change in his feelings for me and hiding behind the excuse of my age, that was cowardice.

By the time I had finished, I was nearly overcome with emotion, and I got up to go into my room before I burst into tears in front of him. Hurt and angry and empty inside, I reached the bedroom door before Medgar caught me by my shoulders, turned me around, and, without a word, placed a tiny box in my hand. I stared at it without moving, fighting against tears, too stunned to know what it meant. When he saw I wasn't going to open it, he opened the box himself. Inside was an engagement ring.

I couldn't speak. Medgar took the ring from the box and put it on my finger. I watched as though I were watching someone else. "I'm sorry I can't afford a more expensive ring, Myrlie," he said softly. "This is the best I can do. But along with it goes all the love I have."

I have never felt quite like I did at that moment. My whole body began to shake. Medgar pulled me to him and asked me what on earth was wrong. I couldn't speak. Not then. I was too torn by conflicting emotions, too spent emotionally, too shattered by all that had happened in the space of an hour. I was furious and deliriously happy, hurt and surprised, shocked and wounded, overcome that one person could do to another what he had done to me. In the tiny corner of my mind that was still functioning as he held me tightly and I let myself go slack in his arms, I knew that I would never forgive him for the last hour. And in that same corner of my mind I knew that I would never let him go.

—— V ——

In the few days between that unforgettable hour and Medgar's return to Alcorn for early football practice I wore my ring only when I was alone. It was a simple enough ring with a single small diamond, but to me it was the most priceless possession imaginable. After Medgar left Chicago, it became even more than that—a tangible promise between us.

The summer about over, I quit my job and spent my last week in Chicago visiting friends from Vicksburg and Alcorn. Then I took a train to Detroit to meet my grandmother and visit my father. Afraid to wear the ring on the train, I packed it carefully at one end of my wardrobe trunk and shipped the trunk to Detroit.

I hadn't seen my father for nearly five years, and we had a joyful reunion at the station. At his home, a basement apartment in a two-story frame house, there was a reunion with Mama. This was a tearful one, though we had been separated only ten or twelve weeks. But Mama had something on her mind besides her joy at seeing me again and, her tears dried, she began pressing for details of my summer. I had written her each week, but I went over the main events again, carefully avoiding any mention of Medgar. Finally she could stand the suspense no longer, and she asked directly about him.

"Oh, Medgar went back to school for football practice a week ago," I said as casually as I could.

"But you saw him this summer, didn't you?" she asked.

"Oh yes. We went out some."

"And how did you get along?" she asked finally, annoyed at my lack of information on the one subject about which she wanted information.

"Oh, we're still getting along," I said and changed the subject. I don't think I fooled her at all.

I liked Detroit much better than Chicago. There were fewer of the tall, grimy apartment buildings that had made Chicago seem so grim and more of the two-story frame houses I associated with Vicksburg. The neighborhood where my father lived was much cleaner than the South Side of Chicago, and seeing him after all these years made everything seem brighter.

Two days after I arrived in Detroit, the Railway Express Company called. My trunk had arrived, they said, but it had been damaged. One end had been knocked out, and it was possible that something might be missing. Would I please let them know as soon as it was delivered? I couldn't conceal my panic about the ring. Both my father and Mama were puzzled by my reaction, which must have seemed wildly out of proportion to the news. When I insisted that we go and get the trunk immediately, they pointed out that we had no way of getting it home, that it was probably already on its way. My father assured me that we could always buy a new one, and Mama nodded in agreement.

"It's not the trunk that's important!" I said impatiently.

"What is it then?" Mama asked curiously.

I could hold it in no longer. "My ring was in it."

"What ring?"

With difficulty I caught myself. "Just a ring," I said. "A ring that was given to me."

Now they were both as anxious as I to see the trunk. When it finally arrived at the house, my heart sank. The end in which I had so carefully hidden my ring was the same end that was crushed. I ran to open it and began pulling things out. At the very edge of the crushed end, right where a good shake would have tumbled it out, was the box with the ring. My relief was so great that the secret, if it was one, was out. I had to show it to them. They were both greatly distressed.

I explained that Medgar and I had set no definite date to marry, that it was something we were determined to do with their permission, but as I chattered on, making this time a speech for which I was not prepared, the two of them just sat there, shaking their heads. Mama couldn't bring herself even to talk about it for several days, but I defiantly put the ring on my finger and I didn't take it off.

When she was finally ready to talk about it, Mama said I was making a terrible mistake, that I was too young, that Medgar was too experienced, that I would be used. It was a thing she had often said, and I never really knew what she meant. I guess I didn't really want to know, for I never asked for an explanation. She was convinced that my grades would go down, and when she had finished with her catalogue of the disasters in store for me, she picked up the telephone and called Aunt Myrlie with the awful news.

A few days later we were home, and Aunt Myrlie and I had a long talk. She was much calmer than Mama and my father had been, and she asked me, finally, if I were sure I was doing the right thing. When I said yes, she seemed satisfied. "Well, Baby," she said, "you've always been a good girl, and if this is something you really want, I'll stick by you.

Whenever you and Medgar are ready, you let me know and I'll give you a church wedding." After that, all of my conversations about Medgar and marriage were with Aunt Myrlie.

I had saved about a hundred dollars from my summer's work, and I turned it over to Aunt Myrlie and Mama for safekeeping before I went back to school. At Alcorn, word about Medgar and me was the big campus news, and we were both assailed by questions. Remembering our weekend arguments of the previous year, nearly all of our friends predicted that the engagement wouldn't last. And, strangely enough, that crazy pattern of breaking up on Friday night and making up on Sunday began again almost immediately. Over the next few weeks that little ring was passed back and forth so many times I don't think it knew where it belonged, in Medgar's pocket or on my finger.

But our disagreements were never serious, and I think we both knew that. We argued about everything and about nothing: how an article should have been written in the school newspaper, how much time I had spent chatting with two boys from Vicksburg, what Medgar was doing walking between classes with another girl. I was usually the one to walk away, after formally returning the ring.

In fact, neither of us dated anyone else, and we got along wonderfully—too well, really. We needed something to argue about, something to put spice in our relationship. And in the long periods when we weren't arguing, we talked about when we would get married. It was still chiefly a question of money.

We even had an argument about money that fall. Medgar collected students' clothes for a dry cleaner in Port Gibson, and one Friday before leaving on a football trip he asked me to take care of about a hundred dollars he had collected.

That would have been fine, but he felt it necessary to add that I was not to spend a penny of it. I felt insulted and said so. I gave him back the money and told him to find someone else to keep it for him if he didn't trust me.

Medgar had always been cautious about money. When we first started dating, he had said that he didn't spend money on women. It turned out to be all too true. I think he took me to dinner just once in all the time we were going together on campus. But he had also said, when we finally began talking of marriage, that when we were married, everything he had would be mine. That, too, turned out to be true.

Though we were engaged and I wore my ring on the campus, Medgar and I were limited by the college rules to two dates a week. There were no rules against studying together, though, and we spent many hours at that. Mama had predicted that we would forget all about our studies and concentrate on each other, and both Medgar and I took this as a challenge to make the best possible grades. I began typing his papers and doing research for him, and he helped me with my toughest subject, mathematics. By Thanksgiving time we had decided to be married at Christmas. Medgar's football scholarship would end after the first semester anyway, and I had found that mine would continue even if I married.

After days of calculating, we decided we could barely make it on our savings, Medgar's job with the cleaner, his G.I. Bill, and what he made driving students various places in his old station wagon. I volunteered to help by taking in typing. We had checked into the cost of Vet City, the off-campus barracks-type apartments for married veterans, and we found it beyond our meager means. But we also found that some couples shared the two-bedroom apartments. If we could make such an arrangement, we could get by. When we left for home before Thanksgiving, I gave Medgar flat orders to stay away from Vicksburg. I wanted to break the news to Mama and Aunt Myrlie by myself, and I did.

Mama was furious. She said she thought we would at least have waited until the end of the school year. With Aunt Myrlie, it was different. She accepted our decision and began immediately to plan for the wedding. Medgar and I had decided on Christmas Eve, and the day after I got home, Aunt Myrlie and I went to the printers to order announcements. From the printers, we went to The Valley, Vickburg's main department store, where we picked out my wedding gown.

It was the most expensive dress I had ever bought, and trying it on, having it fitted, knowing it could not be returned once we had ordered it, I was suddenly overwhelmed by doubts. I knew that I wanted to marry Medgar, but I knew, too, that I could never take him for granted. Remembering his fantastic proposal to me, I shuddered to think what he might do about the wedding. I knew he was a popular young man, and I just couldn't be sure. But the fitting went on, and I concealed my qualms as much as possible from Aunt Myrlie.

I think that Medgar, too, must have had some second thoughts during that short vacation period, because he telephoned one day to ask me if I was positive I wanted to go ahead. With Medgar, my answer was immediate and direct. I was. I left no room for doubt with him.

Back at Alcorn after Thanksgiving, Medgar and I picked up the routine of school. Now there were no arguments, and the ring stayed on my finger. We discussed a short and inexpensive honeymoon. Medgar had investigated and learned of several decent places for Negroes on the Gulf Coast, places where we could stay for a week. Eventually we decided that our tiny bit of money should not be spent on anything so frivolous. Instead, we would visit relatives. I had yet to meet his parents anyway. And then, just before Christmas vacation began, we found a couple from Vicksburg willing to share their two-bedroom apartment in Vet City with us, and we both left school feeling that a run of good luck had begun for us.

Back in Vicksburg four days before the wedding, I found Mama adamant and unresigned. I'm afraid that in the press of activity I just ignored her. Wedding gifts were pouring in, and I tried to keep ahead of them with thank-you-notes. My wedding dress was ready, and when I went to try it on, I was torn between a feeling of joy at its beauty and one of fear that something terrible would happen to prevent my ever wearing it. I guess my doubts about Medgar remained with me right up until the wedding itself, because when he and his mother were two hours late arriving from Decatur the day before, I nearly went into shock imagining all the things that might have happened.

Medgar's mother stayed with us, and I fell in love with her at first sight. My own mother came from Yazoo City, and my aunt arrived from Chicago, and then, all at once, everyone was there and the wedding was upon us.

Among my friends, there were a few that Medgar didn't entirely approve of. They were, in his view, a little too sophisticated. He had often expressed his fears that I might come under the influence of someone who might see that I learned too much about life. He liked me, he used to say, as I was: young and inexperienced. He felt that this way he could bring me up to be the kind of wife he wanted. Usually this sort of thing was said in at least a half-joking manner, but there was never really any question of its being a joke. Medgar meant every word of it. In a way, he was as protective of me as my grandmother, and as fearful of my losing my innocence. There were times when I saw the two of them as unconscious allies, and I enjoyed tormenting Medgar with the thought that I might just know a little more than he thought I did.

Remembering the events of my wedding day, I still find it all hard to believe. I woke that morning with puffy eyes, nervous, unable to eat. It got worse during the day. When I bathed before putting on my wedding dress, I found my body covered by an itching, stinging rash.

An hour before the wedding, it began to rain, altering everyone's plans for getting to the church. In the midst of the confusion, with Mama breaking into tears every minute or so, I managed to dress. Medgar's mother, who had made friends immediately with my family and had taken over the kitchen, was the only one who remained calm.

When it was time for me to leave for the church, a look in the mirror convinced me the whole thing should be canceled. Aunt Myrlie came to my rescue. "You look beautiful, Baby," she said. "No one will even notice the rash. It will probably disappear before the service. Everything is going to be all right. You and Medgar will make it just fine. You'll have problems; everybody does. But I know you'll have a happy marriage. Now stop worrying and be happy."

As though to prove her right, the rain stopped as we started for the church. I crouched in the back seat of a friend's car all the way to keep from sitting and mussing my newly pressed wedding dress. The church was beautiful, a hazy mixture of flowers, candles, and people dressed in their best, listening to the lovely voices of the soloists singing "Oh Promise Me!" and "The Lord's Prayer."

We sent word that we were ready to Medgar, his best man, Julius Ward, and the minister, and then everything fell apart again. Back came word that the wedding ring had been lost! Walking up the back stairs to the church, Medgar had let it slip from his fingers. It had dropped to the stairs and fallen through a crack to the ground below. The three men were out with flashlights searching the ground under the steps.

Before I had time to disintegrate completely, the ring was found and I faced the moment I had dreaded for days. Because my father had been unable to come from Detroit, Mama was to give me away at the altar. But I would have to make the long walk down the aisle to the altar alone. I think it was only the solemn tones of the wedding march and a sense of pressure from the procession I knew was behind me that kept me going—that and the visible nervousness of Medgar, waiting for me.

There was a reception in the church basement after the wedding, and Medgar and I stayed long enough to greet the guests and for me to throw my bouquet. Then, with Julius and Rebecca Green, my maid of honor and best friend at Alcorn, we drove back to my house to change clothes. We found the house locked. None of us had a key. Julius drove back to the church and returned to say that both Mama and Aunt Myrlie had left their keys in the locked house.

Medgar ran next door and recruited a small boy whom he boosted through a bathroom window. My heart stopped as I heard him slip and hit his head against the tub. Then he cried out, and I knew he was at least conscious. In the house a moment later, we rubbed his head and thanked him. He left as Aunt Myrlie, Mama, my mother, and Medgar's mother appeared.

Somehow, in the midst of all the confusion, with a feeling that I wanted nothing so much as to lie down and scream, to send Medgar home and let the whole world forget me, I managed to change to my traveling clothes. In a daze I said goodbye and got into the car with Medgar, Julius, and

Rebecca. Fifteen minutes later we were back at the house. Medgar had forgotten his wallet. The look on my grandmother's face when he reappeared at the door was more expressive than words. She was sure the marriage had already failed.

The drive to Jackson in Medgar's station wagon was uneventful. We dropped Julius and Rebecca at the bus station to catch buses home for Christmas. Then Medgar took me to Jackson's finest hotel for Negroes. My heart sank when I saw it: a poorly lighted, dingy, two-story house in a Negro section of town. Walking in, I tried hard to conceal a feeling of shame and embarrassment. Inside, I felt the eyes of people in the lobby probing us, questioning whether we were newlyweds or, worse, not married at all.

The bridal suite, which Medgar had reserved, was not ready. Medgar didn't argue. I think he felt, too, an enormous need to get out of the lobby and be alone. Taken to a room on the first floor, we unpacked quickly, not looking at each other. Finished, we turned, caught each other's eyes, and laughed, the tension of the day suddenly broken. We were in each other's arms when a knock came at the door. The bridal suite was now ready.

We packed and moved, to find a maid still making up the room. For what seemed hours, we sat across from each other, not speaking, while she slowly finished her work. Then, at last, we were alone. We spent part of the night applying medicine to my rash and listening to the couple next door argue and fight.

We stayed in Jackson two days and then drove to Yazoo City to visit my mother on the first leg of our economy wedding trip to the homes of relatives. The next stop was Decatur, where I saw Medgar's home and met his father. Mrs. Evers took me in as though I were another daughter, and there was never a moment's feeling of strangeness or unfamiliarity. Within minutes of our arrival, I was introduced to the full majesty of Jessie Evers' cooking, and I knew what a formidable job of cooking for Medgar lay ahead of me.

The Evers' house, with all the improvements made since the war, was large and comfortable. Though the street was unpaved, the lawn was green and well kept, and the house was nicely furnished with fairly new furniture. There was a large living room, its old fireplace closed up now by a gas heater. There were a dining room, four bedrooms, one with a working fireplace, a bathroom, a kitchen, and a breakfast nook. The old barn was gone, though there were still chickens and a couple of ducks, and Medgar's mother still maintained a small garden for vegetables.

Medgar's pride in his home and family was obvious, and during the two days we were there, I was inspected by friends and relatives with both friendliness and curiosity. There was, I learned, some feeling in Decatur that Medgar really should have married a local girl. And it was whispered in his mother's church that in marrying a Baptist he had left the faith. I decided I was not going to let either of these feelings bother me, and I didn't.

Our wedding trip ended where it had begun, at my home in Vicksburg. Medgar and I were given the front bedroom, the choicest one. Mama liked Medgar; she respected him; but she also resented his marrying her baby. All of this was implicit in her cool cordiality to him when we returned. It was wildly obvious in her repeated trips to the bathroom all night long that first night. When I asked her about that the next day, she confided that she had done it "to protect me."

Back at school after New Year's Day, it was a full month before Medgar and I could arrange to move into the apartment in Vet City. Meanwhile, we lived in separate dormitories, restricted, because I was a sophomore, to two dates a week. We got around these restrictions occasionally by visiting friends in Port Gibson on weekends.

When we finally moved into the apartment with the other couple, I found we had solved the problem of being together only to face some new ones. For in addition to being a full-time student with a full load of subjects, I was now faced with somehow being a full-time wife as well. I had washing, ironing, and cleaning to do for two people, along with what seemed at first the impossible job of learning to cook on an oil stove and practically no money. The cooking was sometimes disastrous, and on occasion Medgar took over in disgust. I remember particularly what was to be a wild departure from our usually economical bill of fare: fried oysters. They ended up stuck fast to the bottom of the frying pan. During our first five or six weeks of domestic life I lost nine or ten pounds on the diet I was preparing for the two of us. I couldn't understand it, but Medgar gained almost an equal amount over that same period.

My loss of weight must have been obvious, and when we went to Vicksburg for a weekend, it precipitated my first and last open conflict with my grandmother. She opened the door, took one look at me, burst into tears and cried out, "What has he done to you?" It was the beginning for a series of criticisms that built rapidly to a crescendo. She began at once by asking how our grades were, insisting before we could answer that she knew we couldn't study properly living together. Once again she said we should have waited at least until Medgar graduated before marrying. When she learned that I was playing piano for the chorus only part-time now, she accused Medgar of taking advantage of me, of telling me how to run my life, of making me give up everything she had worked so hard to give me.

It was a devastating attack and one for which neither of us was prepared. Medgar was visibly hurt. He tried to explain that he, too, had urged me to continue my music full time, but that I had insisted on giving it up. He said he was doing the best he could for me and that he would always be a good provider. But Mama kept after him, and eventually Medgar disappeared into the bathroom. When he stayed a long time, I went to him. He was badly shaken, and that in turn shook me. I pleaded with him not to take Mama's attack to heart, not to let it bother him, to try to understand that this was merely the bitterness of a fiercely possessive woman. And then, as I came out of the bathroom, Mama made the mistake of continuing. "You were a fool to get married," she said.

My anger flared and for the first time in my life I talked back to her. "I don't think I am a fool, Mama. I think you're wrong. I know what I'm doing. I'm not a helpless child any more. I'm a married woman."

She gasped, and I continued. "You can say anything you want about me. You can call me a fool if you wish. I don't care. But just don't say anything more against Medgar. I love him, and I'm going to stick with him. And from now on, I'm going to do what I think is best for Medgar and me— not what you tell me to do."

I don't know which of us was more shocked: I, at my own voice saying these things to my grandmother, or Mama, hearing her little Myrlie say them. She stared at me in amazement and then turned, speechless, and went off to cry. It was a moment in our lives that has never been mentioned by either of us since. I never apologized. Mama never again said anything against Medgar. And from that moment on, both Medgar and I knew that we were strictly on our own.

We had demanded our independence; it was now up to us to prove we were ready for it.

In a way, we did that almost immediately. Back at school we both worked hard at our studies, and for the first time Medgar made the Dean's List. My grades remained good, and little by little I even began to establish more friendly relations with the oil stove on which I cooked. Those last five months of Medgar's senior year I remember as a quiet, studious, pleasant time, a period of hard work and interesting new adjustments to each other.

Shortly before graduation, Medgar was interviewed on the campus by a representative of the Magnolia Mutual Insurance Company, a new firm founded by Dr. T. R. M. Howard and a group of other Negro business and professional men from the Mississippi Delta. Dr. Howard was well known throughout Mississippi for having founded a medical clinic in the all-Negro community of Mound Bayou. He was probably the wealthiest Negro in the state and certainly one of the most respected.

The new company was felt by many Alcorn seniors to be an ideal place to begin a business career, and there were many that applied for their first jobs there. Medgar was among the more enthusiastic ones, and he awaited the results of his interview and application with great impatience. In fact, the new company was almost the only place for a Mississippi Negro to begin a business career in Mississippi. There were few other Negro-owned companies with many employees in the state. White-owned companies did not employ Negroes in white collar jobs.

Medgar's enthusiasm for the insurance company job was most emphatically not shared by me. I could not imagine a Negro with a college degree and any ambition at all planning to remain in Mississippi. It seemed inconceivable, despite

Medgar's frequently professed love for the state, that he, of all people, would decide to stay, and in the last few weeks of college we had many discussions of these points.

There was never any question that we both planned for me to finish college, but I had hoped that we might move to Chicago where we would both find jobs and that, later, I would finish school, perhaps in Chicago. Medgar, I now learned, had other ideas entirely. He had no use for Chicago, and now that his need for summer jobs was over, he wouldn't consider moving there. He wanted the more leisurely life of the South, he said, not the rat race of Chicago. He wanted to live where there was space, not buildings, where you could hunt and fish and breathe clean air without driving a hundred miles from home. As for a job, he refused even to discuss other possibilities as long as there was a chance of his being accepted by the insurance company. That, he said, was a chance to begin with a new company, to grow and advance with it, the kind of chance every young man looks for but few find. Our discussion ended the day we received word that his application had been accepted and that he was to report for work in Mound Bayou soon after commencement. Medgar was delighted. I was frankly depressed at the thought of living indefinitely in Mississippi. The thought of living in the tiny, all-Negro community of Mound Bayou, miles from a city of any size, was more than I could bring myself to contemplate. I tried to put it out of my mind.

The day before graduation, Medgar and I drove to Vicksburg. His mother had come down from Decatur to spend the night, and we were all to drive back to Alcorn together for the ceremonies the next day. The small house was crowded, and Mama had fixed up a pallet of quilts for Medgar on the living-room floor. After dinner we sat in the living room talking of Medgar's graduation, of his job, of where and how we would live in Mound Bayou. Finally Medgar yawned, and we all prepared to go to bed. His mother, Aunt Myrlie, and Mama said good night and retired to the bedrooms. I stayed behind for a few minutes. In ten minutes Mama was back for me. "Medgar said he wanted to go to bed," she said sternly. "I think you'd better come out so that he can get undressed and retire." This time there was no argument. Medgar and I just laughed. Mama, shaking her head in disapproval, turned and left the room.

# VI

U. S. Highway 61 runs north out of Vicksburg just east of the Mississippi River. Halfway to Memphis, Tennessee, it bisects the small town of Mound Bayou: population 1328. You would not notice Mound Bayou just driving through. If it were not that rare thing, an all-Negro community, it is doubtful that many people even in Mississippi would have heard of it. Its major claim to a place in history is a shameful one. One of its founders, Isaiah T. Montgomery, was a former slave of the brother of Jefferson Davis. As the sole Negro delegate to Mississippi's post-Reconstruction Constitutional Convention of 1890, he voted for the provisions that have prevented the vast majority of Mississippi's Negroes from voting ever since.

Mound Bayou lies in the heart of Mississippi's Delta, a huge triangle of flat, fertile land where an inexhaustible topsoil, sweltering summer temperatures, and a seemingly endless supply of cheap Negro labor have enabled generations of white families to become rich growing cotton. The Delta is still the economic capital of Mississippi, and its racist views of the Negro have dominated the state's politics for generations. It is in the Mississippi Delta that the status of the

American Negro today most closely approximates that of slave. And it was to Mound Bayou that Medgar took me ten days after his graduation from Alcorn A. and M. in July of 1952.

We lived, at first, in a furnished room. After a month or two we went into debt to buy a refrigerator and some furniture so that we could take a two-room apartment with kitchen-sharing privileges. Medgar had already borrowed money to buy a four-year-old car, an absolute necessity in his job, and we soon found that even with my typing job at the insurance company, we had barely enough money to live and make payments from one week to the next. It was, I thought, really beginning at the bottom. Never during the two and a half years we lived in Mound Bayou and both worked for the insurance company did we have an income exceeding $3000 a year.

Medgar's work, which he enjoyed from the beginning, was for me a serious disillusionment. I had always vaguely pictured him, whenever he spoke of going into business, working in an office, sitting at a desk, taking telephone calls, dictating letters to a secretary. I had visualized a working day of nine to five, had seen him in my mind's eyes coming home early in the evening, having lots of time to spend with me. It was never like that.

He rose at dawn to eat hurriedly and drive twenty-five miles to Clarksdale, the city he had been assigned as a beginning territory. There he would park the car and start on foot down a block of houses in the Negro section, knocking on doors, trying to sell hospitalization and life insurance. When he made a sale, the family would become one of a slowly growing number to whom he would return each week to collect premiums. His day was long, rarely ending before seven o'clock, because the best prospects for insurance

—those who were working—generally spent the day in the fields and could be approached only after they returned home.

I hated the long days without Medgar, hated even more the evenings waiting for him to come home. I disliked my own repetitious eight-thirty-to-five job typing at the office, found the incredible heat of a Delta summer debilitating, and came quickly to think of Mound Bayou as an absolute dead end. The town offered almost nothing in the way of entertainment. No one had television at that time; there was a single small movie theater that showed only the oldest pictures; even the magazines at the town's single newsstand were consistently two months old. Few people seemed to read newspapers or take much interest in anything that happened outside the immediate area. What little happened within the immediate area held little interest for me.

Once in a great while when I could stand the monotony of my life no longer, Medgar would scrape up the money and take me to the little town of Cleveland, Mississippi, on a Saturday night. There at least there was a drive-in theater where for a few hours we could lose ourselves in a world far different from the one I had grown so thoroughly to dislike. Even here, though, it was only the world on the screen that was different; the theater itself was familiar: Negroes, permitted to enter by the same gate used by whites, were required to park their cars in the very last row.

Late in September, after two months in Mound Bayou, I had a miscarriage. I had not known for sure that I was pregnant, and finding out in this way came as a shock. The thought that I had lost a baby upset me terribly, and I was quite sick for a while. After more than a week in the hospital and several more resting at home, I returned to work more depressed than ever. The expenses of my illness had made a huge dent in our budget, and it was clear now that any possibility of my returning to Alcorn that fall was gone. Medgar and I pretended that somehow it would be possible for me to go back to school for the term that began after Christmas.

Yet while I was dragging myself through what seemed an endless series of dreary days, Medgar was making long strides in a number of directions. His energy and enthusiasm as an insurance salesman quickly earned him a promotion to district supervisor of the Clarksdale district, and his territory was expanded to include large rural areas surrounding the city. The promotion involved little in the way of money, but the company took it seriously enough to "run a sheet" on him, printing his picture and success story on a flyer that was used to recruit other salesmen. The advertisement began with a quotation, supposedly from Medgar: "If I had to do it all over again I would make a choice of life insurance for my life's work . . . and with Magnolia Mutual." I'm sure that the words, whether or not they were actually Medgar's, represented his sentiments exactly, but I found myself reading with considerable annoyance a line that began: "I've managed to make a good living for my family. . . ."

As the months wore on, it became increasingly clear that what really interested Medgar about his work had less and less to do with insurance and salesmanship and more and more to do with people who were his potential customers: the poor Negroes of the Delta. What fascinated him, what kept him talking for hours after he had made a sale or given up all hope of making one, was the condition of life of these people, a condition that dropped from mere poverty as you left the small frame houses of the Negro section of Clarksdale to absolute squalor as you visited the sharecroppers' shacks on the near-by cotton plantations. Here, on the edges of the cotton fields, life was being lived on a level that

Medgar, for all his acquaintance with the poor of both Mississippi and of Chicago's teeming black ghetto, found hard to believe. In a way, a horrified fascination with it drew him back again and again even as the sight of that long-ago pile of bloody clothing had drawn him to the place in the woods near Decatur where a Negro had been lynched.

Day after day in the weeks after his territory had been expanded, Medgar returned home bursting with stories: of children without shoes, without proper clothing; of adults with nothing to eat; of sanitary conditions no self-respecting farmer would permit in his pigpen. He painted word pictures of shacks without windows or doors, with roofs that leaked and floors rotting underfoot. For a while he had ignored the worst of these shacks, sure that no one could live in them. But then he was sent to one and began to visit them all. "They are all of them full, Myrlie!" he would exclaim as he drove me by a cluster of the worst of them on a Sunday afternoon. "Every one of them! People live in there. Human beings. People like you and me."

But along with his horror at the conditions under which these people lived, Medgar felt a rising resentment that, even under such conditions, they seemed to do little for themselves. "At least," he would say, "they could keep what they have clean. At least they could comb their children's hair. At least they could refuse to keep their children out of school to pick cotton. My parents never kept me out of school to work for any white man!" But, having said this, he would drive home and collect some of his own clothing to take with him in the morning to distribute among the neediest. I think Medgar knew how easy it was for a hopeless people to cease to care about the niceties of life, about soap and combs and school. What angered him was not really their neglect of such things but the very hopelessness that led to it. His anger was not really with them, for he returned to them again and again with gifts and help. His anger was with his own frustration at not being able to change it all.

As the weeks went by, Medgar began feeling guilty about his own role in attempting to sell insurance to people in such circumstances. It was not that any particular persuasion was necessary; most of them wanted the insurance and would have bought it from one of his many white competitors if he had not been there. His justification for continuing was that, unlike the white insurance salesmen, he at least respected these people. He knew, too, that the white salesmen traditionally went to the white plantation owners when Negroes failed in their payments and the owners, happy to bind their sharecroppers closer to them by larger debts, would usually charge the payments against the sharecroppers' credit. That, at least, was something Medgar would never do.

There was a sort of contagion about Medgar's usual enthusiasms, but this new one for the impoverished Negroes of the Delta left me almost untouched. It was not callousness, I hope, or even a lack of human sympathy. It was something more basic: selfishness. I was absorbed in my own unhappiness, my own loneliness. I was too busy feeling sorry for myself to see. Poverty was a subject of no little personal interest to me, but it was my own near-poverty that I wanted Medgar to worry about. Children without food and clothing disturbed me greatly, but it was the thought of my own children to come with perhaps too little of both that disturbed me most. Men who worked from dawn until dark picking cotton in the fields for pennies a day seemed to my shortsighted gaze too little removed from my own husband who worked from dawn until dark selling them insurance and worrying about them. What pity I had, I'm afraid, I kept pretty much for myself.

But even my indifference and self-absorption failed to quench Medgar's growing anger at what he saw around him, and he fed that anger with daily investigation and returned home with even more shocking stories. Little by little, and without really wanting to, I learned from him the basic elements of the system under which the Negro sharecroppers had been reduced to near-nothingness. In essence, as it was practiced in the Delta, sharecropping was almost an exact duplication of slavery. Under it the plantation owner had virtual life and death control over his Negroes, whose work cost him, as it had under slavery, only what it took to keep them alive. And in one sense, at least, the new system was worse than slavery, for under slavery a Negro's life, his body, his health were worth cash money to his owner. Under the carefully calculated debt slavery of sharecropping, the Negro's life was worth nothing to the plantation owner. He could always be replaced at no cost at all, for there was always a surplus of Negro families anxious to find a shack to live in and a plot on which to crop shares.

The sharecropping arrangement was simplicity itself, though it had ramifications it would take an experienced investigator to ferret out. A plantation owner would assign a portion of his land to a Negro family to raise cotton. The rent was a fixed percentage of the crop, usually half. Generally the acreage allotted to a family seemed carefully calculated to keep all of the members of that family, small children included, hard at work from dawn to dark during the growing season. Always the percentage of the crop that went to the 'cropper seemed calculated to keep him and his family on the land forever. If by chance that didn't work—if the 'cropper was more than usually industrious or talented or had a larger family than was necessary and managed to hire out for wages enough to emerge at the end of the crop year with cash left over—well, there were other ways to chain him to the land and assure the plantation owner of an unending source of labor and a constant crop of cotton at a cost of next to nothing.

To begin the year, the sharecropper needed a "furnish"—sufficient credit at a near-by store to buy his seed and materials and keep his family alive until the crop was sold. This credit was supplied by the plantation owner at a store which he himself either owned or whose policies toward his sharecroppers he controlled through agreement with the owner. As the year wore on and the cotton was planted, the amount of credit would be carefully extended, assuring the sharecropper and his family of at least enough to sustain life but rarely much more. If the sharecropper seemed to the plantation owner to be doing better than expected as the year went on—if the crop was unusually large, for example—the price of food at the store would sometimes mysteriously go up. If the 'cropper tried to go elsewhere for his goods, he would find he could not establish credit.

But the ties that bound the sharecropper to his plantation owner were even stronger than that, for there came at the end of each year the final settlement, and many landowners were not above practicing outright fraud to assure that, at best, their sharecroppers broke even when the year was over. This could usually be accomplished with ease, since the owner controlled the store's bills and it was a rare share-cropper who could produce receipts to prove the bills inaccurate. Even with proof, the 'cropper was in no position to push his claim, for the man whose word he challenged was the very man whose grant of credit for the coming year was all that stood between the 'cropper's family and starvation.

Most often, of course, the sharecropper was illiterate, or

nearly so, and hence completely at the mercy of the planta-tion owner. And even this aspect of his defenselessness could be said to be a part of the system, for the schools for Negroes in the Delta were crushingly inferior, and learning for Negroes was widely regarded—even by Negroes—as a senseless waste of time. The rare Negro youth who tried to break out of the pattern and pursue his education was often defeated by his own family's need for his labor in the fields and the fact that the Negro schools were run on different schedules from the white schools specifically to make that labor available. Until very recently in the Delta, schools for Negroes opened late in the fall, after the cotton crop had been picked, and closed early in the spring in time for planting. A six-month school year was not unusual.

As time went on and Medgar had an opportunity to probe deeper into the sharecropping system, he concluded that virtually every aspect of the Delta Negro's life was de-liberately manipulated to produce the results he saw around him. The helplessness of the Negro family in escaping the system, the manipulation of the schools, the collusion be-tween plantation owner and store manager, and the frequent resort to outright fraud all combined to give illiteracy and hopelessness an almost genetic quality. Sharecroppers begot more sharecroppers generation after generation with almost no hope for escape. And beyond all of the built-in controls, beyond the system itself, lay the iron-clad rule that no Negro, sharecropper or not, could win in a showdown with a white. This was the ultimate bond, the final link in the chain that kept the Delta Negro in the cotton fields. The law was white; the courts were white; and beyond even the law and the courts lay white violence that could be forged into a lynch mob on an hour's notice.

Trapped by this system, ensnared by its deceptions and

frauds, the Delta sharecroppers and field hands had become slaves in nearly every sense of the word. Even the possibility of simply picking up and leaving was precluded, for there was nearly always a debt to the plantation owner that could be used with greater legal effect than the old fugitive slave laws to bring the runaway back. Nor was this an unusual occurrence; Medgar himself met Negroes who had tried to escape by flight only to be arrested and brought back to face not only a return to the system but a brutal beating in the confines of a jail cell.

It was a long time before Medgar was able to piece together all of the elements of this vicious system, and there were many aspects that could only be guessed at, but in time he was able to point out to me some of its elements at work. We would be shopping for groceries on a Saturday night, and Medgar would point out a plantation owner huddled with the storekeeper as the sharecroppers made their weekly purchases of meal and flour and lard. "You don't need that, Willie," the owner would tell a ragged Negro, pushing aside a box of cookies or a pound of bacon. "This is enough for you." And the Negro would meekly accept the command, taking, in effect, what he was permitted to take, feeding his family what the plantation owner decided he should feed them.

The vicious and oppressive system of sharecropping, of daily hired hands, of working small children in the cotton fields that produced such beaten and subservient Negroes also produced a small group of fantastically wealthy whites. Just how wealthy could only be surmised, but occasionally there were clues. One such clue appeared in the Congressional Record of July 2, 1955. In an accounting of payments made by the U. S. Department of Agriculture to the owners of Mississippi cotton plantations for their 1954 surplus, it was

84

revealed that five of the larger Mississippi Delta planters received over $2,000,000.

The idea behind the government's support of farmers—originally, at least—was to help a growingly impoverished group of Americans achieve some kind of economic equality with industrial workers in the cities. The result, in Mississippi, has been to subsidize white millionaire racists in their continued brutal exploitation of Negro men, women, and children. Here, in a single year—the year in which the Supreme Court of the United States finally ruled that Negro children had the right to go to decent schools—the United States Government paid just five Mississippi planters a total of more than $2,000,000 for work performed at starvation wages of $3.50 a day and less.

All during that long, unbeliveably hot summer of 1952, Medgar sold insurance and gathered information. He was like a student driven by horror to learn more. The more he learned, the more he had to know, and his hours away from home stretched more and more often into the darkness that falls over the flat Delta in a matter of minutes after the sun goes down. Sometime during that summer his anger reached a peak, and he began organizing chapters of the National Association for the Advancement of Colored People.

The organization was little more than a name to me, a name I had first encountered in a thin paperbound book used as a text for a six-weeks' course in Negro history during my senior year in high school. That course, and the book, were the only exposure I had had in twelve years of public school to the accomplishments of Negroes in America. I don't know today whether the book was supplied by the state, as our regular textbooks were, or whether our Negro teachers somehow included it on their own, but I do know that it was the only antidote to a course in Mississippi history that pictured ante-bellum Negroes as ignorant and happy slaves, dancing, playing the banjo, and picking cotton. Negroes were not even mentioned in the approved post-Civil War version of the state's history.

Even the thin paperbound textbook was hopelessly inadequate, but it had at least taught me something of the way slaves had been brought to the United States on ships from Africa, of the breaking up of Negro families in the slave markets of the South, and of the famous underground railroad to freedom in the North. I learned the names of a few famous Negroes: Crispus Attucks, the Massachusetts Negro who was one of the first Americans to fall before British guns at the Boston Massacre; Harriet Tubman, the escaped slave who risked recapture on recurrent trips South to lead more than 300 fellow slaves to freedom; Sojourner Truth, the Negro woman abolitionist; Mary McLeod Bethune, the great educator; Booker T. Washington; George Washington Carver; Marian Anderson, and a few more.

Where Medgar heard about the NAACP—and how—I never learned; suddenly it was there as a fact of our existence. I'm afraid my chief reaction was a resentment of his using his time to work for the organization. It was one thing more to keep us apart. But then, in November, five months after we had come to Mound Bayou, Medgar and I were drawn together by the knowledge that I was again pregnant. We both wanted children, and the shock and disappointment of my miscarriage made this pregnancy an occasion for rejoicing. Medgar made an obvious conscious effort to spend more time with me. We had little money for luxuries, but we managed to go to Memphis once that fall to watch the Alcorn football team play, and sometimes we would drive to Clarksdale to see the Negro high school team play. Medgar went hunting whenever he could, and after a successful hunt we would have friends over for rabbit stew. Most of our friends were young people like ourselves struggling to make ends meet, and, thinking back, I can see a certain irony in one of our favorite pastimes—the game of Monopoly. The play money distributed at the beginning of each game must have held more than minor unconscious interest for all of us.

And yet even on our Sunday afternoon drives when I had such a desire to be gay and lighthearted with Medgar, we would inevitably find ourselves on the highway to Clarksdale, and somehow the rest of the day would be spent visiting a family of sharecroppers Medgar had met the previous week. They were social visits, really, and I suppose they had the extra motive on Medgar's part of trying to involve me in something that fascinated and angered and drove him to try to find some kind of solution. They were like an obsession with him, these unfortunate people, and even the joy of knowing we were soon to have a child could only occupy his mind for a short time before he was back worrying about their problems. Inevitably those Sunday drives would end with Medgar driving home, his anger heated to a new pitch, his determination to do something renewed. Once more I would sink into quiet despair.

It was during these months that an organization called the Regional Council of Negro Leadership was formed in Mound Bayou by Dr. Howard and a group of other Negro leaders in that part of Mississippi. There were small meetings that led, eventually, to an annual meeting in Mound Bayou, and out of all this grew an issue and a slogan: "Don't buy gas where you can't use the restroom." The organization's immediate goals were as minimal as the slogan indicated, but more and more, as time went by, Medgar and I would see little bumper stickers with those words on the

87

usually beat-up automobiles of Delta Negroes. It may sound silly, but even that sort of protest required a considerable amount of courage.

One of the organization's annual meetings—it may well have been the first—was the occasion for Thurgood Marshall, the renowned attorney of the NAACP, to come to Mound Bayou to speak, and for weeks before the actual event there were massive preparations. A huge tent was rented and set up in a clear area, and the meeting was advertised and discussed for miles around. When the day finally arrived, it was like a huge all-day camp meeting: a combination of pep rally, old-time revival, and Sunday church picnic, with a parade down the main street of town to begin the festivities.

Medgar of course had spoken to all of the plantation Negroes he knew, urging them to come to Mound Bayou for the event, and throughout the day he searched the crowds for the faces of people he knew. Some of them came, but many more did not, and I think that was the first time Medgar really faced the extent of the fear so many of the plantation Negroes had of doing anything that could be interpreted by the plantation owners as hostile. Even among those who came to the meeting, there were many who had slipped into town on some pretense they hoped would stand up under questioning. Only a few displayed the courage to come openly, willing, if necessary, to go back to the plantation and face whatever music was played by the plantation owner.

But if Medgar was brought face to face with the fear of the Delta Negroes on this occasion, he had at least the background to understand it. For by this time he was in little doubt as to the existence of widespread brutality and beatings as the ultimate means of white control over the Negroes. Reports were forever circulating about this or that plantation owner or manager having beaten one or more of his Negro sharecroppers or hired hands, and on investigation most of the reports turned out to be true. Most often it was the younger Negroes who were the targets of this kind of abuse, presumably as a means of preparing them for a life of subservience and near-slavery, and nearly any excuse was sufficient to make an example of a rebellious young Negro boy. There was nothing that could be done about it. A report to the police would often bring a second beating, this time administered by experts who routinely beat up Negroes who drank too much on Saturday nights and found themselves in the hands of the police or sheriff's deputies. In cynical moments Medgar used to say that these regular Saturday-night beatings of Negroes were the way the white man got his exercise, but beneath this bitter attempt at humor was a growing anger and even hatred.

Because Dr. Howard was the sort of man to whom many Delta Negroes came with their problems, he heard more of these stories than anyone. And because Medgar was in almost daily contact with him, Medgar undoubtedly heard more than he picked up visiting the plantations. But even Dr. Howard, with his prestige and money and position, was usually unable to do more than listen to the victim's complaints and bind up his wounds, and this, too, added to Medgar's frustration.

Dr. Howard was a tall, heavy man with a mustache, glasses, and a heavy, booming voice. He had a light skin, a friendly smile, and a hearty handshake, and there was about him an aura of security so lacking among the vast majority of Negroes in the Delta that he stood out as different wherever he went. One look told you that he was a leader: kind, affluent, and intelligent, that rare Negro in Mississippi who had somehow beaten the system. Many Delta Negroes knew from personal experience of his generosity with money.

His income came from a large farm, worked by share-croppers, from the profits of the new insurance company, from the clinic, and from investments. Rumor had it that he regularly increased his wealth by judicious betting at horse races out of the state. He had a lovely home, a gathering place for the social affairs of the few well-to-do Negroes of the area, and he raised pheasant, quail, and hunting dogs for sport. He loved automobiles and always drove the latest model; at the time we were there, it was not unusual to see him sailing down the highway in a red Buick convertible on his way to visit a patient. His wife drove a Cadillac.

There were some Negroes who resented Dr. Howard's wealth, but on the whole he was viewed as a brave man, a spokesman for the Delta Negroes, and it was widely believed that he had at least some influence with the white plantation owners. The truth of it was that there were many whites who despised him for his wealth and success; yet even among these he commanded a certain respect. He was so far from the usual Delta Negro that he had to be regarded as a special case. And to Medgar he remained just that: a special case. Medgar's growing concern and frustration were with the average Delta Negroes, the masses.

I do not know where or when Medgar first heard or read of Jomo Kenyatta, the reputed leader of the Mau Mau uprising in faraway Kenya, but little by little more and more about this man entered his conversation and his thoughts. He must have picked up most of his information from the newspapers: Hodding Carter's *Delta Democrat-Times*, published in near-by Greenville, and the Memphis papers, the *Press-Scimitar* and the *Commercial Appeal*. The stories they published about the Mau Mau must have been brief and few, though Southern newspapers in general have a habit of playing up any news that can be slanted to demonstrate the supposed savagery of the Negro. Yet out of these stories, and out of what was surely the white bias with which they were written, Medgar somehow extracted what he regarded as the true story of what was happening those thousands of miles away in an African colony he had never seen.

Kenyatta, Medgar felt instinctively, was a man driven to violence by the brutal oppression of his people, and the fact that newspapers in Mississippi and Tennessee were reporting the deeds of his Mau Mau army at all could only be interpreted to mean that he was succeeding at least in calling the attention of the world to that oppression. Medgar had always admired men who stood up for what they believed, and while he abhorred violence, his frustration at the seeming impossibility of doing anything constructive about conditions in the Delta gave added stature to the bearded black giant in Kenya. Here was a man, a man educated in white schools and universities, a man who dressed as a European and yet was still an African and had the courage to fight injustice and brutality.

And for a time Medgar himself flirted intellectually with the idea of fighting back in the Mississippi Delta. For a time he envisioned a secret black army of Delta Negroes who fought by night to meet oppression and brutality with violence. He had no illusions about the outcome of open warfare between whites and Negroes; the whites had all the weapons and could bring the full power of the police and even the army against whatever the Negroes could muster. But he also had no illusions about the glaring light of publicity and public attention that would inevitably be focused on the plight of the Delta Negro by such a clandestine war. And without the attention of the rest of the country and even the rest of the world, Medgar saw no way out of the impasse that had kept the Delta Negroes in virtual slavery for generations.

In a way I am sure Medgar never realized, this dream of his of a Mississippi Mau Mau, striking under cover of darkness, punishing the crimes of whites against Negroes, setting itself up as a sort of black vigilante army, writing a new law of an eye for an eye over the brooding flat land of the Delta, was straight out of the Southern tradition. It was the Ku Klux Klan, the lynch mob, the terrorist police turned black. It was the time-honored weapon of the Southern whites against the Negroes, used once with great effectiveness against the occupying armies of the Yankees and utilized sporadically throughout the South ever since when the anger or the fears of the white men exceeded the limits of the law. In a sense, all that Medgar was doing was turning the Southern white man's traditional weapon against him, using darkness and terror to bring about a new balance of power and, hopefully, a new intervention by the rest of the nation.

He was an angry young man, grasping at any solution that might bring an end to the degradation he saw around him, and he fed his seething anger by reading everything he could lay hands on that told more about Jomo Kenyatta and the Mau Mau. I don't know today how much he actually learned about this controversial man or where, exactly, he got his information. We lived in different worlds in those months, he in his world of bitterness and wild plans and I in my own world of loneliness made bearable only by the knowledge of a new life growing inside me. Yet on the subject of Kenyatta, little as I really knew about him, we agreed to some extent; for here, at least, was release from the frustration of doing nothing. I hated the idea of murdering people, even murderers; I shrank from it even as Medgar himself did. And yet there was no doubt about the injustice and brutality around us. It was in the very air we breathed. And there was no doubt that nothing was being done about it. I guess I came eventually to that same dead end that Medgar had reached before me: if it takes violence to change things, it will just have to take violence.

It was strange how the end came to that wild period of violent thoughts, strange and yet inevitable, I suppose. For Medgar, in the turmoil of his mind, recalled some passages of Scripture that his mother had read frequently to him, and he began to pore over the Bible we had received as a wedding gift. He had never been what I would call a deeply religious man; he was a man of action, a man who saw the beginnings of solutions in taking a stand. I think he must have read the Bible more for its thought-provoking qualities, more for its spiritual opposition to the violent ideas that possessed his mind, more, as it were, as the other side in a mental debate with himself, than because it was the word of God. And eventually he changed his mind about a Mau Mau in the Delta, though he never lost his respect and admiration for Jomo Kenyatta.

Recently I have tried to find out more about this man whose image dominated my husband's thinking those many angry months in 1952. I know, of course, that with the independence of Kenya he emerged as the undisputed leader of his country, respected by whites and blacks alike. But I did not know until recently that his association with the Mau Mau terror was never actually proved or how wildly inflated were the stories we read at the time of the Mau Mau violence. In the entire period of the Mau Mau uprising, according to one source, only seventy whites were killed. Forty of them were members of the security force that hunted down and killed nearly 8000 Mau Mau. Only thirty were white civilians. As one author puts it, "During the emergency more Europeans were killed in traffic accidents within the city limits of Nairobi than were murdered by terrorists in the whole of Kenya." I wonder if Medgar knew that.

My pregnancy ruled out any possibility of my going back to Alcorn that winter, and I had little choice but to continue working as long as I could. My grandmother's reaction to the news was predictable: "Now you'll never go back to college."

I managed to work right into my final month of pregnancy, and then my feet swelled so that I couldn't get my shoes on and I had to stop. As the time drew closer, Medgar's excitement rose. He was convinced from the first that the baby would be a boy, and he had his entire family behind him in this display of wishful thinking. All of the Evers grandchildren had been girls, and there was much serious talk of a boy to carry on the name.

I remember sending Medgar off to work with a big smile and a kiss on the last morning of June 1953, just a week after I had stopped going to the office myself. At eleven o'clock I felt the first pain of labor. An hour later I telephoned Dr. Howard, and he sent someone from the hospital to pick me up. After an examination he told me I had some hours to wait and that he would check on my progress every now and then.

They put me to bed in a private room with nurses to watch over me, and by three o'clock I knew the baby was coming. I was much too happy and excited to be frightened, and just fifteen minutes after my final warning to the nurses I was in the delivery room and had produced a fine healthy boy to carry on the Evers name. Dr. Howard arrived just in time.

There was no way to reach Medgar, though I had left word with a neighbor before leaving home that I was going to the hospital. I learned later of the sequence of events that evening when Medgar drove up to our house and found me gone. In a way it reminded me of our wedding day. Finding the house empty, Medgar went outside, where the neighbor told him the news. With great excitement, he leaped into the car, threw it into reverse, and backed into a ditch. When he finally reached the hospital, he was in a state of excitement that made my own pale by comparison. I have never seen a happier man. I think at that moment he felt I had done something no other woman had ever done or would ever do again. And beyond the fantastic feat of having a baby, I had performed that miracle of miracles: I had produced an Evers boy.

Medgar spent only enough time with me to let me know precisely how he felt and to be sure that both the baby and I were well; then he rushed off to spread the news by telephone to our families. I have been told that in Decatur, Mississippi, there was almost dancing in the streets, and I know that in Vicksburg there was an unusual flow of tears of joy and pride. Within minutes of Medgar's call, my grandmother was packing her bags. She arrived in Mound Bayou the following day to envelop my newborn son in the same web of love and protectiveness with which she had always tried to surround me. She was joined shortly by my mother, who came from Yazoo City to help out.

For months before the baby came, Medgar and I had talked and argued about names—boys' names. If it had been a girl, I think I could have had my choice. But assuming, as Medgar did, that the baby would be a boy, I wanted him to be named after Medgar. Medgar was opposed; he felt that every child should have a name of his very own and for his son he had one all picked out: Kenyatta.

I understood and even sympathized with his feelings about

Kenyatta, but I'm afraid the name Kenyatta Evers just didn't sound right to my ears. When the time came in the hospital for me to make an official decision for the birth certificate, I hesitated only a moment and then slipped the first name, "Darrell," in before Kenyatta. Later, when I admitted to Medgar what I had done, he accepted it without argument.

As soon as I felt able to go back to work, I faced an inevitable separation from my new son. There was no choice: we needed money desperately and I had been unable to find a woman to care for Darrell during the day. We drove that weekend to Decatur so that Medgar's parents could see their new grandchild and then, after staying overnight, drove on to Vicksburg.

Leaving Darrell in Vicksburg was like leaving a part of myself behind, and I told Mama repeatedly that as soon as I could locate a baby sitter I would be back for him. Mama herself was torn between her desire to keep Darrell and her conviction that I should give up my job and keep him myself, and as we finally broke away to return to Mound Bayou, there were tears on both sides. I cried all the way back to Mound Bayou, and the next day my eyes were so swollen I couldn't go to work.

We were without our baby for three and a half months, and for me they were months of emptiness and concern. I lived for the weekends when, just after noon on Saturday, we would make the two-hour drive to Vicksburg. We always stayed as long as we could on those weekends, rising at 5:00 A.M. on Monday to drive back to Mound Bayou Each parting from my baby was as hard as the first.

Those weekends were both a joy and a despair for me, for there was always the fascination and amazement and delight at Darrell's progress mixed with an almost overpowering jealousy at his deep attachment to Mama and his almost complete lack of interest in me. Each early morning drive back to Mound Bayou found me stronger in my determination to find a baby sitter and take my baby back.

Eventually I found an elderly woman who could come and stay with Darrell while I worked, and the very next weekend we drove to Vicksburg to get him. Mama had by now become so attached to him that she fought against our taking him, and there were tears and arguments and hurt feelings when we finally left.

With Darrell in Mound Bayou, my life quickly slipped into a harried routine. Early in the morning the baby sitter would come and Medgar and I would both leave for work. Since we lived only a block and a half from the insurance company office, I managed to slip home at least once a day to check up on things. Finally, at five o'clock, I would rush home for good to claim my baby, and for two hours or so, until Medgar came home, I would have him all to myself. Those hours alone with Darrell are almost my only completely happy memories of the years in Mound Bayou. They sustained me through a succession of baby sitters, a job I grew more and more to dislike, and the growing hours of Medgar's absence from home, for his rejection of the idea of a Mississippi Mau Mau had only increased his search for other possible solutions to the problems of the Delta Negroes, and more and more I found I could count on his coming home from work at later and later hours.

## VII

Eventually Medgar's efforts to enlist Delta Negroes in the NAACP began to bear fruit. It required at least fifty members in a single locality before an application could be made for a charter as a new branch, and the first of these to result largely from Medgar's work was at Shelby, Mississippi. As the months wore on, other new branches were formed in the Delta, and together with branches chartered earlier though-out the state, they made up the state conference of branches. By late 1953, the eight-year-old Mississippi State Conference of the NAACP consisted of twenty-one separate branches with a total membership of 1600. It was pitifully small for a state with a million Negroes and the greatest need in all the South, but it was a beginning, and Medgar was already a part of it.

It was late in 1953 at an area meeting of the NAACP in Mound Bayou—a meeting Medgar attended without me—that the state president, Dr. E. J. Stringer, a young dentist who was also president of the Columbus, Mississippi branch, spoke of the importance of an attempt to desegregate the University of Mississippi. In the light of the rioting that was to accompany James Meredith's appearance on the campus of

Ole Miss nine years later, this might seem to have been a revolutionary suggestion; yet in the context of what was happening elsewhere in the South, it was really a conservative start. The pattern of school desegregation suits was by then quite clear, and almost without exception initial breakthroughs in each state had been made at state universities, usually at the graduate school level.

Unlike the suits that led to the historic school desegregation decision of 1954, most of these early school suits sought only enforcement of the Supreme Court's 1896 *Plessy vs. Ferguson* decision that each state must provide facilities for Negroes that, though separate, were at least equal. It was not difficult to prove in most of the states that either permitted or decreed segregated schools that what separate facilities existed were far from equal. In many cases, of course, there were simply no separate facilities at all. Mississippi was not the only state that had no schools for Negroes who wanted to study law or medicine or dentistry or, in my own case, to major in music. Nor was Mississippi alone in having devised a system of state grants for Negroes to study elsewhere in the hope of avoiding the cost of building these separate facilities. It was precisely this kind of evasion that had been attacked with considerable success in other states. With few exceptions, the end result had been not the building of new facilities for Negroes but the admission of Negroes to existing white facilities.

The first of these cases had occurred in Maryland as early as 1935, and by 1951 the states of Missouri, Arkansas, Oklahoma, Kentucky, Virginia, Louisiana, Texas, and North Carolina had all admitted Negroes to previously all-white state universities. In most of the court battles that led to these victories, the NAACP had supplied the legal talent. Dr. Stringer, suggesting that the time had come for a start in

Mississippi, made it clear that such would be the case here as well.

That very night, as the meeting continued and various speakers commented on the suggestion, a young college graduate in the audience made up his mind to be the first Negro to attempt to enter the University of Mississippi. There was no doubt in his mind what graduate degree he would seek: the skill of NAACP attorneys in working these legal miracles in other states made it inevitable that he would choose the law. As a Negro lawyer, he too could play a major role in breaking down the legal barriers that confronted his people.

At an appropriate moment the young man stood up and announced his decision to the meeting. It was, of course, Medgar. His announcement was greeted by wild applause, and after things had finally quieted down, there were hurried conferences and consultations. It was late when Medgar finally left the meeting for home. It was even later when, filled with excitement and enthusiasm, the cheers still echoing in his ears, he woke me to tell me the news. I thought he had lost his mind.

My first reaction, when I finally grasped the implications of what he proposed to do, was one of complete devastation. It was like a personal attack on me by the man I loved most of all people in the world. I felt isolated, lost, alone, let down by the man who had sworn to love and protect me. I could not have felt worse if he had left me a note that he was leaving me. What I heard, as he explained his decision over and over to me, was not that he had taken a courageous step to help his people. What I heard was that he was leaving me and Darrell, abandoning us, going off on his own on some wild mission that could only end in disaster. What I heard was the wrenching, tearing, uprooting of my marriage.

It seems incredible now that in the argument that followed

neither of us even mentioned the possibility of personal danger. The fact is that it occurred to neither of us then. It is possible, I suppose, with the history of similar cases in other states, all ending in victory for the Negro applicant and an absence of violence when he appeared on the campus, that the chance of physical danger had not occurred to anyone. But even more fantastic is the fact that all of my arguments—and all of Medgar's defenses—were based on the simple-minded assumption that Medgar would, in fact, be admitted to the university. Neither of us questioned that assumption for a moment.

What concerned and frightened and angered me, once I found the strength to fight back, was neither the thought of danger nor a sense of the futility of the effort but the incredible fact that Medgar would even consider quitting his job and returning to school at the very time that, with a new son, we needed a steady income more than ever before. I found this thought staggering, and I honestly wondered what kind of dream world Medgar inhabited. We had had our differences before. I had never ceased to resent the time and effort he devoted to soliciting memberships in the NAACP. But this was different. Now, it seemed to me, in proposing to go to law school, Medgar was threatening our very existence as a family. It seemed crazy; it seemed wildly selfish; it seemed fantastically impractical; and I said so.

But Medgar was a determined young man, and for each of my arguments he had an answer. What he was doing, he said, he was doing specifically *for* his family. The barriers he was trying to break down were barriers his children would never have to face if he succeeded. If there were sacrifices to be made along the way, they were necessary sacrifices. Nothing worth-while was ever accomplished without sacrifice. This was something that had to be done. It was something that he had to do. It had been done in other Southern states, and it would be done in Mississippi as well. It is an understatement of considerable proportions to say that none of these arguments reached me.

But the next day Medgar wrote to Alcorn College requesting that a transcript of his record be sent to the University of Mississippi's School of Law. A few days later he filled out an application and signed a retainer requesting and authorizing Thurgood Marshall, special counsel of the NAACP, to act as his attorney. And in the cold silence between us as these actions were taken, there was a frightening quality of bitter hostility.

On January 22, 1954, the story was published. Across the front page of the Jackson *Daily News* the bold, black letters spelled it out: NEGRO APPLIES TO ENTER OLE MISS. Reading it, it seemed to me almost a battle cry.

The next day we read in the same newspaper of the state's response. Dr. E. R. Jobe, executive secretary of the State Board of Trustees of Institutions of Higher Learning, announced that the board would do nothing about the application until it had received a ruling from Mississippi's Attorney General (later Governor and today Federal Judge), James P. Coleman. Dr. Jobe attempted to calm whatever white fears had been aroused by the previous day's headline with a statement that "we don't think applications for entrance into state schools by Negroes is news at all." But lest this sound encouraging to Mississippi Negroes, he proceeded to give away the board's strategy by asking plaintively, "Why don't the newspapers wait until a suit is filed before reporting these cases?" So Medgar's application was already a "case." After that, there seemed no doubt that a lawsuit would have to be filed before the issue was decided.

In the meantime, my private war with Medgar continued.

For the first time in our marriage, an issue had arisen on which we could find no agreement whatever. And this time I refused to accept his decision in silence. When I asked, a hundred times, who would pay the bills to put him through law school, he said he would find a way even if we had to borrow money. When I asked who would lend him money to do such a thing, he said he was sure someone would. When I objected to our being separated while he was at school, he said we could spend our weekends together. And as a lawyer, he added, he would be able eventually to give his family all of the things we deserved. My answer was blunt and to the point and wholly truthful. I would rather live on bread and water for the rest of my life, I said, than to have him pursue some wild dream of becoming a lawyer so that he could give us the things we supposedly deserved. Of one thing I was certain: Medgar was not going to justify his actions as a sacrifice for his family.

Eventually, though it had still not occurred to me that Medgar might fail in his objective of admission to the school, the thought of danger, once he was on the campus, did cross my mind. Medgar's reply was characteristic: a Negro in Mississippi was always in danger, if only of starving to death. Better to live in danger that had at least some prospect of improving things than to accept the finality of oppression. And again; "We have to make sacrifices to make progress."

Woman-like, wife-like, mother-like, hiding even from myself a glowing spark of pride in my husband's audacity and courage, I continued to press him with the inevitable questions: Why did it have to be him? Why did it have to be us? What compelled the man I had married to insist on being the first of his race to enter Ole Miss, that privileged sanctum of white supremacy? Why, if he were set on becoming a lawyer, couldn't he leave the state? Or wait to become the second? Or the third? There were, of course, no answers, or none, at least, that satisfied me. And for weeks as we waited for more news of the fate of his application, we harbored enormous hostility for one another—each certain that the other was refusing only out of stubbornness to understand what was really so easily understood.

And then, suddenly, I had another argument on my side. I was pregnant again. This, it seemed to me, rendered all of Medgar's previous arguments obsolete. This, I thought, would curb his adventurous spirit and bring him back to solid earth. This was decisive, solid, final. But this, alas, was woman's logic. Medgar's was simpler: now he had two children for whom the walls of segregation must be breached. Now he had twice as much to fight for.

When we visited Medgar's parents, I found I had allies in both of them. Both, though proud of their son's courage, had been terribly upset by the announcement in the newspapers and the thought of its effect on Darrell and me. Both tried hard to dissuade him. Medgar was unmoved. When I announced that I was pregnant, his mother became even more upset, and in the heat of the argument I left the dinner table in tears. Medgar's mother followed to console me, and moments later we heard with amazement Medgar's father, always so quiet and dignified, shouting angrily at his son. That visit was a disaster, and Medgar must have been badly shaken by his father's anger, but when it was over, nothing had changed. Even his father's death, just a short time after that angry scene, only served to strengthen Medgar's conviction that what he was doing was right.

We heard by telephone that his father was seriously ill in a hospital in Union, Mississippi. Because I was pregnant, Medgar left me at home with Darrell and fled, a stricken man. He found his father in the hospital basement with the other Negro patients. Infuriated at this kind of treatment but unable to do anything about it, he sat by the bedside watching helplessly as his father's life slipped away. Near the end, his father hemorrhaged and began sinking fast. Medgar, in despair, could do nothing but stand and watch. Suddenly, as he waited, there was a sound of voices, a rush of feet outside the hospital. Torn from his anguish by the noise, Medgar turned to see a white nurse enter the room. "Come quickly," she said, her eyes wide with fear. "We may need your help."

Dazed and uncomprehending, Medgar followed her from the room to another part of the basement. There, in a small room, trembling with fear and shock, lay a Negro man with a bandaged leg. There had been some kind of fracas with a policeman. The Negro had been shot in the leg. Medgar never did get the full story. But through the window he could see a growing mob of whites, milling and muttering, peering through the windows in hopes of catching sight of the Negro. Every few moments a voice stood out from the rest, and the word "Nigger!" hung on the hot, still air. It was an ugly scene, threatening each minute to explode into violence, and Medgar wondered who, if anyone, was attemping to control the mob. There was nothing he could do.

When he returned to his father's room, resolved at the very least to defend him, if necessary, with his own life, he found the older man dying. When the end finally came, the mutterings of the mob were at their height, and Medgar's father, that quiet and dignified man whose courage and manliness had provided the model for much of Medgar's own character, died to the accompaniment of angry white voices and the threat of violence. Medgar never forgot that, and in his sorrow and bitterness afterward, he cited it often as proof that a Negro could neither live nor die in peace in Mississippi as long as things remained the way they were.

As much as anything he saw around him, I think that experience at his father's deathbed convinced Medgar that he had to continue his personal crusade against injustice and segregation. When we visited Vicksburg and both Mama and Aunt Myrlie vigorously opposed his attempt to enter Ole Miss, he quietly told them this story. When Mama tried to change the grounds of the argument and charged him with deserting his family, he said that to withdraw his application would be to desert not only his family but his people. And that, he said, he would never do.

And then, one day five months after his original application, Medgar acquired a powerful added argument on his side of the question. I was at the office that Monday afternoon in May when word swept quickly through the community that the United States Supreme Court had declared public school segregation unconstitutional. The excitement was contagious, though none of us really understood the full implications of the news, and there were arguments about what, precisely, the decision might mean to us and our children in Mississippi. When Medgar got home that evening, he, too, was full of the news, and we sat together and listened to every news report we could pick up on the radio.

It was a frustrating experience, for none of the reports told us half what we wanted to know, but Medgar listened with intense concentration to every word. Between reports, he talked about what he thought it might mean. He had few illusions about how white Mississippi might react to the decision, but he saw it as at least the beginning of a new day for the Negro. With decent educations, he said, Negroes could begin to better their own conditions. And that, he believed, would be the beginning of the end of segregation. "Educated

Negroes, Negroes who have a real stake in their society, aren't going to accept these conditions long. They will know, because history tells them so, that no people were ever given their freedom without a struggle. And a struggle means sacrifices."

In the days and weeks following the decision, the voices of the white South began to be heard, and while there were many that said precisely what everyone expected, there were also some surprises. The very day after the decision, Governor Francis Cherry of our neighboring state of Arkansas announced tersely that "Arkansas will obey the law. It always has." Governor Gordon Persons of Alabama rejected attempts to stampede him into calling a special session of the state legislature, a session that would have tried to circumvent the court's ruling. From Florida came the voice of Senator Spessard Holland, saying, "No matter how much we don't like it, we must not have false ideas of the seriousness." Florida Representative Charles E. Bennett went further: "I think the federal government should be required to take all necessary steps to make the states carry out the ruling."

In the border states and the mid-South there were also encouraging signs. Governor Caleb Boggs of Delaware told his state board of education that it would be "the policy of this administration to work toward adjustment to the United States constitutional requirements." Maryland's Governor Theodore R. McKeldin said, "Maryland prides itself on being a law-abiding state, and I am sure our citizens and our officials will accept readily the United States Supreme Court's interpretation of our fundamental law." Similar statements came from Kentucky, North Carolina, Oklahoma, Tennessee, and West Virginia.

But it was Virginia, the state that later adopted a policy

of "massive resistance" to school desegregation—a policy widely emulated throughout the South—that provided the greatest surprise. Looking back today, it is hard to believe that Medgar and I sat together by a radio in May of 1954 and heard reports that Governor Thomas B. Stanley of Virginia had expressed hope that the decision would be received calmly by his people. He urged Virginians to "take time to carefully and dispassionately consider the situation before coming to conclusions on steps which should be taken." And if this statement seemed calculated to placate both sides, the words of Dowell J. Howard, Virginia's Superintendent of Public Instruction, were not. "There will be no defiance of the Supreme Court decision as far as I am concerned," he said flatly. "We are trying to teach school children the law of the land and we will abide by it."

These were the surprises. There were other statements, of course, that surprised nobody. South Carolina's Governor James F. Byrnes expressed shock at the decision. Georgia's Governor Herman E. Talmadge said with finality that his state would not desegregate its schools. And in the words of one report: "Mississippi officials are unanimous in their reaction: the Court decision will not be accepted." The Jackson *Clarion-Ledger* mourned in an editorial that "May 17, 1954, may be recorded as a black day of tragedy for the South." The Jackson *Daily News* titled its lead editorial "Blood on the Marble Steps." And when Hodding Carter's liberal (for Mississippi) *Delta Democrat-Times* noted on May 20 the "Delta's calm acceptance of the decision," there was good reason to believe that what calmness prevailed among the white people of the Delta sprang from a conviction that the court's ruling would never touch them. Even Representative Frank Smith, the Delta's congressman since 1950 and one of the few Mississippi politicians who seemed to avoid the issue of race wherever possible in his campaigns, was hardly reassuring when he urged "calm consideration . . . of how the ruling will ultimately affect Mississippi."

Ten days after the ruling, Senator James O. Eastland, even then running for re-election as the most worthy possible successor to the state's worst racist, former Senator Theodore G. Bilbo, was on the record as declaring the Supreme Court had shown a "disregard of its oath and duty." On the floor of the House of Representatives, Congressman John Bell Williams, another racist, described May 17 as "Black Monday"—a name that stuck.

Late in May the circuit judge of Brookhaven, Mississippi (population: 7801), Judge Tom Brady, delivered a speech to the Sons of the American Revolution in Greenwood, Mississippi that, published later as a book, became the new Bible of Mississippi racists. Titled *Black Monday*, it was a wild amalgamation of rewritten history, half-digested law, pseudo-scientific anthropology, and raw racism. While it served its obvious purpose of rousing the animal instincts of many Mississippi whites, it also had the unforeseen effect of revealing the depths of depravity of the genuine Mississippi racist in a way that Mississippi Negroes could never have done. To white liberals in the North who clung fondly to the idea that Mississippi segregationists were merely misguided whites, entitled to sympathy and even respect in difficult times, *Black Monday* must have come as a bombshell.

Making the mental leap that seems simple to most white Southerners from school desegregation to interracial marriage, Judge Brady, who for some reason pronounces his name to rhyme with "Daddy," began his book with this judicious distortion of history: "What happened in India and Egypt happened in Babylon—it happened in Burma, Siam, in Greece, Rome, and in Spain. It is the same deadly story—the Negroid blood like the jungle, steadily and completely swallowing up everything." Apparently secure in his judgment that none of his readers would know that India, Burma and Siam are in Asia and thus far from the center of Negro contamination in Africa, Judge Brady continued: "Whenever and wherever the white man has drunk the cup of black hemlock, whenever and wherever his blood had been infused with blood of the Negro, the white man, his intellect and his culture have died. This is as true as two plus two equals four. The proof is that Egypt, India, the Mayan civilization, Babylon, Persia, Spain and all the others have never and can never rise again."

Lest this lament for dead civilizations, some of them remarkably alive, be read as a hopeless acceptance of the Supreme Court's decision, Judge Brady gave the signal for retaliation—not against the court but against the Negro. "Oh, High Priests of Washington," he exclaimed, "blow again and stronger upon the dying embers of racial hate, distrust and envy. Pour a little coal oil of political expediency and hope of racial amalgamation upon the flickering blaze which you have created and you will start a conflagration in the South which all of Neptune's mighty ocean cannot quench. The decision which you handed down on Black Monday has arrested and retarded the economic and political, and yes, the social, status of the Negro in the South for at least one hundred years."

Judge Brady clarified what he meant by that status in the following passages: "The American Negro was divorced from Africa and saved from savagery. In spite of his basic inferiority he was . . . compelled to lay aside cannibalism, his barbaric savage customs. He was transported from aboriginal ignorance and superstition. He was given a language. A moral standard of values were presented to him, a standard he could never have created for himself and which he does not now appreciate." And then, "You can dress a chimpanzee, housebreak him and teach him to use a knife and fork, but it will take countless generations of evolutionary development, if ever, before you can convince him that a caterpillar or a cockroach is not a delicacy."

For those whose need for pornography was not satisfied elsewhere in the book, Judge Brady summoned up the picture most likely to incense the ignorant and potentially violent. The conflagration that would envelop the South if the Supreme Court's decision were implemented, he predicted, would be started by a young Negro schoolboy or veteran. "The supercilious, glib young Negro, who sojourned in Chicago or New York, and who considers the counsel of his elders archaic, will perform an obscene act, or make some obscene remark, or a vile overture or assault upon some white girl." And lest there be any mistake about what white girl the judge had in mind, he put himself on record: "The loveliest and purest of God's creatures, the nearest thing to an angelic being that treads this terrestrial ball is a well-bred cultured Southern white woman or her blue-eyed, golden-haired little girl."

What should be done? The judge had an answer: "As a last resort, a step which no Southern man wants to take, is the declaring of a cold war and an economic boycott. . . . A great many Negro employees will be discharged, and though it will work a grave hardship on many white employers, still it is better 'if our right eye offend us to pluck it out.' . . . The Negro of the South should be forewarned," Judge Brady declared with a nicety befitting a true Southern gentleman, "and when the next case is brought in any of the remaining thirteen states, the economic boycott should begin."

Within weeks of the judge's original speech, the program

he mapped out had begun. In Indianola, Mississippi, less than forty miles from Mound Bayou, fourteen white men gathered in a private home on July 11, 1954, to form the first White Citizens Council. One of them, since given major credit for the idea, was a big man with fiery red hair, Robert "Tut" Patterson, a Delta planter and former football star at Mississippi State College who had returned from army service during World War II to farm some rented land near Indianola. Patterson himself has claimed that he was inspired by Judge Brady's book to devote his life to fighting desegregation, but there is evidence that he was well prepared for the inspiration. Even before the book appeared—even before the Supreme Court's decision—Patterson had been writing for a number of anti-Semitic and anti-Negro publications.

And so the White Citizens Councils with their major thrust at economic intimidation of the Negro joined the ranks of the racist organizations whose histories are in so many ways synonymous with the history of the South. Before the end of the year, Patterson was claiming White Citizens Councils in 110 Mississippi towns, with a total of more than 25,000 members. There was no reason to doubt it.

But while all of this activity was going on in Mississippi, Governor Hugh White apparently thought he saw an easier way out of the dilemma posed by the Supreme Court's decision. After consulting a small group of conservative Negroes, he summoned to Jackson 100 Negro leaders from various parts of the state for the announced purpose of endorsing a proposal to continue segregation voluntarily. This, if it could be brought off, would be a coup of considerable proportions. The governor's bait was a tacit admission of the inferiority of Negro schools. If the Negro leaders accepted his proposal, he promised the state would begin immediately to wipe out the estimated $115,000,000 disparity between white and Negro schools.

On July 29, 1954, the night before the scheduled meeting with the governor, more than ninety Negro leaders met in Jackson to discuss their plans for the following day. Later reports indicated that the session was long and the debate heated. By the next day, however, the Negro delegates were ready. Walter Sillers, Speaker of Mississippi's House of Representatives and a long-time segregationist politician, opened the meeting and introduced Governor White. The governor welcomed the participants confidently and swung into a eulogy of the fine relations between the races that Mississippi had always enjoyed. What it cost him internally to brazen his way through this speech to the very people in the best position to know what a monstrous lie it was no one will ever know, but he appeared, according to later reports, to be enjoying himself. When he had finished, a Negro delegate took the floor with an outright demand for an end to segregation.

That first speaker, Charlie Banks, was followed immediately by others, and their message was the same. Finally, and almost in desperation, Speaker Sillers called out for J. W. Jones, a conservative Negro teacher known to be a friend of the white man. Jones performed as expected, coming out meekly for segregation, and Governor White was seen to relax a little. But Jones was followed immediately by a Negro woman delegate who denounced him roundly and held him up to ridicule as a classic example of the results of segregation.

Again Speaker Sillers broke in. He called on the Reverend H. H. Humes, a Negro minister presumed to be a trusted ally. All eyes were on the minister as he rose slowly and began to speak. "Gentlemen," he said deliberately, "you all should not be mad at us. Those were *white* men that rendered that decision. Not one colored man had anything to do with it. The real trouble is that you have given us schools too long in which we could study the earth through the floor and the stars through the roof." It was a moment in which many of the Negro participants felt for the first time a surging pride in being a Negro in Mississippi.

When the meeting broke up on that note, Governor White declared himself stunned. "I had believed," he told reporters, "that certain elements representing the vast majority of Negroes would go along. Now I am definitely of the opinion you can't put any faith in any of them on this proposition." It was the first time in the memory of any Mississippi Negro that a white official had admitted publicly what every Negro knew in his bones: that most Negroes were bitterly opposed to segregation whatever they might say out loud. The final proof came with the release of a statement signed by all but one of the Negro delegates. Led by Dr. T. R. M. Howard of Mound Bayou, they declared themselves "unalterably opposed to any effort of either white or Negro citizens to attempt to circumvent the decision of the Supreme Court of the United States of America outlawing segregation in the public schools."

When news of the meeting came out, Medgar was exultant. At last, he said, the Negroes of Mississippi were standing up for what they wanted. At last they were throwing off their fears of speaking out. And once again he felt his decision to seek admission to the law school at Ole Miss had been vindicated by events. But as the long, hot Delta summer dragged on without word from the Board of Higher Learning, it became more and more clear that they were stalling.

It was late in August when Medgar was summoned to Jackson by Dr. Jobe, the executive secretary of the State

Board of Trustees of Institutions of Higher Learning. A. P. Tureaud, a Negro lawyer from New Orleans, went along as his NAACP representative. At Dr. Jobe's request, the three of them went to the office of Attorney General Coleman. It was the attorney general who conducted the interview with Medgar.

He asked many questions, most seemingly designed to determine whether Medgar's application was a sincere one. Why, he wanted to know, had Medgar waited until he was twenty-nine to decide to go to law school? And why law? Why didn't he continue in business administration? When Medgar had answered all of these questions, he asked, finally, if Medgar would accept an out-of-state scholarship. Medgar shook his head. He wanted his legal education in the state where he would practice law, he said.

The attorney general paused and then asked, if he were admitted to the University of Mississippi, would he want housing accommodations and meals on the campus? The question was asked in such tones of disbelief that its implications were obvious. Medgar, answering, spoke to them. "Yes, I plan to live on campus in a dormitory," he said, "and to do all the things any other student of the law school might do: use the library, eat in the dining hall, attend classes. But I can assure you that I bathe regularly, that I wear clean clothes, and that none of the brown of my skin will rub off. I won't contaminate the dormitory or the food."

Hearing Medgar's version of this meeting, I knew in my heart that nothing could dissuade him from going through with his plans. Almost as though by agreement between us, we both avoided the subject. There were times, though, when we knew it was uppermost in both of our minds, for neighbors and friends in Mound Bayou had begun to warn us to look out for strange cars following us when we drove, and whenever strangers were spotted in town, word was quickly passed to us to be on our guard. We did not seek this advice or warning; it was simply the Negro community's way of closing ranks around us, trying to protect us. In one way, it gave me a feeling of warmth and security and even a secret pride that my husband meant so much to these people. But the message of their concern was also clear: Medgar was in danger. There were mornings when I watched through the window as he got into the car and drove away wondering if I would ever see him again.

Medgar had sought admission for the fall term, and the fall was approaching. Though I was near the end of my pregnancy, I kept working, convinced that whatever happened we would need every penny we could earn. Medgar's work for the insurance company, combined with his recruiting for the NAACP, still kept him away from home until late in the evening, for the long summer days meant extra time in the fields for the Delta Negroes lucky enough to have work.

One night toward the middle of September, bored and restless waiting for Medgar to return home, I took Darrell and walked the five blocks to the little movie house in Mound Bayou. It was stifling inside and the picture was years old and Darrell promptly fell asleep, but it was an escape for an hour or so. When the movie was over, I carried my sleeping son home. Medgar was still out, and I went to bed with a backache.

In the morning I woke and dressed for work. Medgar, who had come in late, roused himself and began to dress. When the first pain came, I looked at my watch. It was seven-thirty. Forty-two minutes later our second child, Rena Denise Evers, was born. In-between, there was a mad dash to the hospital in which Medgar, wildly excited but insisting he was calm, forgot the suitcase I had packed more than a week earlier.

When Darrell was born, we had had both my mother and grandmother with us for some time after I came home from the hospital. This time Medgar and I had decided in advance to keep the birth a secret for a few days unless I really needed help. I suspect that Medgar did call his mother immediately. But my mother in Yazoo City, and Aunt Myrlie and Mama in Vicksburg heard nothing.

In two days I was out of the hospital, feeling fine. Several days later, when both of us had had a chance to get to know our new daughter, Medgar telephoned my family. My mother was terribly hurt at not having been notified. Aunt Myrlie and Mama were furious. A few days later Mama arrived to take over. By then I was happy to have help.

It was not long before the difference in Medgar's approach to his two children became obvious. With Darrell, he had always exhibited great pride and a kind of loving roughness. With Rena, there was an overwhelming tenderness. When he held her, it was as though he were holding a china doll that might easily break. She was a good baby from the very beginning, easy to care for, happy, undemanding. Medgar remarked about how seldom she seemed to cry, and then, I suppose because she was so placid and accepting, he went on to say that he hoped she wouldn't be as timid as I had been. It was not intended as a rebuke, and I didn't take it that way. What he meant was that he hoped beneath her happy exterior there would develop some of his own sturdy will. In that sense I *was* timid, I suffered in silence things that others wouldn't.

Habitually I avoided arguments, disliked disputes, afraid, I guess, that they would end in something worse. I was never one to demand my rights. But even then I was learning from Medgar that it was possible to argue, to discuss, to debate, without rancor. Even then, I had begun to find that people respected my opinion when I gave it, and on those rare occasions when I finally blew up over something, I had noted an unmistakable glow of pride in Medgar's eyes. If my explosion was at him, he would argue back, and it was obvious that he enjoyed me most when I gave him as good as I got.

On September 16, three days after Rena was born—the very day I came home from the hospital—the Board of Higher Learning announced that Medgar's application to Ole Miss had been rejected. I heard the news with a mixture of outrage and relief.

The excuse given by the board was that Medgar had not, as required by the university, submitted two letters of recommendation from prominent citizens of his county. In fact, he had done exactly that, even to finding two *white* citizens to vouch for him. His mistake, the board said, was that he had secured his letters from citizens of Newton County, where the Evers' home in Decatur was, and where Medgar had been born, had grown up, and had lived most of his life. Instead, they said, he should have submitted letters from citizens of Bolivar County, where Mound Bayou was located and where he had lived for the past two years. It was too bad, the board's announcement implied, and Medgar could of course try again, but it was now too late for a second application to be considered for the fall term.

There was, of course, no explanation of why it had taken a Board of Higher Learning from January to September to locate the two counties on a map, to note on Medgar's application where he lived, to understand that a mistake had been made, if mistake it really was, and to announce its decision. Nor was there any explanation of why the board had not pointed out the error to Medgar and suggested that he round up a couple of new letters in a hurry. No such explanations were necessary. No one in the state of Mississippi, black or white, misunderstood the sophistry of the board's explanation. It was precisely the sort of explanation Mississippians, black and white, had been trained to expect. It accomplished two important goals at one and the same time: it informed the white people that it was really quite simple to outwit ignorant Negroes who didn't know their place and it let the Negroes know that there wasn't a chance that such an application would ever be considered on its merits.

In this instance, the board made certain its intentions were clear by announcing the adoption of a new regulation for the future. Henceforth, each applicant for admission to Ole Miss would be required to obtain character recommendations from five alumni of the school, all of whom had been personally acquainted with the applicant for two years. Since all alumni of the university were, of course, white, the prospect of a Negro's obtaining five such recommendations was, as the board intended it to be, bleak.

For about a week after the board's decision, there were conferences between Medgar and various NAACP officials and attorneys. In the end, and much to my relief, it was decided not to pursue the case in court. Medgar's application was left on file so that a suit could be started at any time, but in the meantime the organization had something else in mind for the young Negro who had volunteered to desegregate the University of Mississippi. A state field secretary was needed if the NAACP were to capitalize on its earlier successes in organizing the Negroes of Mississippi. Medgar, it appeared, was the leading candidate for the new job.

## VIII

In the years that I had been growing up in Vicksburg, cared for by my grandmother and Aunt Myrlie, my mother had lived in a series of small towns in the Delta, supporting herself by working in white homes, as a waitress in restaurants, and finally at a dry-cleaning plant in Yazoo City. About the time I entered eighth grade, she remarried. My stepfather, Lee Mack Sanders, a United States Marine, was stationed for a number of years in North Carolina, and I saw him and my mother only when they came to Mississippi on furlough. Then, after Lee's discharge, they settled in Yazoo City, where my mother went back to work at the dry-cleaning plant and Lee found a job with an oil refinery and drove a taxicab at night.

I had had little chance to know my mother well in my youth, but after my marriage we had become increasingly close. When Medgar was called to Jackson to discuss the possibility of a job with the NAACP, I jumped at the chance to spend some time with her.

We had two days together before Medgar returned, and they brought us closer than ever before. For the first time I heard the details of her life: where she had lived, what work she had done, and, more interesting to a daughter, about her own childhood in Vicksburg. I was fascinated and plied her with questions, wondering as I listened to her answers why she dwelled at such length on mistakes she felt she had made. When I asked, she said forcefully that she hoped I might profit from hearing about them. She told me how lucky I was to have such a good husband, that most girls would give anything for a man of action and courage like Medgar. She said that if he truly wanted to do something—anything—I would be wise to support him in his attempt.

She knew of my opposition to Medgar's plan to break down the racial barriers at the University of Mississippi, and she said flatly that she thought I was wrong. "You ought to be proud of him, Myrlie. You don't know how rare such a man is. He's trying to do something important, something most men would be afraid to do."

I had to admit she was right. And I defended my pride in him. It was just that these drives of Medgar's threatened me, frightened me. I tried in those long talks with my mother to understand why.

I knew that what attracted me most about Medgar were the very qualities of courage and fearlessness of which my mother spoke with such warmth and admiration. I knew that what had always made him stand out from almost all the other men I had known was the fact that he was indisputably a man. And that, at least, was the beginning of understanding, for Southern Negroes are not supposed to behave like men. They are often in mortal danger when they do.

Recently I stumbled on a quotation in a book by Charles Silberman, *Crisis in Black and White*, that helps explain what I mean. "When the Mississippi Constitution was revised in 1890 . . ." he writes, "the purpose of revision was stated quite baldly: 'The policy of crushing out the manhood of the Negro citizens is to be carried on to success.'" This was not simply a nineteenth-century figure of speech to symbolize the denial of the vote to Negroes. Crushing out the manhood of Negro men means that and much, much more. It has been a deliberate goal of both slavery and segregation, and it is a goal that has, in all too many cases, been accomplished.

It is not for nothing that Negro men have for so long been called "boy" throughout the South, that they have been denied the title, "Mister." It is a part of the same deliberate plot that has forced Negro men to step off the sidewalk, to bow and tip their hats, to address all white men as "Sir," in the manner of boys to their superiors. If there is one thing above all else that has been degraded by Southern discrimination against the Negro, it is the concept of manhood in the Negro man.

A man, it is generally accepted in our society, supports his family. The Southern Negro has always been denied this right. Under slavery, of course, he worked solely for his master, contributing nothing to the support of his wife and children. They, too, worked for the same master, deriving their right to life and sustenance solely from him. The destinies of man and wife were separate. Marriage in any formal sense was forbidden. The real meaning of family disappeared.

Under segregation, it has been substantially the same. With only the most menial work available to the Negro man, with the good jobs reserved for whites, he has only rarely had a chance to support his family decently. Not only did his wife usually work, she often had the better, the steadier job. At its worst, her job provided food for her children, even if it were only scraps from the table of the white family for whom she cooked and cleaned. Almost always, the children worked, too, thereby undercutting the importance of their father still further. The sight of six- and seven-year-olds laboring in the cotton fields of Mississippi was not uncommon just a few years ago.

Together, the Negro mother and her children often brought more into the family larder than the father could hope to provide. Even where this was not the case, she was generally the one whose work sustained the family during the frequent layoffs from work traditional for male farm workers. The hopelessness of maintaining his status as head of the family in such a situation has caused more than one Negro husband and father to abandon his family for good.

But a man in our society also protects his family, stands up for its members, defends them from attack. The Southern Negro man has been denied this right as well. Under slavery, his wife and children were as much the possessions of the white master as was he himself. They could be worked, beaten, sold, or raped at the master's discretion. And they were.

The scars of whipping under slavery have long since disappeared, but a casual glance at the skin colors of American Negroes today gives some idea of the frequency with which the master, his sons, or his white overseer made sexual use of Negro slave women. Where there were attempts to conceal this sort of thing, it was only from the white community. The rapes took place under the very eyes of slave fathers, husbands, brothers, and sons. For to lift a hand in protest meant death. My own great-great-grandfather, the white overseer McCain, is a good example of the white rapists most Negroes can count among their ancestors. How can I be sure it was rape? Can sex between a master and a slave be anything else? Is a slave ever in a position to refuse?

Under segregation, it has been different only in degree. There are still parts of the rural South, or were until the recent racial crisis, where the only alternatives open to a Negro woman sought sexually by a white man are submission or flight. She dare not tell her menfolk—her father, brother, husband, or son—for if they reacted as men to defend her, the result, as under slavery, could well be death. And if they withdrew in fear and impotence, the Negro woman's worst fears about the men in her family would be realized. What woman would not recoil from such a test?

No, little has changed, really, except perhaps the frequency of sexual assault under segregation. And assault it still is, even where there is seeming consent on the part of the Negro woman. For who can say that she would have given her consent under conditions of genuine freedom?

The willingness—the ability—of a man to protect his family is probably the basic element in our concept of manhood. The willingness to protect one's women from the sexual advances and assaults of other men is central to it. The man who will not risk injury and even death to protect his wife or daughter from a rapist is no man at all. And it was here, at precisely this point, that the Southern Negro man lost not only his manhood rights but much of his masculinity as well. For in his case it has never been a question of risk. Death has been the universal sentence. And, knowing that, the Southern Negro woman has often protected him by silent acquiescence to the white man's sexual demands.

The degrading effect of this on the Southern Negro man has been incalculable, for it has left him impotent and unimportant in the eyes of his own family. To attempt to assert oneself as the head of a family one can neither support nor protect is, in the end, so much empty bluster. And so it was that both slavery and segregation produced and maintained among Negroes a matriarchal society, family after family in which the mother was indisputably in charge.

There was no escape from it, nor was one intended. For, to the white man, this has always been one of the benefits of slavery and segregation. It has provided him with a plentiful supply of willing male laborers, eager to work for next to nothing if only to prove their manhood to their families. And it has given him sexual access to Negro women whenever he desired it.

The results in terms of the emasculation of the typical Southern Negro man should be obvious: impotent in the eyes of his own family, without status in the Negro community, without even the ties of affection to the white community that sometimes spring up between white women and their Negro maids, he has been virtually cut off from all that manhood means. But the effect on the white man has been no less profound, for having deliberately deprived the Negro man of his manhood and masculinity, the Southern white man began immediately to fear Negro masculinity. It is an odd form of poetic justice, I suppose, the psychological principle that we fear in others what we hate and feel guilty about in ourselves. But that is precisely what happened.

No sooner had the white man successfully removed from the Negro his ability to protect his women from sexual assault; no sooner had he isolated Negro women as safe targets for his own sexual aggression; no sooner had he set up this world with its twisted double standard than he began to feel almost obsessive fears about the sexual safety of his own women. No sooner was the Negro man demasculinized than he became, in the white man's guilt-ridden mind, masculinity run wild. It is the white man throughout Southern history who has played the role of rapist. Yet it is the white man who, at the same time, has obsessively feared the Negro man as a potential rapist of white women. It was, at base, a guilty fear of retaliation.

This is the climate in which generations of Negroes have lived in the South, the climate that has twisted and distorted the Negro family and bred irrational fears in the minds of generations of white men. It is rarely spelled out in detail, and, when it is, it is generally rejected by everyone. The Negro woman rejects it because it reflects on her; the Negro man for the same reason. Whites reject it out of blindness and guilt, and the vicious circle goes on, spiraling into the future.

It has affected every one of us, black and white, who has lived in the South in one way or another. The almost miraculous thing is that some Negro men manage to grow up in spite of it with their virility and manhood intact. Medgar's father, with his refusal to step off the sidewalk for a white man, was surely one of them. Medgar, with his determination to fight segregation in all its aspects, was another. And yet the tensions of this cruel and twisted world of the white man's making had their effect even on him.

I have seen Medgar in an almost uncontrollable rage only twice. Both times the incident that provoked it involved a white man, a Negro woman, and sex. Once, driving home late at night, the headlights of his car flashed over a couple embracing in a parked car at the end of our street. The woman was a Negro, a woman we both knew, recently separated from her husband. The man was white.

My first knowledge that anything was wrong was the violent slam of our car door and the sight of Medgar storming into the house. He was cursing, something he almost never did, his eyes wild with rage. It was a long time before I could calm him enough to tell me what had happened. Then it came out.

"That slut!" he shouted. "That foul, no-good woman! Lowering herself to make love with a white man!" His fury grew even as he spoke. "I ought to get a gun and blow their brains out!"

I had never heard him talk this way, and it frightened me. Why should he care so much?

"What does it matter to you?" I asked. "Do you have some personal interest in her?"

He turned in amazement to face me. "Of course I don't!" he shouted. "What do you think I am?"

"Then you have no right to interfere," I said.

"She's a traitor to her race!" he shouted, whirling and slamming his way into the bedroom.

For a moment I thought he might really go for his gun, but when I heard him pacing, I knew that he wouldn't. Later, in bed, he tossed and turned and cursed under his breath. Before dawn he was awake and pacing the floor again, preaching to the room. I understood only partly what he was feeling then, but I sensed his frustration. It was a frustration, I now know, at his inability—at the inability of all Negro men—to end the long history of this kind of degradation.

The other time I saw him in such a state was at his office during the time we both worked for the NAACP in Jackson. This time I understood better. A young couple that lived not far from us had come in to tell a tragic but all-too-familiar story. The woman worked in a private home for a white family. That day, while the woman of the house was away, her white husband had raped her.

The young woman told her story in such detail it was impossible not to believe her. Her husband sat, head lowered, hearing it now for the second time. Medgar's face was tense with anger as he listened, stopping her now and then to ask a question. When she had finished, Medgar, holding his anger in check, asked the two of them to come with him to the police station to prefer charges against the white man. The husband refused.

"It's no use going to the police," he said. "You know they won't do anything. They never do. All that'll happen is that Ruthie and I will both lose our jobs. We'll be threatened and maybe beaten up. We might even be killed."

Medgar stared at the frightened young man in utter disbelief. "The man raped your wife!" he said. "He raped your wife!"

"I know that," the young man said mournfully. "You don't have to tell me. But you know we can't do anything about it."

Medgar flew into a rage. "Can't do anything about it? We can go to the police! We can make out charges against him! We can insist that the police arrest him! We can publicize it in the newspapers! We can expose him as a rapist! What we *can't* do is nothing! We can't let him get away with it, can we?"

"He's got away with it," the man said dejectedly. "They always get away with it. All that'll happen is we'll both lose our jobs and maybe get beat up."

"To hell with your jobs!" Medgar shouted. "To hell with getting beat up! If a white man touched my wife, I'd fight back or die in the attempt! They'd have to kill me to stop me! I'd be less than a man not to fight back!" And then he stopped and in cold anger spat at the man, "That's what you are. You're less than a man!" The words had the ring of a curse.

Both of those incidents took place later, after Medgar had been working with the NAACP for some time. But a similar one occurred the very night he returned from Jackson to Yazoo City with word that, subject to the approval of the national board in New York, he had been accepted as the NAACP's first Mississippi field secretary.

My mother and Lee had gone to a movie, leaving Medgar and me alone with the children. Walking home, they noticed a car with two white men in it slow down beside them and then cruise along at the curb, keeping pace with them. Finally one of the white men called insultingly to my mother, inviting her into the car. Mother and Lee kept walking. But the white men persisted, and the invitations became more obscene. Eventually the car stopped, and the man on the right opened the car door.

Lee turned to face the car, sending Mother running to the nearest house. It was a white neighborhood, and when the door opened at her pounding, the white men in the car slammed the car door and drove off. Lee joined Mother at the house and together they described to the white owner what had happened. Lee telephoned the police.

Two white policemen came to the house, clearly annoyed to find the complainants Negroes. When Mother and Lee had told their story once more, the policemen began asking questions. Before long, their questions became insulting. Wasn't it possible, one of them asked Lee, that Mother might be having an affair with one of the white men and that he had been angered at seeing her with a Negro?

Medgar was enraged at the story, and he stalked the kitchen as Mother and Lee told how they had left the house and walked home, knowing that nothing would be done. All of us knew, or thought we knew, what would have happened if Lee had not been with Mother. Yet even his presence had not kept the men from stopping. Watching Medgar pace, his teeth clenched, the muscles of his jaw tensed, I felt myself the awful frustration, the terrible impotence of the Negro man in the South, the impossibility of his properly defending his women without immediately risking his life. Lee had been reduced to standing between the men and Mother, and even this had done nothing to stop them. It had been Mother's success in bringing people—white people—to the door that had frightened them away. My heart ached at the torment of frustration Lee must have been feeling.

We talked far into the night, my mother, Lee, Medgar, and I. I recalled a time when I was fourteen and had been walking home from a movie with Aunt Myrlie in Vicksburg. A white man had driven by slowly several times, looking us over, and then he had stopped and offered us a ride. It was clear to me even then that what he was suggesting was more than a ride. Aunt Myrlie pushed me along, her eyes straight ahead. When the man circled the block again, she whispered to me to keep walking, to ignore him. If he stopped the car and got out, she said, I should scream and run as fast as I could. She would take care of herself.

I remembered my fears and questions when we finally reached home safely, and I remembered Aunt Myrlie's evasive answers. In time I came to understand, as all Southern Negro girls do, what that experience had meant, but it was not until the night at my mother's house, as we sat for hours discussing such things, that I really felt the fullness of the horror these experiences had for Negro men. Medgar was furious and Lee humiliated, and as they talked I wept inwardly at the thought of how their helplessness in the face of such incidents must corrode their very souls.

Medgar's news about his new job had clearly pleased Mother, and while I had some fears about the dangers of such work, I, too, found reasons to be happy. It meant, first, that we would leave Mound Bayou, and no wish had been closer to my heart for the past two years. It meant, too, that we would have a larger income, for Medgar's salary of $4500 a year would be a considerable increase over what he had been earning. He had insisted as a condition of his employment that the NAACP hire me as his secretary, and they had all but agreed. That meant not only that I would not have to find a new job when we got to Jackson but that I would be spending more time with my husband than at any time since his graduation from college.

These were all practical reasons for my happiness at the news, but there were others, more important in the long run. My two days alone with my mother had taught me something about myself and Medgar. For the first time, really, I was able to admit openly my pride and admiration for some of the things he had done, things I had opposed because they frightened me. I had begun to understand how important it was for Medgar to have my approval and backing—important not just for him but for myself. I had begun to see how much I had denied myself of him, of his enthusiasms, his thoughts, his dreams, by refusing to share the preoccupations that absorbed him.

There was by now no reason to doubt that Medgar had found a cause that would remain central to his existence for years, and I could see that to remain aloof from it could only mean disaster to our marriage. We had been at odds with each other for more than two years, and more than anything else in the world I wanted that to end.

Even more important, I had at least the beginnings of an understanding of the conflict within myself that had kept us apart. Largely through those long talks with my mother I had begun to understand that it was the very same qualities that I most admired in Medgar that also frightened me. I had grown up in a family that never discussed race, that never complained about discrimination. Until I met Medgar, I had never heard a Negro challenge segregation. Now I was married to a man who did, openly and publicly.

More and more from that time on, I found myself reassessing the things he had done, the things he had said, his almost desperate frustration at the conditions he had found in the Delta, and to find within myself more room for understanding, pride, and sympathy. I never lost my fears, for they were based on reality; I guess I slowly learned to live with them. I think Medgar sensed this change in me even as I myself was becoming aware of it, because he slowly drew me more and more into thoughts he had previously kept private.

My mother cried when we left Yazoo City the next day. It was the first time I had ever seen her cry on parting. Two days later I was called to the telephone at work in Mound Bayou and told by my stepfather that she had died of heart failure.

The next few days are a blur even in memory. We went to Yazoo City, returned to Mound Bayou, and went back again for the funeral services, which seemed interminable. We drove to Vicksburg for the burial. I was sick from within, for I felt I had just come to know my mother when she was taken from me. I felt dazed and bruised but, try as I would, I couldn't cry. A few weeks later, tears came in a flood, and I guess I was on my way to recovering. In a way, my mother's death drew Medgar and me still closer, for he had just lost his father, and we had a common feeling of deprivation.

# IX

Early in December 1954, Medgar learned of his final acceptance by the national board of the NAACP in New York and gave notice to Dr. Howard that he was leaving the insurance company. Gloster Current, the director of the NAACP's branches throughout the country, wrote him from New York welcoming him formally to the national staff. Medgar was instructed to fly to New York on New Year's Day for a ten-day orientation in the national office. Meanwhile, he was authorized to find office space in Jackson, purchase the necessary furniture and equipment, and prepare a budget for the operation of the new office. His job, in essence, would be to act as the national office's representative in Mississippi.

Gloster, who was to become a close friend, also urged Medgar to begin immediately securing affidavits from victims of racial incidents in Mississippi and to continue a county-by-county investigation into the activities of the White Citizens Councils, which he had begun on his own. A good portion of Medgar's work, it was clear, would be investigations of this kind.

But there were dozens of loose ends to be tied up before

he could embark on his new career, the most depressing of which were our debts. To leave Mound Bayou and start fresh in Jackson, we had somehow to pay our bills. Medgar tried to consolidate them with one large loan but could find no one who would advance that much money against his new and untried job. Finally, and with great reluctance, he wrote Gloster about the problem. It had been impossible to break even in Mound Bayou on our combined salaries, and despite the promised increase with the NAACP, we faced the prospect of starting anew with a $500 deficit. Fortunately, the NAACP came through with a $500 advance against Medgar's salary. He agreed to pay it back at the rate of fifty dollars a month.

That settled, he drove to Jackson, found an apartment, and arranged for our few pieces of furniture to be moved from Mound Bayou. When the moving van came, we drove to Vicksburg, and Medgar went on to Jackson to supervise the unloading. He was back in Vicksburg the same day, and on January 1 he took a plane from Natchez for New York. Dr. A. M. Mackel of Natchez, a vice-president of the state conference of NAACP branches, was there with me to see him off, and as we watched the plane leave the ground, he turned to me. "That man has a great future ahead of him in Mississippi," he said. "He could easily develop into another Walter White."

He said it with such conviction, with a deep pride in Medgar, in himself as a Negro, and with a kind of optimism for the future so rare among Mississippi Negroes that I was deeply moved. I don't know what I said in reply, but I remember driving back to Vicksburg with a new sense of my husband's destiny and a desperate impatience to pass on this high compliment to him. Walter White was then the NAACP's executive secretary, with thirty-seven years of work for the association behind him. He was a legend among Negroes, a man whose fair skin and blue eyes would easily have enabled him to escape identification as a Negro, yet a man who had devoted his adult life, as an investigator, as a writer, as an organizer, to the cause of the American Negro.

Medgar's ten days in New York were a heady experience, and it was only slowly after he returned to Mississippi that I gathered together the bits and pieces of it. In his more than two years in the Delta, he had found both a cause and a career, and in New York, with an annual gathering of field secretaries from the other states, he was surrounded by professionals whose full time was devoted to solving the problems that had so frustrated him. It was ten days of talk and listening, comparing observations, experiences, techniques, successes, and failures. There were stories of lawsuits and investigations, of police brutality and private violence, of economic intimidation and threats, of membership drives and publicity campaigns. Everyone was interested in Mississippi, and there was a unanimous belief that it would be the hardest of all the states to change. Not a few of the other field secretaries expressed admiration for Medgar's courage in taking the job. Some expressed doubt that he was wholly sane.

There was time, aside from business, for Medgar to see a little of New York, and he reveled once more in the freedom to eat in any restaurant and sit in any seat at a movie. The association had reserved a room for him at the Hotel McAlpin, on 34th Street and Broadway, and there he literally wallowed in the luxury of room service. When I joshingly expressed jealousy at his extravagant descriptions, he relented slightly. "Your room service is better, Myrlie," he said mock-seriously. "There's usually a little affection to go along with it."

Medgar came back to face a crushing time schedule. When we moved to the new apartment in Jackson, we took Big Mama, my mother's mother, along, for by then we had heard the final word that the association had agreed to hire me as Medgar's secretary, and we needed someone to care for the children while we both worked. Medgar quickly found a suitable office on Farish Street in a Negro neighborhood of downtown Jackson, and on January 23, 1955, the office was formally opened. Gloster Current flew down from New York and Mrs. Ruby Hurley, Southeast Regional Secretary of the association, came from her headquarters in Birmingham, Alabama.

In his speech at the opening ceremonies, Gloster attacked a package of recent legislation passed by the Mississippi State Legislature. Of a law that would permit the abolition of all public schools, he said that the state's Negroes and "thinking white citizens will not sit idly by while misguided politicians destroy the schools." He described a new anti-integration amendment as "not worth the paper it is written on." A second amendment designed to make Negro voter registration even more difficult than it was drew this challenge: "The NAACP will not rest until every Negro in Mississippi who is eligible is granted the right of the ballot." These were strong words in Mississippi, and for Medgar they came to constitute almost a program. When Gloster introduced him to the crowd of Negroes as a dedicated man, I knew in my heart that it was no exaggeration. Medgar Evers, Gloster said, was a man who, "as a veteran, is determined that the democracy for which he fought abroad must obtain in his native state of Mississippi."

Looking back, I can see that our move to Jackson was the beginning of a whole new life for us. Even at the time,

I had something of a sense of beginning. Jackson, after Mound Bayou, was like a big city, and for months I felt a special tingle of excitement at just living there. Our two-bedroom apartment was a vast improvement over Mound Bayou, even with my grandmother as an extra occupant. In spite of the twenty-five dollars a month we insisted on paying Big Mama, we found ourselves much better off than before, for with my salary of just over $2000 a year, we had a combined income for the first time of more than $6500 a year. It left nothing for luxuries, to be sure, but there was no question that we would have plenty to eat.

Medgar faced his new job as he faced almost everything. He had a sort of happy optimism that most problems could be solved with a little effort and that only stubbornness stood in the way of others sharing his various enthusiasms. He assumed, for example, that people he liked were people I would like, that pleasures he enjoyed would be pleasures for me, too. Once, in Mound Bayou, I was sick in bed with flu when friends from Decatur turned up in town. Medgar, without a thought in the world, insisted they come home for dinner. The first I knew of it was when he appeared at my bedside with a happy smile on his face. "Hi, honey," he said brightly. "Look who's here! Come on, get up and fix dinner for us." I did. But he caught it later.

He had the same sort of optimism about most things, and he was always impatient when events proved it unwarranted. He had learned to drive at an early age, and when he met me at Alcorn, he was convinced he could teach me in a few short lessons. It didn't turn out that way. Again and again my lesson would end in a bitter argument about my alleged stupidity. Medgar would grow impatient; he would raise his voice; I would burst into tears of frustration and anger; and months would go by before either of us was ready to try again.

This business of teaching me to drive went on for a long time. One night after we had moved to Mound Bayou, Medgar decided to make yet another attempt, and we drove out to an old highway where there was little traffic. Taking the wheel, I drove for some distance, my confidence growing with every turn of the wheels. Finally, and with a grudging grunt of approval, Medgar pointed to a road into a cotton field and told me to turn in and stop. I executed the turn like a professional.

Medgar got out of the car to make sure the highway was clear and then told me to back up. I put the car into reverse and started back, apparently too fast for him. "Wait! Slow down! Put on the brakes!" he shouted. In my confusion I slammed my foot down hard on the accelerator and backed the car neatly into a ditch. Medgar was furious.

It was dark and silent at the side of the highway, the silence broken only by Medgar's explosions and my sniffling back the tears. Eventually we started walking down the highway together, looking for help. Two miles and many bitter words later, we found a farm house, and after much persuasion Medgar succeeded in getting the Negro farmer to dress and drive his tractor back to our car. With the car back on the highway, Medgar reached in his pocket and gave the man what he thought was two dollars. It wasn't until he had parked the car at our home that he took out his money in the light and found he had given the man a five-dollar bill and a single. It was more than a minor mistake, for it left us with only two or three dollars until payday. Medgar, now totally out of patience, really let go. He called me stupid, said I would never learn to drive, and slammed out of the car and into the house, leaving me sitting there fuming.

I resented being called stupid, and I resented being blamed for his mistake with the money. Most of all, I guess, I resented not being able to make the car do what I wanted it to do. As I sat there clenching my fists, I made up my mind that no mere automobile was going to defeat me. Screwing up my courage, I started the engine and began to practice backing. When I could back without difficulty, I left the house and drove around the silent town of Mound Bayou, backing up at every opportunity. It was hours later when I came home and went to bed. Medgar was sound asleep.

Next morning, up ahead of him, I dressed quickly and drove the car to the office. I expected him to be furious at having to walk to the office to get the car, and when I saw him get into it and drive off to work without coming inside, I was sure he was. But that night I found him more pleased with my determination than anything else. Medgar was like that; I think he admired determination more than any other single quality.

When we opened the NAACP office in Jackson, I learned about another side of this man I had married. Though the office staff consisted of just the two of us, Medgar had firm ideas about how things should be done. From the beginning, he insisted that if we were to work together, we must behave in the office strictly as employer and employee right down to addressing each other as Mr. and Mrs. Evers. I came finally to accept this largely as evidence of Medgar's determination to make good in the job and avoid any possible charge that my employment was simply a way of taking more money out of the organization, but I must admit I found it hard to adjust to this kind of formality for eight hours each day. Once or twice, when there was no one around and the work was caught up, I went into his office and sat on his lap. He was abrupt and businesslike.

"No, Myrlie. Not here."

"Oh Medgar," I said. "Who's going to know? Even if someone walked in, it isn't important. We *are* married."

But he would firmly push me off his lap and explain all over again that the association was paying us to work and run a dignified office, and that was what we were going to do. The arrangement was successful, for it meant that we never discussed personal problems until we left the office, and as far as I know, there was never a complaint about my working for my husband. But we were teased unmercifully by visitors from the national office in New York. Roy Wilkins, then the NAACP's administrator, and Gloster Current both thought it was the strangest thing they had ever heard when Medgar addressed me as Mrs. Evers. But Medgar, being Medgar, never budged from his position no matter what anyone said.

It wasn't long before I came to prize my job as Medgar's secretary for much more than the additional income it brought us. Without it, I would scarely have seen my husband at all. Even with it, I saw little enough of him, for he began early to make a habit of leaving me with all the office work and walking out. Later I would look out the window and see him on the sidewalk below, mixing and chatting with people. When I mentioned it in something less than approving tones, he explained patiently that he was "making contacts." "Good public relations, Myrlie," he said. "Good public relations."

At first I had my doubts. It seemed too much like fun to be work. But as time went by I learned that this was an important part of Medgar's job, for the very mention of the NAACP was enough to frighten many Mississippi Negroes, and the sight of a smiling, friendly young man who openly introduced himself as the association's Mississippi field secretary could not help but reassure people.

The fear that many Mississippi Negroes had of association with the NAACP was not entirely unreasonable, for known membership in the organization had proven more than ample cause for dismissal from a job, loss of a mortgage or farm loan, or even threats of violence. Medgar quickly learned the details of many such incidents and came to have an even greater respect for the Negroes who dared to accept positions of leadership throughout the state. He was insulated against economic reprisal by being an employee of the national office; they, on the other hand, were volunteers, men who had to make a living in other ways.

With the growth of the White Citizens Councils, economic pressure on Negroes known to favor desegregation quickly became a brutal fact of life. Even before Medgar assumed his new position, Roy Wilkins had announced publicly that the association was working to find ways of combating this new racist tactic. Two days before Christmas of 1954, Dr. Channing Tobias, chairman of the board of directors of the NAACP, had wired President Eisenhower urging a conference with him on the growing problem. "Negro leadership in Mississippi is being subjected to undisguised economic intimidation admittedly designed to curb civil rights and particularly to discourage registration and voting and to force abandonment of efforts to secure peaceful compliance with the May seventeenth ruling of the U. S. Supreme Court outlawing racial segregation in public schools," the telegram read, in part.

"Reports from members of our staff in the state indicate banks and other private credit institutions are conspiring to put the squeeze on Negro farmers, businessmen and homeowners who are active in the NAACP by foreclosing their mortgages, demanding full and prompt payment of indebtedness, and refusing credit."

The telegram pointed the finger of blame at the White Citizens Councils, quoting State Representative Wilma Sledge of Sunflower County, Mississippi, to the effect that the councils were "organized for the sole purpose of maintaining segregation of the races" through the "application of economic pressure to troublemakers."

Dr. Tobias's telegram ended with a plea to President Eisenhower: "We believe that a public statement from you followed by corrective action would be a proper exercise of the moral suasion inherent in the high office of the Presidency of a free people." The plea apparently fell on deaf ears, for no public statement was made.

Meanwhile, the NAACP set up its own way of providing economic relief for Mississippi Negroes denied credit within the state, and on January 6, 1955, while Medgar was still in New York, the plan was announced. It called for the association and other sympathetic organizations to deposit reserve funds in the Tri-State Bank of Memphis, a Negro-owned institution, and for the bank to utilize these funds solely for loans to Negro victims of economic reprisal in Mississippi. Within two weeks the bank had extra assets of $40,000—$20,000 from the NAACP, and $10,000 each from an insurance company and a strong NAACP backer. It began immediately to process applications for loans.

By January 20, three days before the formal opening of our new office in Jackson, the NAACP had filed with the White House a number of sworn affidavits accusing representatives of federal financing agencies of joining in the economic pressure tactics of the White Citizens Councils. The affidavits named two white agents of the Farmers Home

Administration, an agency of the U. S. Department of Agriculture, as individuals who had refused federal assistance to Negro applicants entitled to loans.

One applicant, the owner of seventy-three acres of rich Mississippi Delta soil, a farmer whose property included a seven-room house, a barn, and a tractor, swore to his inability to get loans for operating the farm. "Because of my activities in bringing in about 25 members in the NAACP branch," he wrote, "economic pressure is being exerted on me." Although his tract produced as much as a bale and a half of cotton per acre, he was being pressed for immediate payment of a $3500 mortgage. "Anyone belonging to the NAACP," he wrote, "is deemed unworthy of financial assistance and is termed a troublemaker in the community."

As far as we ever learned, these protests to the White House were ignored, for the pressures increased, both from individuals and companies in Mississippi and from agencies of the federal government. It was, in fact, about this time that Dr. T. R. M. Howard of Mound Bayou was ordered by his draft board to state why he should not be reclassified 1-A. He was then forty-seven years old.

If anyone wanted to know how the White House really felt about the problems of Negroes in the United States, he had only to read of the incident involving the U. S. Navy's aircraft carrier *Midway*, which visited Capetown, South Africa, that same month of January 1955. Despite protests from both Negro and white Americans, the 400 Negro, Filipino, and Japanese crew members of the *Midway* were sent ashore with instructions to obey South African apartheid laws and carrying special permits to drink in segregated Negro bars. The philosophy of the Administration was clearly to abide by the customs of the country, whether in South Africa or in Mississippi.

## X

Medgar had not been at his new job many weeks before we both knew that he had joined the national organization of the NAACP at a time of crisis for Mississippi. It was not long before we began to see the effect this crisis would have on Mississippi's Negroes.

Before the Supreme Court's 1954 school desegregation decision, most Mississippi Negroes had slumbered along under a system of segregation that was a part of the fabric of their lives. There were a few Negro voices of protest to be sure, but those that were not quickly silenced in one way or another too often took on the sound of a cry in the wilderness, too fragile and isolated and certainly too dangerous to be listened to.

When thoughts of resistance to segregation, or even to one aspect of it, did arise, there was almost always a recent event to turn such dangerous thoughts aside. Somewhere in the state a Negro had disappeared, had been murdered or lynched, had been railroaded through the white man's courts to a living death in the state penitentiary at Parchman. There was nothing in the law to prevent a Negro from hating individual aspects of segregation, but there were few voices to help him make the important connection between the general poverty and hardship of his life and the system that, in fact, perpetuated them.

Then came the court's ruling that segregated schools were inherently unequal. Suddenly there was a voice, more impressive and resounding than that of any Negro leader, the voice of the highest court in the land, and it was saying in unmistakable language that segregation was wrong, was illegal, was intolerable, and that it must be ended. It was a voice that echoed through Mississippi's Negro communities all the louder for the relative silence that had preceded it. It was a voice of change, of impending liberation, of challenge to the central fact of any Negro's life. It was a voice that demanded decisions.

Negroes had to make up their minds. In the face of the state's announced decision to resist, Mississippi Negroes were going to be forced to take sides. If it were not their fellow Negroes who demanded it, it would be the state's whites who insisted on it. Sides were being chosen for a battle to come, and woe to the individual caught in the no man's land between them.

The NAACP's decision to hire the state's first field secretary, to open an office in Jackson, and the accompanying step-up of the organization's activities in Mississippi forced the issue on many Negroes. For the first time, really, there were *Negroes* who wanted to know just where other Negroes stood.

For most of Mississippi's Negroes it was a difficult decision. The enormous weight of proof, of history, of the facts of their own individual lives were all on one side. They knew from long experience what happened to Negroes who stepped out of line. On the other side lay—what? A hope? A fragile promise? Some few educated Negroes knew it was a promise made almost a hundred years before, a promise abandoned and forgotten. There was little question which side of the scales held the overwhelming weight of history.

And yet, for the first time in generations, there was hope. For the first time in memory there was activity. Suddenly now there were men and women, Mississippi Negroes, quietly stepping out of line and beginning to walk toward this new voice that called out from far-off Washington. What was a Negro to do?

The crisis of decision continued for years. Many were those who changed their minds again and again as events appeared to tip the scales first one way and then another. Many more were those who put off any decision, who held back as long as they could. But there were some from whom an answer was demanded almost immediately. Medgar's presence on the sidewalk below our office urging people to join the NAACP, his public statements, his speeches to various groups, and his help in setting up new NAACP branches— all these activities put the question before them. And there were not a few who responded with opposition to the organization that was thus demanding that they make up their minds.

Many of these were teachers who knew that even a whisper of a connection with the NAACP could mean loss of jobs. Beyond that, some of them actually feared an eventual desegregation of schools. It was at least conceivable to them that the state might someday permit some Negro students to attend white schools. It was inconceivable that Negro teachers would be allowed to teach in those schools. And the Supreme Court, after all, had said nothing in its decision about teachers.

There were others who opposed the efforts of the NAACP for other reasons. A few, undoubtedly, actually favored segregation, for under it they had fared relatively well—relative, that is, to the masses of Mississippi Negroes. These were usually Negroes who had so ingratiated themselves with whites that they had been rewarded with the better jobs, the better acres of land, or the better chance to escape the unequal justice of the state. They included, in places where Negroes were permitted to vote in small numbers, Negro politicians who swung whatever segment of the Negro vote they controlled to candidates selected by their white patrons. They included Negroes who had worked loyally, sometimes for generations, for a single white family of substance and who had thereby earned the protection of that family, a protection too precious to jeopardize in the dangerous times that clearly lay ahead.

They included the rare Negroes who served as spies in the Negro community for the white political powers, those obsequious traitors to their people who sold bits and pieces of information for the crumbs of privilege such intelligence was considered to be worth. They included sometimes a Negro school principal or college president, a Department of Agriculture county agent or a minister, whose reward for helping to keep their people down was to be raised above the majority of them.

There were probably hundreds—maybe thousands—of Mississippi Negroes who were actually bought and paid for by the whites in various communities. They included the gamblers and bootleggers who bled their own people of their paltry share of the state's paltry income—always with the connivance and on the orders of the local sheriff or police chief. They included the out-and-out criminals whose price for being permitted to prey on the Negro community invariably included a large percentage of the profits of their crime paid to their white protectors.

In a segregated society there was always room for a few Negroes willing and able to justify their racial treason to work in the interest of the white man. Nor were all of them always conscious of the degree of their defection. Some, like the Negro minister whose church performed the function of draining off the frustrations of his flock, probably served a mental health function among the Negroes while at the same time helping to keep the system working smoothly. Anything that kept the Negro in his assigned place, anything that turned his anger inward, anything that channeled his aggression toward his own people and away from the whites served the system. And it was in the very nature of the system that all of us, at one time or another, served it somehow. There were a few that served it willingly.

One could live a lifetime of such service to segregation and not be found out, for almost invariably those Negroes who, for services rendered, had the ear of important or powerful whites were the very ones who, in the Negro community, were turned to for help in time of need. To many Negroes they seemed the leaders of the Negro community where leadership had always meant, first and foremost, the ability to appeal successfully to powerful forces in the white community. And these Negroes were, of course, often opposed to the NAACP and all its goals, for progress toward those goals meant the inevitable loss of their privileged positions. The whites would not long stick with a Negro who could not prevent his people from petitioning for school desegregation, who could not supply the information necessary to make examples of the newly emerging crop of genuine Negro leaders, or who could not continue to drain off the frustrations, energies, and tiny incomes of the Negro community into harmless channels.

These were facts of segregation, rooted in understandable

human foibles and ambitions, and they would appear in retrospect easy enough to detect. And yet it was not easy at the time. Segregation had stood, immovable, for generations. It was the system one was born into, the system one grew up under, the system in which one lived and worked and married and reared children and died. For the vast majority of Mississippi's Negroes there was no other system, and it remained as unquestioned as the sun that rose at dawn and set at dusk, immutable, inexorable, as much a part of nature as the air one breathed. Even those Negroes who became pawns of the whites through ambition or greed or simply through faithful family service often did not recognize their roles. For if the system were fixed and unchangeable, then they were merely operating within it according to the generations-old standards of all Americans: following the drive to get ahead, seeking personal and family security and a little profit on the side. And it is undeniable that they were performing a service for the Negro community as well, even if that service were simply to supply a link in the chain of appeal to the white powers of the community.

Yet, for all of this, there were many, many more Negroes who refused or were unable to serve the white-imposed system of segregation than there were those who would sell out their people for forty pieces of silver. The real choice came when segregation suddenly seemed no longer quite so immutable. Then, with a tiny light of hope at the end of the long dark tunnel, many Mississippi Negroes were forced to make a conscious choice. The real traitors were those who persisted, in the face of that hope of change, to serve their narrow self-interests. And as time went by, it became clear that they would be in the tiny minority. Evidence of this fact never failed to astonish the white community, and all sorts of irrational explanations were offered to explain it. Communists, outside agitators, Northern politicians, secret and subversive elements were blamed for the defection of Negroes previously thought to be safely bought and paid for, or at least sufficiently intimidated.

But if the defection of Negroes from the whites surprised them, the refusal of Negroes to join a movement that was clearly their own surprised and appalled Medgar. He had no sooner taken over his new job than he was attacked by a Negro newspaper editor. Early in April 1955, Percy Greene, editor of the Jackson *Advocate*, published an editorial that left no doubt as to his allegiance.

The editorial dealt with the state's multi-million dollar "school equalization program," the very program Governor White had unsuccessfully attempted to use as bait for Negro agreement to voluntary segregation. It had been sold to white Mississippians as a means of preventing school desegregation on the theory that having got away with separate and unequal schools for decades, perhaps now they could avoid desegregation by belatedly making the schools equal.

As new Negro schools were built, of course, it became clear that equality was to be confined strictly to the shell of the buildings. The books in the libraries, the teacher load, the equipment and facilities never approached equality with the white schools.

There are today in Mississippi Negro schools whose playground equipment was bought and installed by Negro parents. There are high schools whose model chemistry laboratories have no connections for hot and cold water or gas. The state's belated provisions for equal *state* tax money to white and Negro schools made good propaganda only for those who did not know that the *local* school tax expenditures were flagrantly unequal. In Hinds County, which encompasses Jackson, for example, the local per pupil expenditure for schools was $80.24 for white children and $10.41 for Negroes. Nor was that the worst example. Yazoo County, in the Delta, spent $245.55 of local money to educate each white child. The equivalent amount for each Negro child was $2.92.

It should not have taken an exceptional mind to foresee these results. Mississippi had always cheated its Negroes. Nor did it take great genius to read in the white newspapers the openly avowed purpose of the so-called equalization program. The NAACP had pointed this out in a statement characterizing the program's goals of avoiding desegregation as "mere wishful thinking." Percy Greene's editorial read in part: "It can be safely stated as a fact that 85 per cent of the Negro school patrons in Mississippi, and the South generally, are hoping and praying that no attempt will be made to enforce the Supreme Court decision. They know full well the nature of the trouble that would follow and they also realize that the matter could become so bitterly controversial that there would be no public schools at all for Negro children.

"Insofar as Negroes in the South are concerned, the NAACP is an enemy of the Negro race."

This editorial, which infuriated many Negroes and led Medgar to say that it might as well have been bought and paid for by the state of Mississippi, was immediately picked up and published by the white newspapers of the state. The Jackson papers gave it a big play, but one of them, inadvertently, gave it an accurate title: "The Voice of A Negro." Wishful-thinking whites no doubt hoped it was the voice of *all* Negroes. It wasn't.

The punishment some Negroes endured to support the NAACP was truly astonishing. Medgar learned of many such cases early in his new work. Dr. E. J. Stringer, who was president of the state conference of branches when Medgar applied for admission to the University of Mississippi, was a good example. A young dentist from Columbus, Mississippi, he had helped build the conference from twenty-one branches in 1953 to thirty-one in 1954. Membership in the state had grown from 1600 to more than 2700 in the same period, and in his own branch in Columbus, where he also served as president, Dr. Stringer had exceeded his own 1954 membership goal of 150 to end the year with a whopping 400 members.

None of these gains had been made without sacrifice, often the kinds of personal sacrifice that Medgar was forever lecturing me about. Dr. Stringer had lost the use of his automobile when his liability insurance, required by state law, was suddenly canceled. Creditors who previously gave him a reasonable time to make payments on dental supplies began to require immediate payment. A Negro schoolteacher who had paid Dr. Stringer for her dental work by check was accused of making a donation to the NAACP when someone at the bank passed the word to a white school official. It required a sworn affidavit from Dr. Stringer that the check was in payment for dental work to keep her from losing her job.

Mrs. Stringer had been a teacher in the Negro public schools in Columbus, one of the few who held a master's degree. After the publicity surrounding Medgar's application for admission to Ole Miss, she lost her job. But the economic pressure, difficult as it made the Stringers' lives, was nothing compared to the terror. Day and night there were anonymous telephone calls, obscene threats, murder warnings. At night, cars would drive slowly past the Stringer house, and the knowledge that one of them might contain a man carrying a home-made bomb forced the Stringers to sleep in their middle bedroom.

In the midst of this harassment, Dr. Stringer was suddenly called in by the Internal Revenue Service for an audit of his federal income-tax returns. It might have seemed an isolated incident but for the fact that a number of outspoken critics of segregation were suffering the same fate at the same time. What this suggested, of course, was that still another department of the federal government was being used by racists to make life difficult for Southern opponents of segregation. It was not until later, when a 1958 survey of thirty-four prominent white and Negro desegregationists in the South was made public, that it finally became known that the federal income-tax returns of these men and women had been audited at almost four and a half times the normal rate. One of those who by that time had also been subjected to this new kind of harassment was Medgar.

Because few men could withstand this kind of pressure over a long period of time, Dr. Stringer had declined to run for a new term as state president at the end of 1954. Replacing him was another dentist, Dr. A. H. McCoy of Jackson, a man of equal courage and somewhat greater economic security. Dr. Stringer, far from retiring completely from the firing line, became one of four vice-presidents who supervised NAACP affairs in various sections of the state.

Within a few weeks of the opening of our office in Jackson, Medgar began visiting NAACP branches throughout Mississippi. He returned from each of these trips with new stories of harassment and economic pressure and new evidence of courageous commitment. At one branch he was told of a meeting with the local school board after a petition had been presented asking for an end to school segregation. The white chairman of the school board, after reading the petition aloud, had singled out a young Negro in the back of the room. "There is a nigger back there who is a sharecropper," he said, pointing. "Nigger," he continued, looking straight at the young man, "don't you want to take your name off this petition that says you want to send your children to school with white children?"

The NAACP leader who told Medgar the story chuckled: "The young man was badly frightened, and he shook all over until the shaking got to his head, and then he shook that 'no.'"

In Belzoni, Mississippi, in the Delta, a new NAACP branch had recently been formed and had elected as its president Gus Courts, who owned a grocery store and operated a bus. A few months before Medgar's first official trip to Belzoni, Courts had been summoned to the local bank, where he had a small loan outstanding. A bank official demanded to see the books of the NAACP branch. Courts refused, unless, as he put it, the official could cite some law that required him to turn over the records. "In that case," the banker said, "we will tie up your bus and tie up your store. We will run you out of town." To the astonishment of the bank's officials, Courts quietly paid off his loan before it fell due.

But the pressure did not end. In the early months of 1955, Courts lost the income he had made hauling field hands to and from the cotton fields in his bus. Then, one by one, the wholesalers from whom he bought supplies for his grocery store refused him credit, demanding cash payment on delivery. When the squeeze had come close to forcing him out of business, Courts turned for help to a close friend and colleague in the local NAACP branch, the Reverend George Lee, a Baptist minister.

Like Courts, Lee owned a small grocery store. Both men

had managed to get their names on the official list of qualified voters. For some years both men had tried to vote. They had been prevented by the county sheriff's refusal to accept their poll-tax payments. Then in 1953 Courts, Lee, and a small group of other Negroes had complained about this refusal to federal authorities. The sheriff, Ike Shelton, in the face of possible federal prosecution, agreed to accept the payments in the future. But there were other ways of preventing Negroes from voting and other means of dealing with men like Gus Courts and George Lee, and it was not long before they were tried.

On the afternoon of May 7, 1955, Gus Courts dropped in at George Lee's store to continue a discussion that had gone on for weeks. Both men had been under heavy pressure. That very afternoon Lee had received an anonymous threat of death if he did not remove his name from the voting rolls. Courts was by this time dangerously close to losing his grocery business, and try as they might, the two men had found no way to raise a fund to tide him over the economic squeeze. As Courts turned to leave his friend's store, Lee sighed heavily. "Well, Courts," he said, "I've got a funny feeling."

"You're not afraid, are you?" Courts asked.

"No," said the minister. "I'm not afraid."

That night at midnight, the Reverend George Lee was driving his car through the Negro section of Belzoni. Two gun blasts shattered the night stillness, and the Buick sedan swerved over the curb and rammed into a frame house. With the lower left side of his face gone, Lee staggered from the wreckage. He died on the way to the Humphreys County Memorial Hospital.

Within an hour the telephone rang in our apartment in Jackson. For the rest of the night, Medgar was too busy making telephone calls and plans for the full impact of the news to reach him. He called Mrs. Hurley in Birmingham and members of the national office staff in New York. He telephoned Dr. McCoy and took calls from newspapers and wire-service reporters. And he talked several times with Gus Courts, assuring him that he and Mrs. Hurley and Dr. McCoy would be there in a matter of hours.

By the time the three of them arrived in Belzoni, the local police had concluded their investigation. Reverend Lee, they said, had lost control of his car and died as a result of the crash. The lead pellets found in what remained of his jaw tissues were said to be dental fillings, mysteriously dislodged in the accident. There was no need for an autopsy. Already the state's newspapers were carrying the story as a "freak accident."

But Mrs. Lee had asked two Negro physicians, Dr. Clinton Battle of Indianola and Dr. Cyrus Walton of Yazoo City, to examine the body. Dr. McCoy examined it after he arrived. All three reported that the fifty-one-year-old minister's jaw tissues contained pellets fired at close range from a high-powered gun. Dr. McCoy noted what appeared to be powder burns. Later, inspecting a tire removed from the death car, he found evidence of more pellets.

In a long day of investigation, with the weight of evidence gradually accumulating, Medgar, together with Dr. McCoy and Mrs. Hurley, inspected the house hit by the car and talked with dozens of people. Slowly, as eyewitnesses to various moments of the crime were found, the true story of what had happened emerged. George Lee had been followed by three men in another car. A rifle shot had punctured the right rear tire of the minister's Buick. As he slowed, the other car pulled parallel and a shotgun was fired point-blank into his face. There were even descriptions of the three men, with tentative identifications.

But even as the true story began to be discussed around town, the police were readying a new version. Humphreys County Sheriff Ike Shelton announced that Reverend Lee had probably been killed by "some jealous nigger." Rumors were started that the minister had been having affairs with other women. But the sheriff's theory could not have been taken seriously by anyone who knew that Mrs. Lee herself had not even been questioned by the sheriff or the local police. She never was. As the days wore on and tension continued to grip the town, sheriff's deputies began patrolling the Negro section. One by one, eyewitnesses changed their stories or refused to talk at all. One disappeared altogether. There were never any arrests.

The FBI is supposed to have investigated the murder of George Lee, and I suppose that to some degree it did. There was never any public report or even a solid rumor as to what it learned. None was really expected by Mississippi's Negroes, who had come to regard the FBI as irrelevant at best and as an ally of white supremacy at worst. But if the Negroes resented the refusal of the FBI to take a stand for justice, white Mississippians resented even the report that the FBI had begun an investigation of white terror against Negroes.

A month after Lee's murder, the Jackson *Clarion-Ledger* carried a column by Tom Ethridge that illustrated this feeling. Negroes who read it assumed, rightly or wrongly, that it conveyed the sentiments of most Mississippi whites. It began, strangely enough, by admitting that Lee had been murdered:

"The FBI is still investigating that murder of a Negro preacher at Belzoni, to which the nation's press has given considerable publicity. We can't help but wonder why the

FBI never seems to investigate violence and breach of civil rights in labor troubles.

"Some poor workman trying to support his loved ones can be beaten to death by labor goons up East, merely for refusing to join a union against his will. Thugs and terrorists can paralyze the business life of an entire area, indulging in violence and vandalism to their heart's content, yet nobody ever demands federal intervention.

"In Harlem and other metropolitan Negro centers, whites are beaten, robbed, raped and murdered by vicious hoodlums almost with impunity. Taxi drivers actually refuse to take white people into Harlem after dark. You can enter Central Park after nightfall at your own risk. Brutal crimes occur there every night, yet the Department of Justice seems unconcerned with such a shocking situation.

"But just let a couple of Southerners whip a colored person, or let a Negro get himself killed under unusual circumstances and every pressure group in the land promptly howls for FBI action, plus rigid laws that would destroy our basic liberties. Whoever said 'Justice Is Blind,' certainly knew the score."

The delusions of persecution that underlie this column are too obvious for comment, but it is of some interest to note that to a writer like Ethridge a poor workman in the North is "beaten to death by labor goons," while a Negro in the South "gets himself killed." The implication is clear that he was doing something he shouldn't have been doing. In George Lee's case, of course, it was trying to vote.

The brutal murder of George Lee hit Medgar hard. He had read of lynchings and murders, had even seen a lynch mob in his youth. But this was a man he had known, a man he had liked and respected for his courage, a man who was doing in his community what Medgar himself was trying to do throughout the state. Reverend Lee's murder was a cold-blooded answer to the demands for equal treatment that more and more Mississippi Negroes were making. It was a warning, a threat, an example, and it was backed by the blatant lies of the sheriff's office and the local police.

As the days went by after Medgar's investigation in Belzoni, the cumulative effect of the murder and its bland cover-up weighed more and more heavily on Medgar. He reacted with anger and long periods of deep brooding silence. Alone in the bedroom, at his desk in the office, or seated at the breakfast table, he would sit with a deep frown on his face. Then, suddenly, he would boil over, striking the table with his fist as though he were striking someone. If I were there, he would begin all over again, telling me how unfair it was, how unjust, how obscene that nothing would ever be done to find the killers.

He would rage on in an indictment of the killers, of the police, of the white community's knowing acceptance of obvious lies, until the futility of speech struck him once more. Then he would fall silent again, and that haunted, brooding look would cover his face like a mask, and he was off in some world of despair that no one could enter. He was a man with his anger bottled up inside him. His only release was to strike something, to talk, to rage, and, finally, to throw himself back into his work.

It was torture seeing Medgar like this, the torture of not being able to help a loved one in pain. There was literally nothing I could do but listen patiently to his tirades, listen and wait. No one ever seriously accused Medgar of a lack of commitment to the cause for which he worked, but no one, I think, ever knew as I did the emotional depth of that commitment. Medgar felt the deprivation of every Negro as though it were his own. He suffered with every Negro whose suffering he knew. And beginning with George Lee's murder, I witnessed the many deaths that Medgar died as the shotgun and the revolver became more and more the weapons with which some Mississippi whites retaliated against Negroes who wanted something better for themselves and their families and were not afraid to say so.

I remember that after George Lee's death we all began to take more seriously something that had come to be called the "death list." It had begun with a full-page newspaper advertisement in a Delta newspaper, an ad that attacked by name nine Negro leaders. Shortly after the ad appeared, the White Citizens Councils began passing out at their meetings a list of these same names. The Reverend George Lee's name had been one of the nine, and now there were eight. One of the eight was Medgar's.

---- XI ----

On May 31, 1955, three and a half weeks after the murder of George Lee, the Supreme Court handed down its implementation decision in the school cases. The South had waited a year to learn how desegregation would be carried out. Now it had at least the court's answer: "with all deliberate speed."

To many of us, that seemed equivocal at best, susceptible of whatever interpretation one cared to place on it. But the words of the decision that called for "a prompt and reasonable start" seemed clear enough, and on June 5 the state board of the NAACP urged all Mississippi branches to ask local school boards to take immediate steps to desegregate.

The state's answer came two days later when the twenty-four-member Mississippi Legal Education Advisory Committee, composed of such people as Attorney General Coleman, Dean Robert Farley of the Ole Miss Law School, and a sprinkling of state representatives and senators, met in Governor Hugh White's office to announce that Mississippi would "never compromise on racial segregation."

In its report of the meeting the Jackson *Daily News* quoted the statement of one participant, making clear to anyone who could read what tactics would be used. "It's been

75 years since the U. S. Supreme Court said Negroes would vote," he said. "Mississippi, with half of its population Negro, still has only 7500 Negro voters. This has not been the result of what the court ordered, but what Mississippi did to handle its own affairs."

What Mississippi had done to handle its own affairs, of course, was systematically to harass, intimidate, threaten, and, in the case of the Reverend George Lee, murder Negroes who even attempted to exercise their constitutional right to vote. Presumably, then, these were the tactics by which school desegregation would be resisted.

The following week the *Daily News* made this stand its own in an editorial headlined: *"Yes, We Defy the Law."* The key sentence was: "If the Supreme Court decision is the law of the land then we intend to violate the law of the land."

In the face of this defiance, Medgar and the state NAACP leaders pushed ahead. Speaking at one branch meeting after another, Medgar explained the meaning of the court's decision and the rights it gave Negro parents to petition for an end to segregated schools. There was no need to emphasize the inferiority of Negro schools; everyone at the meetings could point to dozens of inequities.

Still there was some feeling that with the state's school equalization program underway, it might be better to wait and see. In a few places, Negro principals had used the 1954 court decision to pressure a school board for new books, inside toilets, or even a new building. There were cases where such requests had actually been granted.

Medgar fought the arguments of those who counseled delay with facts. He quoted the statements of Mississippi's leading racists, pointed to past promises that had never been kept, cited the Supreme Court's own decision that "separate educational facilities are inherently unequal." He pleaded that for a parent to ask for less than the Supreme Court of the United States had decided was just would be to deprive one's own children of their birthright.

Negro teachers in particular held back, fearful of losing their jobs if they were identified with such a move, certain of losing them if the schools were in fact desegregated. And here, with the Negro teachers, lay a special problem that could only be discussed with the greatest tact, for one of the basic inequalities of Mississippi's segregated schools was the inferior training of the Negro teachers themselves. A large majority were products of the very schools in which they were now teaching; few had advanced degrees or schooling outside the state. It was a vicious circle of inferior schools producing inferior teachers who then helped perpetuate inferior schools. Some Negro teachers were willing to admit this; many were not.

At the meetings called to discuss desegregation, Medgar skirted this issue to concentrate on the more obvious, more generally accepted inequities: the leaky roofs, the unsanitary privies, the torn and tattered books, the lack of transportation. When all of the audience's questions had been answered, a petition would be read and explained. Local leaders then called for volunteers to sign it. It was an act of raw courage for a Negro parent to put his name on one of these petitions, and everyone knew it. Much as Medgar wanted signatures, he insisted that people know exactly what they were signing, what would be done with the petition, what were the possible consequences. Even after parents signed, he made it clear that they were under no obligation to leave their names on the petition if the pressures became too severe.

Still there were Negro parents who signed and signed

eagerly, and each of them filled Medgar with pride. On June 18, 1955, less than three weeks after the Supreme Court's implementation decision, the NAACP branch in my home town of Vicksburg filed with the school board a petition signed by 140 parents calling for "immediate steps to reorganize the public schools on a non-segregated basis." A week later, seventy-five parents filed a similar petition in Natchez. The next day forty-two parents followed suit in Jackson. Within weeks, parents in Clarksdale and Yazoo City, both Delta towns, had joined the growing movement.

White reactions were not long in coming. In Vicksburg, after conferring with State Attorney General Coleman, the school board issued a statement of its finding "that the communication is not a petition, wholly fails to meet the requirements for a petition and actually presents the board with nothing upon which to take action." This was the rough equivalent of saying that the people who signed the petition were not people or that the paper on which it was written was not paper, but such problems have never bothered Mississippi whites in their dealings with Mississippi Negroes. The school board added that "the matter therefore will receive no further consideration from us and the incident is closed." Though school boards in the other cities acted similarly, the White Citizens Councils soon made it clear that in their opinion the incidents were far from closed.

In Natchez a new chapter of the White Citizens Councils was quickly formed. The Natchez *Democrat* published the names of the petition signers, inviting readers to "check" them. In Yazoo City the Yazoo *Herald* published a paid advertisement listing names, addresses, and telephone numbers of each of the fifty-three Negro petitioners. The last line of the ad read: "Published as a public service by the Citizens Council of Yazoo City."

The toll of petitioners in Yazoo City began immediately. Jasper Mims, treasurer of the local NAACP, had been a carpenter for thirty years. He had earned up to $150 a week. Months later he reported he had not had a call for work since the now-famous ad had appeared. The income of Hoover Harvey, a plumber whose customers were mostly white, was soon down to twenty dollars a week. Both Mims and Harvey removed their names from the petition, but there was no letup in the pressure.

Nathan Stewart had been Yazoo City's most successful Negro grocer. His income had reached as high as $300 a week. He, with two other Negro merchants, had signed the petition. Immediately their white wholesalers refused to supply them. Stewart was told by the Delta National Bank to come and get his money. All three merchants gave in to the pressure and took their names off the petition. It did them no good.

Arthur Berry, president of the Yazoo City NAACP, reported more of the disaster: "John Covington took his name off the petition, and Ben Goldstein, the junk dealer, fired him anyway. Mrs. Lillian Young signed the petition and the McGraw Lumber Co. fired her husband Harry. She went in the A & P a few days after her name was published and picked out $10 or $12 worth of groceries. The man who operates the meat market came to the front of the store and said, 'this nigger woman is one of the signers of the petition,' and the clerk refused to sell to her. The Youngs went to Chicago in the early part of September."

By the time it was over in Yazoo City, fifty-one of the fifty-three signatures on the petition had been removed. The two that remained belonged to people who had left the county for good. And that, generally, was the story in all of the cities where petitions were filed. In the weeks and months it took for these local tragedies to unfold, Medgar drove from city to city, spoke at meeting after meeting, urging petitioners to stand firm, to hold out a little longer, to chip in and help those hardest hit by economic pressure. It was like trying to hold back a flood with his bare hands.

As each petitioner faltered, the NAACP was presented with a new case of need. A cry for help went to the national office, and before long our office in Jackson became a distribution point for food and clothing for distressed petitioners. Medgar fought both the offensive and defensive battles with a furious sort of desperation.

The effort in my own town of Vicksburg also brought personal tragedy. There one of the leaders of the petition drive was a bright and aggressive young Negro named George Jefferson, son of a well-known and highly respected Vicksburg family. When he threw himself into the effort to desegregate Vicksburg's schools, George was well on his way to becoming that Southern rarity, a successful Negro businessman with a burning desire to help his people. He had expanded the already successful funeral home owned by his family and had branched out on his own into real estate. He had a vision of building a really nice group of homes for Negroes in a lovely section of town, and over a period of time he had put all of his money, all of his wife's inheritance, every cent he could borrow into buying up the necessary property.

He was ready to begin building when the petition was submitted to the school board. His building loans evaporated. Overnight the up-and-coming businessman who could command money from many sources saw all the sources dry up. In a month payments that could not be met fell due.

Worse, petitioners whose names were ranked with George's on the petition began to ink them out. George scurried from house to house trying to prop up the timid, persuade the frightened, and console the defeated. When he was not pleading or cajoling fellow petitioners, he was desperately seeking loans, in town, out of town, in the state, and out of the state.

Then, in the midst of the two struggles, illness struck. George collapsed. Though his family managed to save the funeral home, George and his wife lost everything. Sick and bitter, guilty and helpless, he literally grieved himself to death. I think he was still in his thirties when he died.

All of these stories came to me piecemeal. Medgar would return from a trip to the Delta and dictate a report to the national office before racing off again to some other town. At breakfast he would remember the tag end of a story he had started days before. Both of us picked up bits of news through telephone calls, letters, stories in the newspapers, and from the constant flood of people in various kinds of trouble who by this time were seeking Medgar day and night. It seemed at times that we lived at the vortex of a whirlpool of personal disasters, and it was both touching and frustrating how much confidence everyone had that, whatever the problem, Mr. Evers would come to the rescue.

People called about everything. A woman had received threatening telephone calls; a man had been put off a plantation; a young boy had talked back to his white boss. They called about voting problems and police problems, money problems and even marital problems. And there was always a small but steady stream of people, mostly men but sometimes whole families, who had fled their homes after a threat or a shot in the dark or a fight with a white man or an argument with the police. Sometimes they needed a place to hide and calm their nerves for a day or so. Occasionally they were fleeing the state forever. Always, it seemed, they made a beeline for the NAACP office in Jackson or for our home.

Sometimes Medgar would bring home such a fugitive from one of his trips—a witness, perhaps, who had to be protected from pressure until the time came to testify—and I would feed him and bed him down for the night. When these people left us for a safer haven or to return home, they often went with money from Medgar's own pocket, a gift he could ill afford but could seldom resist giving. But he always exacted a price for his services, and it was always the same. No one who came asking for help was ever denied it, but no one got away without facing two blunt questions: Are you registered to vote? Are you a member of the NAACP? Medgar kept no record of the answers, but the many negative responses began to show in his face.

We learned quickly that first year, Medgar and I, that his job was not to be one of those happy occupations where well-laid plans lead naturally to execution and finally to fruition; where a man can leave the office at the end of a day's work knowing he has proceeded from A to B and that tomorrow's work will lead inevitably to C. It was more like tending a caldron that could explode at any moment and often did and then exploded again before the fire from the last explosion had been extinguished. Through it all, there were reports to get out as well as the more frequent emergency calls to Ruby Hurley in Birmingham and Gloster Current in New York when someone was arrested or murdered or threatened or starving.

Medgar was in the midst of the school petition drive, still trying to push an investigation of the Lee murder, getting food and clothing to victims of economic pressure, fighting for time to read the Mississippi newspapers and send important stories to the national office for use in their campaign of pressure on Washington to take a stand against the erupting racism in Mississippi. He was driving hundreds of miles a week to help start new NAACP branches, shore up faltering ones, investigate new incidents of threats, harassment, and arrests. He was passing along requests for loans from victims of economic reprisal, sending their applications to the Tri-State Bank in Memphis, answering their complaints, explaining procedure, apologizing for delay, soothing ruffled feelings when a loan was turned down.

The case of a Negro accused of rape pulled him one way; the case of one beaten by police pulled him another. The case of a thirteen-year-old Negro girl raped by two white men who were immediately released on bond sickened him and forced him to drop everything else to investigate and protest. There were fund-raising events to be planned and carried out, voter registration drives to be organized, and, in the midst of that, a report from Yazoo City that the number of Negro registered voters, already small, was dwindling as the result of personal pressure on individuals to remove their names.

Then murder struck again.

On Saturday morning, August 17, Lamar Smith, one of those unusual Mississippi Negroes who was registered to vote, was shot dead in broad daylight on the Lincoln County Court House lawn in Brookhaven. None of the Mississippi newspapers noted the coincidence, but few Negroes heard the news without recalling that Brookhaven was the home of Judge Tom Brady, author of the racist tract, *Black Monday*. Medgar was in Brookhaven within hours of the murder.

Smith, he found, was more than merely registered to vote. Along with his wife, daughter, and brother-in-law, he had actually voted in the primary election eleven days earlier and was actively distributing circulars to Negroes explaining how to vote by absentee ballot and thus avoid the possibility of violence at the polls. The sixty-year-old farmer had been threatened with death if he did not slow down on his political activities, but, according to his family, he had ignored the threats.

Though the murder had taken place at ten o'clock on a Saturday morning, a time when the court house square was normally jammed with people, officials claimed no witnesses could be found. Then a white farmer, Noah Smith, was charged with the murder in a warrant filed by a courageous district attorney. Eventually two more white men were arrested, but when the grand jury met in September, it failed to return an indictment.

Even before that predictable end, almost as though the state of Mississippi had officially declared an open season on Negroes, murderers struck again. This time the victim was a fourteen-year-old Negro boy from Chicago, Emmett Till, visiting his uncle in the Mississippi Delta. The purported reason for the killing, widely disseminated by the press, was that Till had asked for a date with a married white woman seven years his senior.

There were, of course, embellishments on this theme, though no one ever charged the youth with more than a lewd suggestion or a "wolf whistle." But because of the overtones of sex, by which Mississippi often justifies its use of violence against male Negroes, it could have been just another Mississippi lynching. It wasn't. This one somehow struck a spark of indignation that ignited protests around the world. Kidnaped forcibly in the middle of the night, pistol-whipped, stripped naked, shot through the head with a .45-caliber Colt automatic, barb-wired to a seventy-four-pound cotton gin fan, and dumped into twenty feet of water in the Tallahatchie River, young Emmett Till became in death what he could never have been in life: a rallying cry and a cause.

Two white men were arrested for the sadistic murder: J. W. Milam, thirty-six, and his half-brother, Roy Bryant, twenty-four. Both were identified as the men who took young Till at gun-point from his uncle's home. Both admitted having taken him but only for the purpose of frightening him. Indicted and tried for murder in Sumner, Mississippi, they were acquitted by an all-white jury that deliberated one hour and seven minutes. Two months later a grand jury in Greenwood refused even to indict them for the abduction both had publicly admitted. Two months after that, in case anyone was still in doubt, reporter William Bradford Huie, in an article in *Look*, quoted both men on the exact details of the murder they now calmly described. Acquitted once, they could not, of course, be tried again.

These were sensational climaxes to a sensational murder, but, even before they were reached, the Till case attracted the kind of world and national attention Medgar had brooded about those many months before when he had speculated privately about a Mississippi Mau Mau. For weeks before the murder trial, newsmen from all over the country probed the psyche of the Delta, interviewing whites and Negroes, turning up some of the conditions of the benighted area. Angry and frustrated over this particularly vicious killing, Medgar made it his mission to see that word of it was spread as widely and accurately as possible. Publicizing the crime and the subsequent defeat of justice became a major NAACP effort.

Those were weeks of frenzied activity, weeks of special danger, for Medgar made many trips to the Delta, investigating, questioning, searching out witnesses before they could be frightened into silence. There were wild night drives to Memphis, where witnesses were put on planes for safer places until their presence would be needed at the trial. And, more than once, there were chases along the long, straight, unlighted highways that led from the Delta back to Jackson.

Medgar was by this time well known throughout the state, and his car was often sighted by police and sheriff's men minutes after he entered a Delta county. Frequently he was followed throughout his trips around the Delta. He had already begun to make it a practice to return to Jackson each night if possible, as much for the safety of the people he would otherwise have stayed with as for himself. Several times, when he started back after dark, he had to jam the accelerator to the floorboard to "shake the car's tail," as he put it, in the faces of anonymous pursuers.

Medgar never pretended he wasn't frightened at such experiences, though he often concealed the details from me. Usually I found out later, when the subject came up at the office with someone else or when a friend who had been with him let the secret drop. There was no hiding the extra precautions he sometimes took. When Emmett Till's body was found, Medgar and Amzie Moore, an NAACP leader from Cleveland, Mississippi, set off from our house one morning with Ruby Hurley, down from Birmingham, to investigate. All of them were dressed in overalls and beat-up shoes, with Mrs. Hurley wearing a red bandanna over her head. To complete the disguise, Amzie had borrowed a car with license plates from a Delta county. Watching them leave, knowing the tension and hate that gripped the Delta, I lived through the day in a daze of fear until their safe return that night.

While Medgar worked in the Delta, I was swamped at

the office with telephone calls from the press, from friends, from unknown Negroes who wanted to know what was happening. I had to buy and read six or seven newspapers a day, clipping every word about the Till case for our own files and for the national office in New York. If Medgar's name had been mentioned in one of the papers, I could anticipate a spate of obscene and abusive telephone calls.

Looking back, I know that from that time on I never lost the fear that Medgar himself would be killed. It was like a physical presence inside me, now subdued, now alive and aching, a parasite of terror that woke to remind me of its existence whenever things were particularly bad. Medgar would leave the house for one of his trips to the Delta, and I could feel my stomach contract in cold fear that I would never see him again. When he was home, when he spent a whole day in the office, it was like a reprieve, for I somehow had the absurd idea that nothing could happen to him if we were together. It was about this time that I began trying to live each day for itself, to count as special blessings those days when I knew he was in no special danger. It is a philosophy more easily preached than practiced, but I made a thousand conscious attempts to live it in the years that followed, knowing that the only alternative was some kind of breakdown.

I never completely understood what it was that made the murder of Emmett Till so different from the ones that had preceded it. In part, I suppose it was his youth. Medgar was convinced that the existence of our office in Jackson and the enormous efforts of the NAACP to get out the news made a tremendous difference. Whatever the answer, it was the murder of this fourteen-year-old out-of-state visitor that touched off the world-wide clamor and cast the glare of a world spotlight on Mississippi's racism. Ironically, the deaths of George Lee and Lamar Smith, both directly connected with the struggle for civil rights, had caused nothing like the public attention attracted by the Till case.

And perhaps that was the explanation. George Lee and Lamar Smith had been murdered for doing what everyone knew Negroes were murdered for doing. Neither murder had the shock effect of the brutal slaying of a fourteen-year-old boy who had certainly done nothing more than act fresh. The Till case, in a way, was the story in microcosm of every Negro in Mississippi. For it was the proof that even youth was no defense against the ultimate terror, that lynching was still the final means by which white supremacy would be upheld, that whites could still murder Negroes with impunity, and that the upper- and middle-class white people of the state would uphold such killings through their police and newspapers and courts of law. It was the proof that Mississippi had no intention of changing its ways, that no Negro's life was really safe, and that the federal government was either powerless, as it claimed, or simply unwilling to step in to erase this blot on the nation's reputation for decency and justice. It was the proof, if proof were needed, that there would be no real change in Mississippi until the rest of the country decided that change there must be and then forced it.

It was toward that end that the NAACP published in November 1955 an eight-page booklet that infuriated Mississippi's politicians. Titled, *M is for Mississippi and Murder*, every word of it was true. It began with a section called "Backdrop for Murder," which recounted recent news stories originating in Mississippi.

One, from an AP dispatch dated September 9, 1954, read in part: "White men who want to keep segregation in force are banding into 'citizens councils' throughout Mississippi, several legislators said today.

"The peaceful approach was emphasized by several leaders in Washington County. . . . But some other legislators from the Delta and other 'black counties' where Negroes outnumber whites predicted bloodshed. . . .

"One said 'a few killings' would be the best thing for the state just before the people vote on a proposed constitutional amendment empowering the Legislature to abolish public schools.

"The 'few killings' would make certain that the people would approve the amendment and 'would save a lot of bloodshed later on,' he added."

A reporter for the Memphis *Press-Scimitar* wrote from a Citizens Council rally on August 12, 1955, quoting Senator Eastland: "On May 17 the Constitution of the United States was destroyed. . . . You are not required to obey any court which passes out such a ruling. In fact, you are obligated to defy it."

In a speech at Greenville, John C. Satterfield, president of the Mississippi Bar Association and a member of the board of governors of the American Bar Association, listed three methods of continuing segregation. Though he said it was "abhorrent," one of them was "the gun and torch."

Frederick Sullens, editor of the Jackson *Daily News*, was quoted in a speech before the American Society of Newspaper Editors in Washington, D.C.: "Mississippi will not obey the decision. If an effort is made to send Negroes to school with white children, there will be bloodshed. The stains of that bloodshed will be on the Supreme Court steps."

In a front-page editorial in Mr. Sullens' paper, Dr. A. H. McCoy, state president of the NAACP, was described as "insolent, arrogant and hot-headed." The editorial continued,

"The fanatical mouthings of McCoy have reached the limit. If not suppressed by his own race, he will become the white man's problem."

An editorial in the Yazoo *Herald* at the height of tension over the Till case read: "Through the furor over the Emmett Till case we hope someone gets this over to the nine ninnies who comprise the present U. S. Supreme Court. Some of the young Negro's blood is on their hands also."

Finally the booklet cited a New York *Herald Tribune* story by Homer Bigart, quoting Robert P. Patterson, executive secretary of the Mississippi Citizens Councils: "Sir, this is not the United States. This is Sunflower County, Mississippi."

Summarizing the news stories, the NAACP booklet said: "In this climate of opinion which derides the courts and the rule of law, which harps on violence, sometimes nakedly and sometimes through the device of repeated disavowal, three persons were murdered in Mississippi between May 7 and August 28, 1955." It then recounted details of the murders of George Lee, Lamar Smith, and Emmett Till.

Medgar had just received copies of the booklet from New York when an urgent call came from Belzoni with word of yet another shooting. His heart sank as he heard the name: Gus Courts, the Negro grocer who had been president of the NAACP branch when George Lee was murdered in Belzoni less than seven months earlier. Within an hour, Medgar had alerted the press, the national office, Ruby Hurley in Birmingham, and the state officers in Mississippi. Before daybreak he was off to Mound Bayou, where Courts lay critically wounded in the hospital.

Gus Courts' story was simple and straightforward, and though he was in serious condition, he was conscious and able to tell it. Medgar made sure it was related in detail to the press. "I'd known for a long time it was coming, and I'd tried to get prepared in my mind for it," Courts told one reporter. "But that's a hard thing to do when you know they're going to try to slip up and steal your life in the night and not out in the bright."

Courts was sixty-five and in pain, but he knew the importance of telling his story. "They shot me because I wanted to vote," he said simply. "They said I was agitating to put Negroes in the white schools, but that ain't so. I was just advocating for the vote. I felt I ought to have my rights."

Courts told the long story of his attempts to vote, of the complaint he and George Lee had filed with the Justice Department two years before when Sheriff Ike Shelton refused to take their poll taxes. He told how he had finally become one of not quite a hundred Negroes in Humphreys County who were registered to vote. "About twenty of us went to vote in the July primary in 1954," he said, "but instead of giving us ballots they gave us questionnaires. We were supposed to answer questions like 'Do you believe in integration?'"

None of them got to vote, Courts said. No Negro had voted in Humphreys County since Reconstruction. And after the White Citizens Council put the screws on them, most of the registered Negroes took their names off the registration list. "Finally it got down to eight or nine of us," Courts told the reporter. "Since that was so few I guess some white folks figured it wouldn't hurt to shoot that eight or nine. But I made up my mind to stick on the list."

Courts said that when he had finally registered, "one of the council members brought the list around. He said, 'If you don't take your name off you're going to be put out of your store.' Three days later the landlord said, 'I've got another use for the building,' so I had to move."

He told how he had reopened his store across the street in a building owned by a Negro who had also left his name on the registration list. A few days later a white planter prominent in the council had walked in. " 'Courts, I want to speak to you,' he told me," Courts said. "I walked out and got into his car. He had the list with him and was holding it up like he was reading it. I saw my name was on it. It had a V marked by my name. I said, 'What does that V mean?' He said, 'That means you're qualified to vote. Do you intend to vote?'

" 'It's not against the law, is it?' I asked him.

" 'No, it's not against the law,' he said.

" 'Well, I intend to vote,' I said. When I was leaving the car to go back to my store, he asked me, 'Have I threatened you?' I said no.

"A few days later, my wholesaler said the Citizens Council had threatened not to buy any goods from him if he sold anything to me on credit. He said I could have my credit back if I took my name off the list. I paid cash. But the second time I went for groceries he said he couldn't sell to me at all—credit or cash."

Courts told how he had lost his business hauling field hands to the cotton fields and then went on. "Along at this time, a council member told me, 'You're relying on the federal government but it don't do anything—you just as well do like we want you to do.' Everyone on the council usually would talk nice," he explained. "Any threats of harm to me would come only in a roundabout way."

Finally he told of the night of the shooting, how he had been at the store, standing at the cash register. He had just sold Savannah Luton a dime's worth of kerosene and was shuffling through some bills and chatting with his wife and a woman customer. "All at once I heard gunfire—it seemed like two shots at the same time. When the shots hit me I knew what had happened. Savannah and my wife and me looked out and saw a car that looked kind of grayish green. One of the women said, 'Yonder it goes.'"

Courts said a call had been placed for Sheriff Ike Shelton but that he couldn't be located. "Then Mr. Nichols [Belzoni's police chief] came and my wife and Savannah told him about what happened. But I didn't feel like talking right then."

Deliberately avoiding the Humphreys County Memorial Hospital where the buckshot that had killed George Lee had been identified as dental fillings, friends drove Courts sixty miles to the Negro-owned and staffed hospital at Mound Bayou. There Dr. J. R. Henry, chief surgeon, removed two pieces of flattened metal, one from Courts' left arm, the other from his abdomen. "I suppose they were bullets," Dr. Henry told reporters cautiously, "but I don't know much about that sort of thing."

Meanwhile, Sheriff Shelton was complaining loudly to reporters. "They took Courts across two counties, though we have the best hospital in the world. They didn't even give him first aid. I'm not going to chase him down. Let the NAACP investigate. They won't believe anything I say anyway." In Cleveland, Mississippi, county seat of Bolivar County where Courts had been taken, Sheriff J. W. McClellan said he had not been officially notified of the shooting or of the presence of a gunshot victim in his county. He said he did not plan any action until the case was reported officially. "It's not my case," he said.

Back in Belzoni, Sheriff Ike Shelton was asked if he thought Courts' voting activities had anything to do with the shooting. "Hell no," he said flatly. "Some nigger had it in for him, that's all."

On November 30, five days after Courts had been shot,

the New York *Post* carried an interview with Shelton. He denied he was ignoring the case. "That's a damn' lie," he was quoted as saying. "Why, we been combing the country-side looking for the fellow who shot him. Some folks believe we don't try to solve these shootings. It's my duty to get 'em solved."

Why hadn't he questioned Courts? the reporter asked. "Well," the sheriff explained, "I called up the hospital Friday night and some woman said he was in critical condition. Then I read in the paper Saturday he was still critical. I figured there was no use to drive way up there and not get to talk to him."

Next day came news of an FBI investigation. C. E. Piper, agent in charge in Memphis, said two agents had been sent from the FBI's Greenwood office to Belzoni on Sunday, two days after Courts was shot. Their investigation did not include questioning of Sheriff Shelton, though they talked with Courts. "We made preliminary inquiries on Sunday and then we quit," Piper said. "We've made our report to the Department of Justice in Washington. It's up to the Department of Justice to determine if there has been a violation of federal civil rights laws and if it wants further investigation."

The following day, Gus Courts came home from the hospital. No one was ever arrested for shooting him.

On December 8, 1955, six days after Courts returned to Belzoni, a Negro named Clinton Melton was shot dead in Glendora, a few miles from the place where Emmett Till had been murdered and dumped into the Tallahatchie River four months earlier. The bodies of Negroes murdered by Mississippi whites were beginning to pile up.

Melton was thirty-three, married, the father of five children. He worked for a white gas-station owner, Lee Mc-Garrh. Elmer Kimbell, the white manager of a cotton gin, had an account at the station.

McGarrh told this story: "I was in the service station when Kimbell drove in with a Negro, John Henry Wilson. I told Clinton to go out and fill Kimbell's tank.

"Clinton came back in a few minutes and said Kimbell was threatening him because he'd filled the tank and Kimbell wanted only two dollars' worth of gas.

"Kimbell came into the station and said he wanted to close out his account. He said I had a smart Negro working for me.

"I told him to get going. As he left, he said to Clinton, 'I'm going to kill you.'

"Kimbell drove away, but came right back and began shooting at Clinton. I heard the Negro in Kimbell's car yell, 'Don't shoot him. He ain't done nothing.'

"The Negro with Kimbell jumped out of the car and ran into the station. He begged me to hide him."

When he was arrested, Kimbell claimed that Clinton Melton had shot at him first. McGarrh flatly denied it. "There's one thing I know about this: Clinton didn't have a gun at any time during the quarrel."

Clinton Melton, the murdered Negro, was well liked in town. He had lived there all his life. Kimbell, his white killer, had lived in Glendora only a few months, was known by few white residents, and was rumored to be a close friend of one of the killers of Emmett Till. For once, white people spoke out against the killing of a Negro. The local Lions Club adopted a resolution branding the murder "an outrage." Medgar's investigation turned up the fact that the club had given the widow twenty-six dollars. A local white minister gave her sixty dollars. Mrs. Melton, fearful that justice would not be done if the NAACP interested itself in the case, told Medgar she didn't want the organization to become involved. Her wishes were respected.

The results repelled even some white Mississippians. Hodding Carter compared them to the Till case in an angry editorial in his *Delta Democrat-Times*:

"Last fall, in the glare of world-wide publicity, Mississippi gave a sorry demonstration of an inadequate legal system that produced such flimsy evidence and presented an attitude of so little concern that even the people most convinced that two half brothers were guilty of murdering a young Negro boy from Chicago, had to admit that the case was not proved.

"Three months later a close friend of one of the defendants in the Till trial was implicated in another slaying of a Negro. From accounts presented by witnesses other than the killer, it was an even more senseless slaying.

"The Negro was no out-of-state smart alec. He was home-grown and 'highly respected' according to a resolution in his behalf by the Glendora Lions Club.

"There was no question of an insult to Southern womanhood. There was only an argument about some gasoline.

"There was no pressure by the NAACP, 'credited' with the outcome of the Till trial. There were no flashbulbs popping, no television cameras, no reporters from all over the world milling around. This was, in fact, very little ado about the trial compared to the attention the Till case drew.

"And the matter was quickly handled, the evidence was presented, and the witnesses were called. It was the word of three men, one white and two Negro, against the accused. Only the accused said that 'somebody, I don't know who' shot at him from out of the darkness before he blasted Clinton

Melton to death. His own wife's testimony conflicted with his. But the jury believed him, or indicated they did.

"So another 'not guilty' verdict was written at Sumner this week. And it served to cement the opinion of the world that no matter how strong the evidence nor how flagrant is the apparent crime, a white man cannot be convicted in Mississippi for killing a Negro."

Hodding Carter's editorial must have angered many white Mississippians, but there were none that could dispute his facts. I remember somewhere toward the end of that bloody first year of Medgar's work for the NAACP seeing a slogan, I suppose of the National Safety Council, that chilled my blood with its unconscious irony. It read: "Stay Alive in '55." I wondered if anyone else had ever read those words in quite the same way I did.

## XII

Late in that violent year of 1955, we moved our offices from Farish Street to the Negro-owned Masonic Temple Building in a part of town that includes Jackson's two Negro colleges, Jackson State and Campbell. Medgar found a wry amusement in the fact that the state office of the NAACP in Mississippi was now on Lynch Street. Pressed for an explanation, of course, he was forced to admit that the "Lynch" in question was not the well-known act of violence.

Actually there should have been something inspiring about being on Lynch Street, for it had been named for a famous Negro, John R. Lynch, Speaker of the Mississippi House in 1872 and later a three-term member of the United States House of Representatives. Though we were not taught this in our segregated schools, John Lynch was one of many Southern Negro legislators during the Reconstruction era whose ability and integrity were beyond question. At the end of the 1872 session of the State Legislature, Lynch was praised by a white Mississippi Democrat "for his dignity, impartiality, and courtesy as a presiding officer." It is one of many incidents redounding to the credit of Negroes deliberately omitted from the massively rewritten history of the Reconstruction South.

We had hardly settled in our new offices when Medgar left, in January, for the NAACP's annual meeting in New York. In his absence I tried to cope with requests for help in securing loans from the Tri-State Bank, with complaints of intimidation by school petitioners, with an unending flood of office visitors, and the sickening report of the beating of a pregnant Negro woman by a Hattiesburg policeman.

Looking now at a letter to Medgar in which I listed these developments, I find also the sentence: "Things are quiet in Mississippi at present," and I wonder at the state of mind that could have led me to such a conclusion. But these were run-of-the-mill events in those hectic days, and I suppose what I really meant was that there had been no reported murders in the few days Medgar had been gone.

That same letter indicated that I had received two telephone calls with no one on the line, that someone had been tampering with the lock on the office door, and that Big Mama had been having nightmares every night. But all of this, too, was by then quite routine.

And yet it never really became routine. In the course of the next year, the strain of trying to hold down a job at the office and be an adequate wife, mother, and house-keeper at home—all of this under a kind of tension impossible to describe—became almost too much. The office was never quiet; even on those rare occasions when there was nothing urgent to do, it was filled with people. Then at five, or often much later, I would start home to face housework that was never quite finished.

Moreover, my daily separation from the children was having an obviously bad effect both on them and on me. I felt I was missing most of the fun of being a mother, and while Big Mama was an enormous help, she quite naturally did things differently. In addition, there was the fact that there were simply too many of us in our small apartment, and more and more, as time went by, there was an atmosphere of strain at home.

Medgar and I talked frequently about these problems, and sometimes our discussions developed into real arguments. I wanted to quit my job and stay home with the children, and while he understood that, while he recognized the need for it, he also knew that we needed the money I earned. More than that, he feared he would never find anyone to help him in the office in quite the same way that I had.

I suppose he was right about that. Because I was his wife, because I loved him, because I worried about him and the terrible strain under which he was working, I went out of my way to take burdens from his shoulders in a way no ordinary secretary could be expected to do. And because the end of the working day generally meant simply that we moved our headquarters from the office to home, where the same people gathered, the same telephone calls came in, and the same problems were pursued, I think Medgar sensed that his loss of my presence at the office would mean at least a partial loss of participation in his work at home. So, for a time, I kept at it.

Medgar was just home from the annual meeting in New York when the attorney general who had played so large a role in opposing the school petitions, James P. Coleman, became Mississippi's fifty-first governor. In his inaugural speech he pledged that the United States Government would never force racial integration on Mississippi. He promised that segregation would be maintained without violence because, as he put it, "Mississippi is a state of law and not of violence."

Like all Mississippi politicians, Governor Coleman had a way of ignoring unpleasant facts. "We must keep cool heads and calm judgment in the face of all the provocation being hurled upon us from almost every direction," he said. In a vague allusion to the murders of the previous year he declared that "despite all the propaganda that has been fired at us, the white people of Mississippi are not a race of Negro-killers."

His message to Mississippi's Negroes was succinct and threatening: he would give sympathetic consideration to "any of your problems which desire the assistance of the state government. If you accept this opportunity, it will mean better days for all of us. If you reject it, the responsibility is yours." Then, to make sure the white people understood that this implied no diminution of segregation, he added, "I have not the slightest fear that four years hence when my successor stands on this same spot to assume his official oath, the separation of the races in Mississippi will be left intact and will still be in force and effect in exactly the same manner and form as we know it today."

Two months later Southern members of Congress issued their famous "Southern Manifesto," signed by nineteen United States senators and seventy-eight members of the House of Representatives. The declaration, which gave immediate aid and comfort to racist organizations in the South, labeled the Supreme Court's 1954 decision "a clear abuse of judicial power" and commended "the motives of those states which have declared the intention to resist forced integration by any lawful means."

The Jackson *Daily News* pointed with pride to the role of Mississippi's congressmen in issuing the defiant document. Senator Stennis, it reported, was a member of the committee that drafted the statement. Congressman Colmer was chairman of the informal House Southern Group that played a leading part. And the manifesto was also signed by Senator Eastland and Congressmen Abernethy, Whitten, Smith, Williams and Winstead—the entire Mississippi delegation in Congress. Medgar's reaction was to work harder.

But the work that year was almost completely defensive. Under the pressure of economic intimidation and reprisal, membership and financial contributions fell. A special cash relief fund of more than $5000 set up by the national office was distributed to those hardest hit. Branches in Natchez, Greenville, Indianola, and Yazoo City all but ceased to exist, and it became impossible to find sufficient applicants to institute a school desegregation suit.

For a time, Medgar and the state officers concentrated on voter registration drives, emphasizing that the ballot was one of the most effective means of combating segregation. In the counties where Negro registration and voting were permitted—and there were a few—Negro registration rose. In other areas, and especially in the Delta, prospective registrants were summarily turned away.

Two years earlier, in 1954, the legislature had drafted an amendment to the state constitution to make Negro registration more difficult than ever. It required, among other things, that a registrant "be able to read and write any section of the Constitution of this State and give a reasonable interpretation thereof to the County Registrar." To become final, the proposed amendment required ratification by the voters in the November election. That October the newspapers made sure the voters knew what the amendment really meant.

"If Mississippians go to the polls in any numbers November 2," the *Delta Democrat-Times* had reported, "it will be to

vote on a constitutional amendment to increase the requirements of voter registration. The Legal Education Advisory
Committee is expected to give some attention to publicizing
the amendment as a long-range method of keeping segregation. The proposal was designed to slow down Negro
registration and a number of committee members have said
they feel any long-range success in keeping whites and Negroes separated lies in keeping whites in control of the ballot
boxes."

On the day before the voting, the Jackson *Daily News*
wrote that "the amendment would raise voting requirements
and its proponents admit it is designed to check the increasing number of Negro ballots." To write of an "increasing
number of Negro ballots" was to resort to scare tactics,
pure and simple, for Negro registration—not voting—then
stood at precisely 22,404, about four per cent of the adult
Negro population. Actual voting was much lower.

In the forefront of the movement to push the racist
amendment were the White Citizens Councils. Robert Patterson, then executive secretary, said, "We must use and
unite our ballot that the squeak of certain insidious minority
pressure groups will be drowned out by our mighty roar."
He admitted publicly that the amendment's "sole purpose is
to limit Negro registration."

James P. Coleman, at this time still the state's attorney
general, explained why the amendment was necessary: "Under the present setup, if a circuit clerk refuses to register a
person who can read, then he is liable for damages in court
for depriving that person of his right. A clerk in Oklahoma
got sued and had to pay $5000. This has scared some of our
clerks in Mississippi, and, as a result in several counties, the
Negroes have been voting in large numbers.

"In other words the only defense we now have is now

crumbling and we need additional requirements that the clerks can legally impose. The time is short. The Citizens Councils in each community are in a position to perform a great service for our cause if they assure the passage of this amendment."

As expected, the white voters in Mississippi approved the amendment, and in January 1955 the state legislature inserted it into the constitution. The following March they implemented it with a law striking from the registration lists all voters who had registered since January 1, 1954. The *Delta Democrat-Times*, which had opposed the amendment, reported: "An estimated 30,000 Mississippians have had their voter registrations nullified and the blunt truth is that county registrars will decide which ones will be allowed to re-register successfully.

"A written three-page exam which a Constitutional lawyer could flunk, if the Circuit Clerk wanted him to—awaits registrants from here on out."

That was the situation in 1956, a year in which other Americans were going to the polls to elect their President. In October, President Eisenhower, running against Adlai Stevenson, issued an invitation to the Soviet Union to send representatives to the United States to observe our free elections. In some quarters it was hailed as a master stroke of American propaganda. Mississippi Negroes saw it differently. The state Conference of NAACP branches promptly fired off a telegram to the White House with copies to the press:

"Mr. President:

"You have expressed your profound and very deep interest in free elections throughout the world, so much so you have invited Russians to come to this country to observe our system of free elections.

"We call upon you, Mr. President, to send the Russian observers to Humphreys County, Mississippi, where the Reverend Mr. G. E. Lee was killed and Mr. Gus Courts was shot because they tried to vote as Americans. Send them to Jefferson Davis County where more than one thousand persons, who have been qualified voters frrom three to ten years, were disfranchised because they were Negroes. Send them also to Hattiesburg, in Forrest County, where there are less than twenty-five Negroes registered when there are twelve thousand Negroes in the county.

"Mr. President, we feel that a more accurate and objective view will be derived from a visit in these counties, and the majority of Mississippi counties where no Negroes are permitted to vote in our great democracy."

I have no doubt that sending the telegram made Medgar and the others feel better. It did get some publicity. It may even have embarrassed the White House. But it changed nothing.

Two years later, Medgar was still trying to reach President Eisenhower with a plea for federal help, for the hopes of Negroes throughout the United States that the wartime leadership of the famous General of the Armies might be turned to peace-time leadership toward racial justice were slow in dying. Negro leaders throughout the United States had been hesitant to criticize their first Republican President since Herbert Hoover, though the years of his administration had dragged on without measurable progress.

Time and again after the Supreme Court's school decisions, President Eisenhower had responded to questions about his attitude toward the decisions with equivocations. He spoke of the need to change men's minds and hearts before changing their laws. He said it was not his business to approve or disapprove of Supreme Court decisions. He denounced "extremists on both sides" of the racial crisis.

The extremists on one side were easily identified: the Ku Klux Klan, the White Citizens Councils, the murderers of Emmett Till and George Lee and Lamar Smith and Clinton Melton. They were Judge Tom Brady, with his *Black Monday* comparison of Negroes to chimpanzees, the county voting registrars of most of Mississippi's counties with their blatant violations of the Fifteenth Amendment.

But who were the extremists on the other side? Were they the NAACP lawyers who laboriously fought civil rights cases through the courts to win, eventually, before the highest court in the land? Were they the Negro parents who petitioned for school desegregation after the court had decreed it? Were they the silent, often fearful Negroes who filed hopelessly into the voting registrars' offices for the fourth or fifth time only to be confronted once again with an adamant rejection of their persons as full citizens of the United States?

Or did the President of the United States perhaps refer to Medgar and those like him who spent their waking hours investigating the horrors of segregation's depths, who fought the uphill fight to make them known, who toyed with and rejected as extremist the concept of a Mississippi Mau Mau? Were these the extremists he had in mind?

In anguish and in anger, Medgar finally challenged the President's inactivity and indecision in the only way he knew. In June 1958 he wrote President Eisenhower: "As a former soldier under your command in the European Theater of Operations . . . and in view of the menacing evils of communists and their vicious propaganda, I hereby urge you, as President and Chief Executive of the United States, the greatest democracy on earth, to speak out vigorously in urging national compliance with the Supreme Court rulings of 1954 and 1955 as it regards to segregation."

The reply came from E. Frederic Morrow of the White House staff: "The President is always pleased to hear from any soldier who served under his command. He faces current problems of this country with the same courage he faced similar problems during the war, and he will meet them with his best judgment and determination." It was no answer at all.

From the beginning of his work with the NAACP, Medgar had insisted that we trade with Negro businesses wherever possible. He would drive miles to buy gasoline from a Negro service station, and he insisted that I do the same. For a while I bought my groceries at Kroger's, a chain owned and operated by whites. When Medgar objected, I pointed out how cordial and courteous they were. "They can afford to be courteous," he said. "They're getting your money. They're happy to have you stand in the check-out line with whites. But they wouldn't hire you as a checker."

He insisted that I trade at the Valley Street Grocery, now Smith's Supermarket, a store owned by the Reverend Robert L. T. Smith and his son, Robert, Jr. The Smiths were strong supporters of the NAACP, and Medgar was eager to support them. I argued that Kroger's was closer, that it had a larger selection, and that the food was actually cheaper, a matter of some importance to our budget. Medgar was adamant. The Smiths were Negroes, he said, struggling to make a success against tremendous odds. "Of course their prices are higher. They're small and they buy in small quantities. When they grow, their prices will come down. But they need our help to grow." I changed stores.

Medgar and young Robert Smith were already good friends, and as time went by I came to know and like Robert and his wife, Kenny. Robert's father, who had started the business, was the minister of a small church in Jackson and the father of eleven children. The grocery store had begun in a small building near the railroad tracks in a field where potatoes, onions, cabbage, tomatoes, and greens were grown. Times had been hard when Robert was growing up, and he remembered days when he had gone into his father's vegetable field with a box of salt and made a meal out of tomatoes picked fresh from the vine. His father had also held down a job as a postman and dabbled in real estate. Medgar, of course, proved to be right. By 1960 the store had grown into a modern supermarket, and with the beginning of a selective buying campaign by Negroes, its business thrived.

But there were other reasons for avoiding white-owned shops and stores, and it did not take me long to understand them. Shopping for clothes in the white stores on Capitol Street could be a degrading experience. The white clerks would often wait on you only when there were no white customers. Almost without exception they would try to sell you cheap and flashy clothes, the kind they clearly felt was fit for Negroes. If you were charging your purchases, they would ask your name. "Mrs. Medgar Evers," I would say. "Well, but what's *your* name? I need *your* name," the clerk would insist and, when I gave it, would write "Mrs. Myrlie Evers" on the sales slip.

Once a clerk knew your first name, it was all he would use. "Well, Myrlie," one would say, "do you want to pay cash today?" More than once I left the merchandise on the counter and walked out.

Many of the clothing stores would not permit Negroes to try on clothes, either at the stores or at home. One store refused even to allow Negroes inside the door except to pick up packages for white employers.

I remember one incident in a shop on Capitol Street that illustrates a typical attitude of white merchants. I needed a new hat and, after window-shopping, stepped into a hat shop. For a while I stood quietly looking around, waiting for a clerk to help me. They all ignored me, waiting on white customers who had come in after me. Finally I asked a clerk to help me. She gave me a cold stare and said frostily that she'd be with me when she had time.

By this time it had become a contest, so I walked to a mirror and tried on a hat. The clerk dashed over. "You can't try that on!" she said angrily.

"Oh," I said. "Why not?"

"We don't allow *you* to try on hats except with Kleenex inside them," she said, taking the hat and lining it with tissue.

"Why is that?" I asked coldly.

"Because you people always have such greasy hair you ruin the hats," she snapped, handing the lined hat back to me.

"Well, I'm not interested in your hats," I said, tossing the hat onto a counter and walking out.

Negroes faced some variation of this insulting behavior wherever they went. I remember at the age of twelve being taken by Aunt Myrlie to my first white doctor, a specialist. His office had two doors, labeled "White" and "Colored," with separate waiting rooms to match. I came to take this sort of thing for granted; indeed, I was uneasy if for some reason the signs of segregation were not clearly marked. A doctor's office without a sign meant moments of uncomfortable hesitation before you finally stuck your head in the door to ask, "Where do I sit?"

Often segregated waiting rooms were visible to each other,

and there was always a noticeable difference. The room for Negroes was always smaller, more crowded, less well lighted, and there was often something dingy and dirty about it. Even the magazines were older. Worse still, a white doctor would sometimes see all his white patients before admitting the first Negro. Then, after hours of waiting, an assistant would call you by your first name.

I came, largely through Medgar, to resent this kind of treatment and to resist it. As an adult I chose to go to Negro doctors wherever possible. When Darrell developed an allergy, however, Dr. A. B. Britton, our family doctor in Jackson, sent us to a white allergist. His office was in a modern, one-story building of doctors' offices, and since I saw no separate entrance, I took Darrell in the front door. We walked through the waiting room to the receptionist, and I told her my name. She asked us to sit down "in the waiting room right over there," pointing to a small, neat, but quite separate room. As we waited, a Negro assistant came in, said hello, and suggested that next time we use the side entrance.

I said I hadn't seen one, and she said she would show it to me when we left. The doctor, when we saw him, was pleasant and helpful. He addressed me as "Mrs. Evers." When we left, though, the Negro assistant jumped up to show me the side door. As she reached to open it for us, I thanked her, took Darrell by the hand, and left by the way we had come in. Each time we visited the doctor after that, we came and left by the front door. Nothing was ever said about it, but it was a partial triumph at best, for we always had to wait in the segregated waiting room.

A white dentist I met much later handled the problem differently. His offices were in a large medical center, and many of his colleagues in that building were known members of the White Citizens Council. When I first went to him, I found he had but one waiting room. He scheduled his appointments to allow twenty minutes between patients, and he insisted that you arrive and leave on time. In all of my visits to him, I never saw another patient.

Eventually we discussed the subject, and he admitted that many of the doctors and dentists in the building were White Citizens Council members. Most frowned on taking Negro patients at all. "I don't agree with them," he said, "but I don't feel I can flaunt my views. I won't have separate waiting rooms, so I worked out this system. It wastes time, but it works, and no one has complained."

In its own way, the shoddy treatment Negroes received from white business and professional people helped to build a small Negro business and professional community in Jackson. Houston Wells, who with his wife, Jean, and their five children, later became our next-door neighbor, was a good example. Houston learned the furniture business working for a white company. Then, with thirty-five dollars and a prayer, he went into business for himself. Like the Smiths with their grocery store, Houston prospered by providing a friendly atmosphere in which Negroes could shop with dignity. Like the Smiths, he began by selling the cheaper brands, expanding as his customers increased in number and demanded better merchandise.

Houston made it a point to get you anything you could buy elsewhere. He would take customers all the way to Memphis wholesalers to pick out and order what they wanted. And, like the Smiths, he was active and interested in the NAACP, a leader in the Negro community.

Medgar sought out people like Houston Wells. Nolan Tate, who was in charge of sales for Fuller Products Company, a cosmetics manufacturer, was another. Nolan and his wife, Hattie, had five children, and Hattie worked as a secretary at Jackson State College. They, too, became close friends.

Cornelius Turner, when we first met him, headed the Jackson area office of the Universal Life Insurance Company. Later he formed his own construction company. With his wife, Marian, and their four daughters, he joined our growing circle of close friends.

When the men got together, there were long and sometimes heated arguments about politics, civil rights, national leaders, and such activities as voter registration and selective buying campaigns. All of the men were strong advocates of progress for Negroes, but they had their differences on tactics and timing, and they argued vociferously. Even when husbands and wives met together for a party, a wide-ranging, male-dominated discussion was inevitable, with the wives sometimes battling to express their views.

Hattie Tate, who was often annoyed at seeing a party turned into a political debate and whose sense of humor was both broad and infectious, would sometimes interrupt these heated sessions by entering the room, raising a steel whistle to her lips, and deafening the combatants with a blast that left hearts pumping double time. Then, if we women could arrange it, we would turn the discussion into calmer channels and sometimes even persuade our husbands to dance, with available teenage children serving as tutors in the latest steps.

Medgar's great relaxation was fishing, and as often as possible, he and Robert Smith would slip off on Saturday, sometimes with others of the crowd, to one of the many lakes within driving distance. These expeditions required great planning, for the men would leave at three or four in the morning, and they all expected their wives to get up and pack lunches for them. Medgar usually wanted a hot breakfast as well.

Stribling Lake, about forty miles northeast of Jackson, was the home of a legendary bass that Medgar had once hooked and then lost. If the men had gone there to fish, there was usually a tall story or two about the sighting of the fish and his real size. They were a congenial group, the men, all with similar problems, all with wives and children to support, all working under a good deal of pressure, and those long, lazy days together were occasions of great relaxation and pleasure they all needed badly.

Except for fishing and hunting, Medgar had little chance to get away from his work. If he were near a telephone, someone with a problem would find him. At home I often tried to protect him from calls, taking the telephone off the hook or trying to take the calls myself. But Medgar had a fear of missing something important and a compulsion to be available to the people who needed him. I was not often successful.

He was not a club man, not a joiner, and for several years after we were married, he resisted even joining a church. It was not that he was not a religious man, though he had been surfeited with churchgoing as a youth. He had a quiet, personal faith by which he tried to live. He read the Bible every night before turning out the light and, when times were difficult, he seemed to draw strength and comfort from this lifelong habit. We both knelt to pray, and I remember one night when it seemed he was on his knees and up again in no time that I made the mistake of teasing him about it. "What kind of a prayer was that?" I asked.

He looked puzzled. "What do you mean?"

I laughed. "I just don't understand how anyone can pray so fast."

I could tell he was annoyed. "Myrlie," he said, climbing into bed, "I don't have to stay on my knees all night to make contact with God. It's not the length of time on your knees but the sincerity and meaning behind it that counts."

Medgar attended church on Sundays when he could, but he made it a habit to visit different churches to meet new people and hopefully draw more ministers into the work of the NAACP. Often he went to my church, New Hope Baptist, where I played on Sundays for two different choirs. Our minister, the Reverend G. C. Hunte, like other Negro ministers in Jackson, had long hoped to snare Medgar as a member, and more than once he took him aside and spoke to him about it. "You're a young man with a growing family, Medgar," he would say, "and with a position like yours you should take a more active part in the church. For one thing, it's important for you to be seen at church more often." That was usually as far as he got. Medgar would explain that he was often out of town on Sundays and that he visited other churches. He didn't argue. But I knew from experience that this was not the approach to use with him.

He had been under other pressures to join a church— any church—for appearances' sake. Once word even came quietly from the national office in New York that it would not be a bad idea for the NAACP's field secretary in Mississippi to be a church member. Each time the subject arose, Medgar's resistance seemed to increase. He would attend church services in the hope of stimulating interest in his work, but he would not join one for that reason.

Then, one Sunday in January 1956, Medgar brought the children with him to church. I was playing for the youth choir, and the sight of the three of them sitting together in a pew made me proud and happy as always. When the service reached the point at which new members are invited to join, Medgar stood quietly and walked to the pulpit, leaving the two children sitting together in the pew. I was not the only one to be astonished.

A woman's voice called out, "Praise the Lord." She was answered immediately by enthusiastic "Amen's" and a patting of feet in every corner of the church. This was more than the usual enthusiasm, and I sensed an almost palpable feeling of joy in the congregation as Medgar shook hands with the minister and took a seat in the row of chairs beside the pulpit reserved for new members. I had difficulty holding back the tears.

After the service, Medgar was a center of attention and congratulations. It wasn't until we were on the way home that I had a chance to tell him how pleased and surprised I was. "Why didn't you warn me?"

"It was something I worked out by myself, Myrlie," he said. "I hadn't really decided when I was going to do it until just before I did." I found that hard to believe, but I was too happy to argue. I think the real reason he kept it a secret was out of a strong desire to do it completely on his own.

Several Sundays later, Medgar was baptized. When the service was over, he stood with the minister as the deacons came forward and shook his hand. After the deacons came all of the other church members, and as I finally reached him, I held his hand a little longer than usual, happy that we were now a complete family in the same church.

But joining the church did not change Medgar or his habits. He continued to visit other churches to make contacts, and when church members tried to involve him in the men's club and other church activities, he politely explained that he was too busy. His religion remained a highly personal thing to him. It was his dedication to freedom that he shared with all who shared his convictions on that subject.

—— XIII ——

The tide of progress toward full civil rights, which ebbed and flowed through the rest of the South in those years, caused only minor ripples in Mississippi. Mississippi was a backwater. Mississippi stagnated. The activity, the progress seemed always somewhere else.

In December 1955, Negroes in Montgomery, Alabama, united and began a boycott of city buses that shocked the white South and started an unknown young Negro minister on the road to international acclaim and a Nobel Peace Prize. With the emergence of the Reverend Dr. Martin Luther King, civil rights became a movement with the challenging philosophy of non-violent protest, and the Montgomery tactic was soon echoed by boycotts in Tallahassee, Florida; Tuskegee, Alabama; Orangeburg, South Carolina.

The following year the Supreme Court ordered the University of Alabama to admit its first Negro student, and Autherine Lucy became the focus of rioting mobs. She left the campus in a matter of days, but the university remained under court order to admit qualified Negro students.

In 1957 the long, bitter trial of Little Rock began, and for the first time the full weight of the federal government was thrown into the battle to enforce the orders of the Supreme Court. American troops surrounded an American school, and five Negro students broke the color line in the capital of Arkansas. Little Rock schools were closed the following year, but in September 1959 they opened again and desegregation was an accomplished fact.

In 1960, young Negro students entered the struggle with a completely new tactic: the sit-in. Beginning in Greensboro, North Carolina, sit-ins swept across the South, leaving in their wake drugstores, lunch counters, and restaurants where Negroes could eat side by side with whites.

That same year, school desegregation came to New Orleans, and the nation saw television pictures of the twisted, hate-filled faces of white mothers screaming invective at Negro schoolchildren. In 1961, Charlayne Hunter and Hamilton Holmes were quietly admitted to the University of Georgia. The Freedom Rides began.

With each new evidence of segregation's crumbling defenses, Medgar took hope. As state after state of the old Confederacy loosened its grip on the legacies of the past, he waited expectantly. But it was all happening somewhere else. Mississippi stood still.

Those years that marked the beginning of the end of racist laws in other states brought, in Mississippi, their full quota of murders and lynchings, beatings and disappearances. The telephone would ring, and Medgar would be off on a dangerous trip to a dangerous investigation that would lead, in the end, to bitter frustration. I waited in silent terror that this time, or the next, he would not return.

I remember the names of the victims of those years of terror, unfamiliar at first, then burned into memory by the repetition of the cold, brutal facts of death and torture. I remember the towns whose violence drew Medgar, towns whose names came to stand in my mind for a murder, the rape of a Negro schoolgirl by white men, the beating of a Negro woman by white police.

A map of Mississippi was a reminder not of geography, but of atrocities, of rivers that hid broken bodies, of towns and cities ruled by the enemy. No spot was safe, no road without its traps, and Medgar was a constantly moving target.

I remember the years by the names of the victims. Nineteen fifty-six was Edward Duckworth, shot to death by a white man who claimed self-defense. It was Milton Russell, burned to death in his home in Bloody Belzoni; no one arrested.

Nineteen fifty-seven was Charles Brown, shot to death by a white man near Yazoo City.

Nineteen fifty-eight was George Love, killed by a twenty-five-man posse. No arrests. It was Woodrow Wilson Daniels, who died of a brain injury nine days after a beating by a white sheriff; the sheriff tried and acquitted of manslaughter.

Nineteen fifty-nine was Jonas Causey, killed in Clarksdale, with fifteen policemen accused of the crime. No arrests. It was William Roy Prather, fifteen years old, killed in what whites called a "Halloween prank."

But, mostly, 1959 was Mack Charles Parker, lynched in the old-fashioned way, dragged by his heels down concrete stairs from an unguarded cell in Poplarville where he had been charged with the rape of a white woman; then shot to death by a lynch mob, his body dumped into the Pearl River. Everyone in town knew who did it. The FBI turned over names and evidence to Governor Coleman. There were no arrests. Some years later, a Mississippi judge, speaking in Connecticut about the wonders of our state, was asked if he thought the lynchers of Mack Charles Parker would ever be caught and tried. He said he didn't think so and then added without thinking, "Besides, three of them are already dead." *Everyone* knew who did it.

If the years were stamped with the names of the murdered, the months were inked with those of the beaten and maimed. Affidavits testifying to the routine cruelty of white Mississippians toward Negroes piled up in Medgar's files. Each represented an hour, a day, a week of Medgar's life in a surrealist version of Hell.

I, [a Negro man], on November 3 came down Whitfield Mills Road and just as I made it to Grandberry Street I heard someone holler "Hey." I looked and saw it was two policemen. I then pulled up by the barber shop and stopped. . . . I sat there in the car until they got there, then one came to my door, opened it and snatched me out of the car, hit me back of the head with a flashlight, then I remember falling. That's all I remember until I came to.

Then they told me to get in the car, so I got in and they took me to jail. While in jail my side and head hurt me all night. After my release from jail I went to the VA hospital for an X-ray and was told I had three broken ribs.

I was told also that while I was lying unconscious on the ground the police kicked me in the side.

On the night of November 26 . . . about six o'clock in the evening, the phone rang and I [a pregnant Negro woman] answered it. The party on the line wanted to speak to me. He asked me if —— —— was hiding out in my house. I told him, "No, I haven't seen her." He said he was coming by my house to search it. I told him to come on. I told him to get a search warrant and help himself because she was not there and hung up the phone. About an hour and a half later someone knocked at the door. I answered the door. He said to me, "Open this . . . door or I will knock it down." I asked him if he had a search warrant, he said, "Yes" and hit me in the head with a club and said "You black s-o-b, you are under arrest." He punched me, hit me in the mouth almost knocked out three of my teeth halfway. About that time my kid ran out of the kitchen and started to cry. He didn't hit me any more. He told me to come and go to jail with him. I then asked him to let me call someone to keep my baby before I go. He said, "H— no," so I went on out with him. They carried me to jail. He asked me my name, then my age. I told him I was thirty. He said to me, "You asked me if I had a search warrant didn't you." I said, "yes, I did." He said, "Here it is and you can get it as many times as you can stand up to it," and started hitting me on my head. I asked him if he wouldn't hit me on my head. So he stopped hitting me.

The jailer who was sitting at the desk said to me, "Let me see your head," and I took my hand to part my hair to show him the operation place on my head. He said, "It is," and hit me as hard as he could with a bunch of keys he had in his hand. They stopped and started cursing me for everything. "Black smart-a— b—" and said they were going to kill me. I asked him, "Kill me for what?" He said, "For what you said to me over the phone." I said, "I didn't say anything I thought was wrong." He said, "You said to me over the phone to get a search warrant and come on out." I said to him, "It's a crying shame, and I am two months pregnant and will be three on December 23." He said, "You stay that way you black no good b—." He hit me in my back as hard as he could, on my hip, hand, arms and shoulder. Then he said, "Lock that d— n— up, I ought to kill her." When I was walking in the door to the jail cell the jailer kicked me as though he was kicking a dog who was trying to bite him.

On the morning of November 27 . . . about five-thirty

or six o'clock, the jailer came and called me. I said, "Sir" and he said "I guess your d— a— is sore, and you tell it I will kill you." At ten o'clock the jailer came and told me I was released.

On December 3 I lost my baby as a result of this inhuman brutality.

I, [a male Negro], a student at Jackson State College, Jackson, Mississippi give the following statement of my own free will and accord.

On Friday night . . . at about 10:00 p.m., as I left my cousin's house . . . I was stopped by two (2) uniformed policemen of the Jackson, Mississippi, police department. I was asked by one officer if I knew "of anyone selling whiskey?" My answer was "no sir" he then said, "yes you do know of somebody selling whiskey on Deerpark." The officer then told me to "stand on one foot" which I did, then he told me to "walk up the street fast." Because of a previous case of polio I was not as mobile as he thought that I should have been so they took me to the City jail and charged me with being "drunk," fact of the matter is, I don't drink whiskey. I was kept in jail from the date of the arrest November 17–20. . . . I was only permitted to make a telephone call the day that I was released. My fine was $15.00 which was paid by a friend.

I [a Negro woman] left Indianola, Mississippi about 8:20 a.m. . . . via Trailway Bus enroute to Newton, Mississippi. I had no trouble until I got to Eupora, Mississippi. When I got to Eupora I asked the bus driver if I could get off and use the rest room and he told me sure and to go right in. I went in the bus station and asked a white gentleman if I could use the rest room. This white gentleman . . . told me that Negroes could not use the rest room in the bus station. He then directed me to a rest room across the street at a Standard Oil Service Station. . . . I followed the sign and the arrows which directed me to the rest room. After I used the rest room and was about to come out a white man came in on me and beat me over the head and cursed me and asked me didn't I know that no Nigger Woman could use that rest room. I told him no and that I was sorry and that the white man across the street directed me to it. He said he would teach me a lesson not to use white ladies' rest room. He put his hand over my mouth. I tussled and got loose from his hand over my mouth. I pushed the door open with my foot and hollered three times. No one came. He caught me around the waist and pulled up my dress and hit me with his hands like you would a child. I tussled loose and came out of the rest room door. I walked approximately three feet and asked him if I could go and get my hat and articles he made me lose out of my pocket book. He told me hell no and to get the hell away from there as quick as I could. . . .

I, [a Negro woman], twenty years of age . . . after being duly sworn according to law, deposes and says:

That on Friday, December 1 . . . at about 1:00 p.m. while I was working (baby sitting) . . . Mr. _____ came into the living room where I was folding baby diapers and he sat down, (the baby was asleep, Mrs. _____, was at work) he . . . looked at television for a while, then he left the room, went to the back porch.

When he came back he went into the back bedroom of the house, and he called me saying, "_____, come here, I have something to show you." I went to see what he had to show me, at that time he locked the bedroom door. He then asked me, "Have you ever been with a white man?" I told him "no" he then said "you are going with one to-day, because, you are going with me, pull your clothes off," when I said "NO SIR" he pushed me down on the bed, pulled my half slip and panties off, and when I started crying he told me "shut up" I then asked him to "let me talk with him first" and at that time he sat down on the bed.

I asked him "do you do your other maids this way," he said "naw" and then I jumped up and ran to the door (which was locked).

Mr. _____ got up and got a shotgun and said "if you run I will shoot you in your damn back." He then put the gun down near the door and threw me on the bed, raped me and finally at about 2:30 p.m., he left me alone.

I asked him "what his wife was going to say" and he said "you had better not tell my wife, if you tell it I will kill you, and if I see you walking the streets I am going to kill you anyway."

He then left the bedroom and went back into the living room, and at that time (when he got back into the living room) the baby had started crying, I went into his wife's bedroom picked the baby up, and he told me "give the baby to me, go wash your face—you look like a damn tramp." Before I left the room to wash my face, I told him, "If I come up pregnant I am going to tell my mother what you did to me," he replied, "you had better not, put it on somebody else," I then went to wash my face and he told me "go take a douche" and after that he left the house.

At about 3:00 p.m., the two little children came in from school, one of the children asked me "what have you been crying about?" I told her "nothing" and then she asked me if I was coming back to work, I then told her "no" and left the house and went home.

When I got home at about 4:00 p.m. I told my mama what had happened, she told my sister to "call the police."

About fifteen minutes later two (2) policemen (dressed in plain clothes came to our house, questioned me in the presence of my mother) and told me to "come and show us where Mr. _____ lives." My sister went with me. At that time they did not go in his house, they circled around the block, then put my sister in another police car and told her "she can go home, because she didn't know nothing about it."

I was then taken to the . . . court house, where I was questioned by another policeman (in plain clothes) and I gave an affidavit to a policewoman and I signed it.

After that I was taken to the . . . hospital, where I was examined by a Doctor (name unknown) and the Doctor told me "you're alright."

Immediately I was taken back to the . . . court house; this time the man who had attacked me was there, he said, "_____ why don't you tell the truth, and tell the police that I asked you for some, and you gave it to me" at that time I answered him and told him "you are telling a damn lie," and he said "I gave her a dollar," to which I replied "I put that dollar on the table." No one else asked any questions, the policemen carried me home.

I had worked for the _____s for only three (3) days, they have four children and one daughter about sixteen years of age.

I feel that since this man has threatened my life, and has assaulted me already, that this should be thoroughly investigated. He told me that "if I see you walking on the streets I will kill you," even if he does not try to kill me. I feel that another maid would have to go through the same thing.

Please help me.

"Please help me." It was a cry that Medgar heard in his sleep, a cry that haunted him, that drove him to frenzies of activity, that took him into danger and brought him back weak with rage at his powerlessness. It was the plea that rang with every telephone, the yearning that scrawled itself across ruled school paper in the crudely lettered words of an elderly Negro who had barely learned to write. It was the call that ran through the stumbling words of every affidavit, the look in the frightened eyes of a man in a jail cell, the hope in the face of a Negro child too young to know what "Negro" meant in Mississippi.

Medgar did what he could. He placed himself between the wounded, the beaten, the frightened, the threatened, the assaulted, and the white racist society that invariably had everything its own way. He investigated, filed complaints, issued angry denunciations, literally dragged reporters to the scenes of crimes, fought back with press releases, seeking always to spread word beyond the state, involve the federal government, bring help from the outside. It was not always easy to get word out, for Mississippi's brutality toward Negroes was an old story, and unless there were some new twist to make it newsworthy, the Northern newspapers would ignore it.

There were always stories that remained untold. There were counties where killing was all but approved, where to be a Negro meant abject surrender or the threat of instant death. White men were elected to office on the unspoken promise that such would remain the case: the bigger the brute, the larger the vote.

Long before the world had heard of Philadelphia, Mississippi, of Neshoba County, of the awful triple murder of Michael Schwerner, Andrew Goodman, and James Chaney in June of 1964; before the pictures of Sheriff Lawrence Rainey with his cheek full of Red Man tobacco and his grin in the face of arrest and arraignment; long before that, Medgar knew.

There was the Sunday night in October 1959 when Mrs. Hettie Thomas sat in a friend's car on Pine Street in Philadelphia, Mississippi, with Luther Jackson, a friend from out of town. According to Mrs. Thomas' sworn affidavit, this is what happened. A police car drove past and stopped. Lawrence Rainey, then a city policeman, got out, walked back and ordered the two Negroes from the car.

Luther Jackson got out first, and Rainey pushed him in front of the car and around the side, out of sight. As Mrs. Thomas was getting out she heard a shot. She ran toward the sound, and there was another shot. When she reached Rainey, Luther Jackson was lying in a ditch, dead.

Mrs. Thomas protested, "You have shot him for nothing!" She knelt by the body of her friend. Rainey hit her, and she leaped up and struck him back. He forced her into the back seat of the car, walked to his police car, called in on the radio. Mrs. Thomas heard him say, "Come on down here. I think I have killed a nigger."

Two officers arrived, and later Police Chief Bill Richardson and Mayor Clayton Lewis. The police chief ran to where Mrs. Thomas was sitting, sobbing. He asked what she was saying. She said that Luther Jackson had been killed for nothing, and the chief hit her with his pistol, breaking her glasses. Once again she struck back. This time the chief slugged her with a blackjack.

Forced into a police car with the chief and two other policemen, Chief Richardson tried to hit her again. He was talked out of it by one of the officers: "We are in deep enough as it is."

At the jail Mrs. Thomas cried and cursed the officers. The jailer's wife said, "Let me have her. I can shut her up." Mrs. Thomas warned the white woman not to hit her.

The jailer's wife let a white man out of a cell and locked Mrs. Thomas in it. She was kept there without medical attention until the next morning, when she was tried for drunkenness, resisting arrest, and assault and battery. She was found guilty and fined forty dollars. Luther Jackson was buried. A coroner's jury ruled that the killing was justifiable homicide.

Four days after that incident, Medgar drafted a letter to the Attorney General of the United States, William P. Rogers, asking for an investigation. Within a week he had a reply: "This matter will receive our careful consideration and should it develop that a violation of federal law is involved, appropriate action will be taken." Less than a month later came final word from the Justice Department: "Careful consideration has been given to all of the evidence developed in the investigation which has been conducted into the circumstances surrounding Mr. Jackson's death. The evidence does not, however, indicate the violation of any federal statute. For that reason, there is no basis for any action by this department."

Two and a half years later, in May 1962, Lawrence Rainey's name appeared in another sworn affidavit. Now he was a deputy sheriff, on his way up. The story began when Willie Otis Nash, a twenty-seven-year-old Negro epileptic who had previously spent three years in the state mental hospital at Whitfield, got into an argument with his brother. The brother, fearing Willie's "mind had gone bad again," called Sheriff Barnett.

The sheriff and two deputies, one of them Rainey, came to the house and took Willie to jail. Willie's father, Levie Nash, a farmer, was told to come in the morning to get papers signed for Willie's commitment to Whitfield. Next day just after noon, Nash handed the papers to the sheriff and saw his son handcuffed and put in the back seat of the sheriff's car. He had reason to fear for his son's life, for on the last such trip to the hospital he had heard Sheriff Barnett say of Willie, "If I ever get that son-of-a-bitch in my car again, I am going to kill him."

Levie Nash asked Sheriff Barnett and Deputy Rainey if he could go along. The sheriff said, "Hell no, we can take care of him." Two hours later, Willie Nash was dead.

Mr. Nash asked to see his son's body. He was told at the white funeral home to which it had been taken that it was so badly shot up it could not be seen until just before the funeral. At the funeral the casket was closed. The funeral director refused to open it. Nash never saw his son's body. No one did. News reports said that Willie had been shot when he tried to open the glove compartment of the sheriff's car. Mr. Nash, who saw the three men enter the car, knew that Willie had been handcuffed in the back seat. There was nothing he could do. There was nothing anyone could do.

Nor were instant brutality and murder the only weapons used against Negroes who somehow offended Mississippi's racist officials. There were more sophisticated ways of destroying a man. Two Mississippians, one Negro, one white, were framed on charges of homosexual conduct during those terrible years. One, Aaron Henry, then state president of the NAACP, was vindicated by the Supreme Court of the United States. The other, William L. Higgs, a young white attorney who had graduated first in his class at Ole Miss and had turned to civil rights work, was vindicated by a sworn affidavit signed by the young white boy used by the Jackson police to frame him.

But the worst case of all, one that extended over many of the years of Medgar's job, was that of a quiet, brilliant, soft-spoken young Negro named Clyde Kennard. I don't know exactly when Medgar first met Clyde, but I know that he was active in NAACP youth work in Hattiesburg and that Medgar came to have an enormous respect for him.

Clyde had been born in Hattiesburg and came from a farm family. His father died when he was four. Five years later, his mother remarried. At twelve, Clyde went to Chicago to live with an older sister and attend school.

After graduating from high school, he joined the Army, served in Germany and Korea, became a paratrooper. It was one of the ironies of his life that he, a Mississippi Negro, was assigned to teach an Army de-nazification course in democracy to German youths. When he left the Army in 1952 after seven years of service, he enrolled at the University of Chicago and used some of the money he had saved for a down payment on a small farm near Hattiesburg for his mother and stepfather.

He had only a year to go for his college degree when, in 1955, his stepfather became disabled. Clyde left the university and returned to Hattiesburg to run the farm. It was a bitter disappointment, made more bitter by the presence in Hattiesburg—just fifteen minutes' drive from his farm—of Mississippi Southern College (now the University of Southern Mississippi), a college he could have attended if he had been white.

Clyde was a gentleman, a man with a firm belief that intelligence and reason could achieve desegregation in Mississippi without court action. He first approached the president of Mississippi Southern, a former army general, William D. McCain, in 1956, and for two years, off and on, the two men discussed the possibility of Clyde's enrolling at the college to finish his education. Clyde made clear to everyone that his interest was education and not provoking a court test of segregation. He refused legal aid from the NAACP, saying, "These people at MSC are more liberal.

They're not like the old ones. I'll get in without the courts."

President McCain, who must have given Clyde this impression, was regarded by many white Mississippians as a sort of silent liberal on the question of race—his silence dictated in part, at least, by his responsibility to a state board of trustees and his dependence on the state legislature for appropriations. He said later he found Clyde "courteous at all times." He also managed to stave off formal replies to three applications from Clyde. Then, in 1959, according to Clyde, "Dr. McCain came by my chicken farm one day and said the governor wanted to talk to me."

The governor was James P. Coleman. "When we arrived at the Capitol in Jackson," Clyde said later, "the governor dismissed all his staff and said he set aside the entire afternoon to discuss my case. Just the governor, Dr. McCain, and I talked. We made no deals. This was mid-semester and the governor told me he had no choice but to close the school if I insisted on enrolling because he agreed that I was qualified. He asked me to wait until after the primary elections that summer when the subject would not be a political issue. I agreed. My main concern was not to do anything that would close the school."

Governor Coleman also urged Clyde to choose any college in America that would accept him and said that the state would pay his expenses. Clyde explained that he couldn't leave the farm. Coleman replied that the political situation was difficult—he had a handpicked successor in the primary—and that time would take care of things. He would, he said, try to work it out. Clyde asked when. The governor had no answer.

When Governor Coleman's candidate lost the primary to Ross Barnett, Clyde resubmitted his application. In it, and in a letter published in the Hattiesburg *American*, he reviewed the traditional arguments for segregation, opposing each with logic and eloquence. On the question of alleged Negro immorality, he wrote: "No thinking person would pass lightly over this problem; for it is no secret that the percentage of Negroes who are accused of crime is often higher than their white counterpart. I admit that we have had and still have, to a large extent, lower economic and moral standards than many of our white neighbors. However, we must realize this condition is not the cause but the effect of segregation and discrimination. The more segregation and discrimination we have in our community the more we shall have ignorance and immorality. Teach men to do a job and then give them the job to do, and high morality will follow as the day follows the night."

Of the vaunted school equalization program then underway, he wrote: ". . . I have not been quite able to understand what possible good a vast equalization program could serve, if no sincere plans are made to equalize employment opportunities. If there are to be no jobs in government, science or industry, in vain is time and money spent in educating the child. The big question seems, then, to be, what part will the educated Negro play in our society in future years?

"Questions of this kind," he concluded, "have led me to request of you that you permit me to enroll at Mississippi Southern College, without a court order to do so. I am a solid believer in the ability of the States to control their own affairs. I believe if the State should lead out with only the smallest amount of integration, it would never have to worry about Federal intervention."

The ability of the state of Mississippi to control its own affairs was demonstrated almost immediately. Attempts to persuade Clyde not to resubmit his application having failed, Tuesday, September 15, 1959 was set as the date of his formal interview. In spite of the warning of a local civil rights leader that Dr. McCain was working with the local White Citizens Council, Clyde continued to trust him. McCain telephoned as Clyde was leaving his home that morning to ask when he expected to arrive at the school. Clyde told him. At the college he parked and locked his car, walked directly to the president's office.

There, with McCain, he found Zack J. Van Landingham, chief investigator of the State Sovereignty Commission, Mississippi's official guardian of segregation. The interview lasted fifteen minutes, and Clyde's application was rejected. A letter dated the previous day gave three reasons: lack of a transcript of Clyde's records from the University of Chicago, a "false and fraudulent" medical certificate "indicative of a lack of good moral character," and an alleged refusal of the University of Chicago to readmit him. The last was completely false; William Van Cleve, registrar of the University of Chicago, said, "Kennard was never refused readmission. In fact, the University expected him to resume studies in the winter of 1957. He left here with a clean slate."

The charge of a false and fraudulent medical certificate was later explained by McCain. Kennard had, he said, advanced the dates on both his medical certificate and character recommendations. Both, of course, had been prepared for an earlier application, the one Governor Coleman talked Clyde out of making, but McCain's attitude toward this understandable updating of valid documents was clearly expressed in his statement that "Mississippi Southern does not deal in forged documents." Mississippi Southern's president had no such difficulty with questions of simple fact, for he told a reporter flatly that he had no knowledge of a meeting with Governor Coleman and denied any communication between the college and the Sovereignty Commission.

But the simple rejection of Clyde's application was apparently not enough. Returning to his locked car after the meeting, Clyde was arrested and charged with reckless driving by two waiting constables. He handed them the keys to his car, watched while they opened it, showed them how to start it. One constable drove Clyde's car while the other drove Clyde in a police car. As Clyde was being questioned at police headquarters, one of the constables entered the room with a paper bag containing five half-pints of liquor. It had been found, he said, under the front seat of Clyde's car.

Clyde, who neither smoked nor drank and who denied any knowledge of the liquor, was charged with reckless driving and possession of liquor, illegal in dry Mississippi. He was released on a $600 bond, his car impounded. Later, he was convicted before a justice of the peace and fined $600. As is usual in such unrecorded hearings, Clyde's attorney put up no defense, saving his witnesses and evidence for an appeal to a higher court. But, even here, Clyde was tricked.

Given misleading information by the district attorney, the justice of the peace, and the jailer, neither Clyde nor his attorney were present when the time came and passed for his appeal. Twice, Mississippi courts refused to reopen the case. Eventually the Mississippi Supreme Court overruled the lower courts, but by that time the entire question was academic. A more permanent punishment had been decided on for the Negro who dared believe that "these people at MSC are more liberal."

If there was one thing that Clyde Kennard had proved, it was that he was not lightly to be turned aside. Persistence in a Negro of Clyde's abilities clearly worried Mississippi's racists. There was still nothing, after all, to prevent his correction of the supposed defects of his application and filing it once more. He had Governor Coleman's own word that he was qualified to attend Mississippi Southern. Few Mississippians who knew about the case doubted that Clyde would try again.

The solution, clearly, was to find some means of rendering Clyde permanently ineligible for admission to the college. Mississippi law provided the answer. According to a state statute, entrance to state schools is forbidden to convicted felons. To convict Clyde of a felony ought to be easy in a county that had already contrived to frame him on a misdemeanor.

At 4:40 A.M. on Sunday, September 25, 1960, an illiterate nineteen-year-old Negro, Johnny Lee Roberts, stole five bags of chicken feed worth twenty-five dollars from the Forrest County Cooperative warehouse where he worked. He was seen by the night watchman who made no attempt to stop him. The watchman noted the license number of Roberts' car and called the police.

Roberts drove with the stolen feed to Clyde Kennard's farm and put it in the unlocked egghouse. He was arrested shortly afterward. By eight-thirty, Clyde had been arrested, though it was not until noon that police returned to Clyde's farm to search for the stolen feed. They found it, they said, in the feed hoppers; the sacks and feed tickets identifying it as the stolen feed were found on a trash pile.

But something more was clearly needed, for possession of stolen goods is still a misdemeanor. If Clyde could be shown to have been an accomplice in the theft, he could be convicted as an accessory to burglary, a felony. For that, the testimony of Johnny Lee Roberts would be necessary. It has rarely been difficult to provide such testimony in Mississippi.

Clyde was charged with being an accessory, and at the trial Roberts testified that the whole thing had been Clyde's idea. He claimed that Clyde had paid him ten dollars for the feed. Yet, on the witness stand, Roberts told a confused story of when and how Clyde had suggested the burglary, a crucial point because it would establish whether or not the idea could possibly have come from Clyde. The frightened young man was led through his testimony by District Attorney James Finch, a sour, skinny man whose devotion to the racist cause was well known in Hattiesburg. But even the dogged Finch had difficulty getting Roberts to place the time of the supposed conference where he wanted it.

There was, of course, no doubt in the minds of the twelve white men who made up the jury. In ten minutes they returned a verdict of guilty for both Clyde and the frightened Roberts. Judge Stanton A. Hall sentenced Clyde to the maximum of seven years. He placed Roberts on probation for five years, leaving him free yet under an obvious restraint against changing his story. The employer from whom he had admitted stealing five bags of chicken feed promptly hired Roberts back.

The well-oiled machinery of Mississippi justice—of frame-up and perjury and threat and reward—had found another victim, and Medgar publicly condemned the outcome as a mockery of justice. Judge Hall declared Medgar in contempt of court and sentenced him to thirty days in jail and a $100 fine. Medgar appealed, but by the time Judge Hall's contempt citation was thrown out by the Mississippi Supreme Court, Clyde Kennard had already served the first seven months of his seven-year sentence at hard labor in the Mississippi State Penitentiary at Parchman.

Still the story was not over, for Mississippi not only punishes Negroes like Clyde Kennard. If it can, it tortures them. While the NAACP raised money to save the Kennard farm from foreclosure, while its lawyers vainly fought the case all the way to the United States Supreme Court, Clyde began complaining of abdominal pain and weakness.

On March 19, 1962, he was sent from Parchman to the University of Mississippi Hospital in Jackson. A large lesion was found in his left colon. Given medication and returned to prison, he was brought back the following month, operated on, and found to have cancer. Eleven days after major surgery, with a diagnosis of cancer, he was returned to Parchman. In June, two months later, he returned to the hospital for a check-up.

In a letter to the prison superintendent, hospital medical record librarian Mary Senter reported that the diagnosis gave Clyde a twenty per cent chance of living five years: ". . . it is my opinion that he should be eligible for early parole, if such could be arranged, because of the extremely poor prognosis in this rather young patient. I have talked with him at length in this regard as well as to his mother, who is incidentally almost totally dependent upon the patient, and have told them that I would write a letter to the Prison Superintendent requesting parole if such were feasible.

"In summary, it is our medical opinion that because of this patient's extremely poor prognosis a recommendation for a parole would be in order from the medical standpoint. However, whether he is paroled or not, we would like to follow him at this hospital in the Tumor Clinic at three month intervals for at least five years, assuming that he lives that long. . . ."

That report was written on June 21, 1962. Seven months later Clyde had neither been paroled nor returned to the hospital for the requested check-ups. Forty pounds lighter in weight than when he entered the prison two years earlier, he was still being forced to labor in the prison's farm fields from dawn to dark.

By early 1963, national publicity about the Kennard case threatened to elevate it into another embarrassment to the state. *Jet*, the Negro weekly, had maintained a steady drumbeat of stories over the years. *The Reporter* had published an article by Ronald A. Hollander about the case. Medgar had lost no opportunity to publicize the incredible injustice to Clyde and his family. Students at Tougaloo College began a campaign for Clyde's release.

Eventually Governor Ross Barnett capitulated. Clyde was first transferred to the University Hospital and later given an indefinitely suspended sentence. He went to Chicago, where he died early that summer, a victim more of Mississippi justice than the cancer that caused his death.

# XIV

The Kennard case is still too little known outside of Mississippi, but it was one of the long wracking pains of Medgar's years as Mississippi field secretary. He knew Clyde well and loved him. After Clyde went to prison, he came to know his mother well, too.

I remember the night of the annual NAACP Freedom Fund banquet in Jackson when Clyde had already spent a year in prison. Medgar, along with Aaron Henry, the state president, had been making awards to various branches for outstanding work during the year. Afterward, Medgar, who had just come from a visit in Hattiesburg with Mrs. Kennard, began telling the assembly about their talk.

He had barely begun when he was forced to stop. Sitting next to him at the head table, I could tell he was choked with emotion. I prayed he'd be able to continue. Medgar had always looked on crying as a weakness in men. Over and over he had told Darrell, "Men don't cry."

Regaining control, he started again, then stopped. It happened three times. Finally tears streamed down his face as he spoke, and he just gave way. He stood there in front of hundreds of people and cried as though his heart would break. Hundreds of us cried with him.

Aaron Henry stood up beside him. "That's all right, Medgar. Let me take over."

Medgar shook his head. "No. I can make it."

A woman called out, "That's all right, son. We all feel the same way," and Medgar, nodding, began once more. This time he finished what he had to say, and, by the time it was over, hundreds of us had cleansed our hearts with tears.

Medgar, it seemed to me, was continually torn between love and anguish. Of the state, he told a reporter from *Ebony*, "This is my home. Mississippi is a part of the United States. And whether the whites like it or not, I don't plan to live here as a parasite. The things I don't like, I will try to change."

Returning from a regional meeting in North Carolina in March 1958, he changed buses in Meridian, Mississippi, deliberately sitting in the front. When the bus driver ordered him to move, he refused. The police came and took him to the police station. "You know how things are done here," they told him. "Yes," Medgar said proudly, "I was born just thirty miles from here in Decatur."

When they let him go back to the bus, he again took a seat in the front. The driver ordered him to move, and again he refused. Three blocks from the terminal, a white cab driver flagged the bus to a halt, got on, and hit Medgar in the face. The driver ordered the cab driver off, and the bus started up again. "I came all the way to Jackson in the front of the bus," Medgar told me proudly.

When he learned on television that Mack Charles Parker's body had been dragged from the Pearl River, he smashed the bedroom dresser with his fist. "Why?" he cried. "How can people do such things?" His body shook with sobs, and he stood up and shouted, "I'd like to get a gun and just start shooting!"

Ten minutes later he was showered and dressed for the office. At the door he turned, "Somebody's going to pay for this," he said grimly. "And I'm not leaving. I'm going to stay here and fight until someone does the same thing to me."

When members of the national office flew down for a speech or a meeting or to investigate a murder, he took them with him, showed them the best and the worst of his state. When they offered him a job in California, he declined. "I belong here," he said.

We bought a house in 1957, as though to prove it. I had by that time quit my job at the office, and my grandmother had gone back to Vicksburg. There was now more room in the apartment, and it was safer than a house, but when a new Negro subdivision opened, the first in Jackson to be developed by a Negro builder, we drove out to look. The houses were tiny—three small bedrooms, a bathroom, a small kitchen, a living-dining area, and a carport—but the desire to own our own home was strong. The homes sold for $9500—$300 down, if you qualified for a G.I. mortgage. We were still in debt, but Medgar borrowed $300 from a bank.

The subdivision attracted mainly Negro teachers, and we had no sooner put our money down and begun to count the days until our house would be completed than we began hearing rumors of a petition to keep us out. There was nothing personal about it; it was just that Medgar's work and his notoriety threatened some of the more timid. There was talk that the wrong house might be burned down by mistake, that to have us in their midst would be dangerous for the whole community. Medgar tried to track these stories down but could never find anything definite. There was probably never a formal petition, but there was plenty of fear.

Nor was the fear exclusively that of our neighbors-to-be. In choosing the site for our house, we had both been drawn to a corner lot, larger than most, which could be bought for the same price. Talking about it together, Medgar pointed out that the corner lot was more exposed, less protected by other houses, closer to the main highway, and hence easier to reach and get away from. It may seem incredible to the average American home buyer, but security from attack was a consideration we discussed at length, and in the end it dictated our final choice of a lot tucked securely between two other houses.

"It may sound funny," Medgar told the *Ebony* reporter, "but I love the South. I don't choose to live anywhere else. There's land here, where a man can raise cattle, and I'm going to do that someday. There are lakes where a man can sink a hook and fight bass. There is room here for my children to play, and grow, and become good citizens— if the white man will let them."

*If the white man will let them:* that was always the question. Our children asked, as all children do, if they could go places and see things they saw advertised in the newspapers or on television. We would tell them they couldn't. They asked, as all children ask, why not. We would tell them that they were for whites only—or that whites and Negroes were segregated there. Medgar refused to pay money to be segregated.

They asked, as all Negro children eventually ask, why a movie or a park or a swimming pool was for whites only. I was always at a loss to answer such questions.

Medgar would begin at the beginning, tailoring his words to their ages, making sure they understood, at least for the moment. He would begin with slavery, telling how the Negroes were brought here from Africa on great slave ships; how many of them died on the way. He would explain how families had been broken up, both in Africa and here, how wives were separated from husbands, children from their mothers, in the unspeakable horror of the slave market.

"It was wrong," he told them. "It was evil, and there was great suffering. And to justify it, to seem to make it right, the white man told himself that Negroes were inferior, that they were fit for nothing but to be the white man's slaves. It was a lie, but many people believed it. Many people still believe it. But it is still a lie.

"Not all of the white men believed in slavery. Many knew it was wrong and worked hard to end it. Finally a great war was fought over that question, with the North trying to free the slaves and the South resisting. The North won that civil war, and the slaves were freed. But the white man in the South had been taught that Negroes were inferior, and he still tried to keep them from being equal. He told them where they could live and where they could not live, where they could work and where they could not work, where they could eat and where they could not eat.

"He called it segregation, and like slavery, it, too, is evil. Like slavery, many white people knew that it was wrong. But the North, having won the war, forgot about the Negroes and let the Southern white men have their way. Some of them knew it was wrong, and some are working now to change it. But mostly it is Negroes themselves who have to change it. That's what I am doing; that's what my work is: changing segregation to freedom. I'm working so that you can go to any movie you want to, swim at any swimming pool, play in any park, go to any school. And if you ever hear a person say that you are inferior to white people, that you're not as good, you'll know it is a lie. God made us all, and He loves us all, and the color of our skins isn't important."

Still, the children's questions never stopped. They arose again in different ways, under different circumstances. A block away from our house was a section of white homes. The unwritten law of the neighborhood was that our children never played with theirs. It was not that we didn't want them to know white children; we did. It was just that in Jackson, Mississippi, it was too dangerous. An altercation, a childish fight could be magnified into race war. We all knew who would win such a contest.

The boundary was Missouri Street, a block from our house, and across that line catcalls and names were sometimes hurled between white and Negro children who generally didn't know what they were saying or why.

One day when Darrell was four, he came running into the house. "Am I black, Mama?" he asked.

They had been rolling a ball across Missouri Street, the white children on one side, the Negro children on the other, playing with each other but still observing the boundary line in that wonderful way that children have of subverting adult idiocy. An older child had seen them and had broken up the game, reminding them of the unwritten code. They had responded with name-calling, and a white boy had called Darrell black.

I found his box of crayons and a piece of paper. With the black crayon I made a mark on the paper.

"What color is that?" I asked him.

"It's black, Mama," he said.

We held it up to his arm. "Are you that color?" I asked. He shook his head.

"You are brown-skinned," I told him. "The boy who

called you black was being naughty. That's a name some white-skinned people call Negroes.

"But there's nothing naughty about the word 'black.' Black is a lovely color because it blends with every other color."

I told him he shouldn't worry about the color of his skin, that it was not important. "What is important is the kind of boy you are and the kind of man you become. So don't worry about it if a boy calls you black. You know you're not black."

"Anyway," Darrell said triumphantly, "Billy Henry called him a poor white peckerwood!"

Later that afternoon the whole gang of children sat on the grass in our backyard eating popsicles and discussing the verbal battle. Through the kitchen window I heard them discussing the color of their skins. Several were quite fair-skinned. Darrell had decided he was brown. One boy was quite dark. But after much discussion and comparison, they decided unanimously that none of them was black. Billy Henry boasted of having called the white boy a name, and a small girl declared defiantly that the next time a white boy called her black, she was going to call him a poor white cracker.

I don't know where or when Darrell first heard the word "nigger," but he must have known instinctively it was a fighting word. He has fought over it, even with other Negro children. And somehow, out of these experiences, he developed very early a disturbing sensitivity to color. He would describe his young friends by the color of their skin, and I thought I detected a preference for those who were lighter. Once he asked why he and Rena, whose skin was a good bit lighter than his, were different colors, and later, when our third child, James Van Dyke, was born in January 1960, he inspected him carefully when I brought him home from the hospital. Medgar, amused, asked him how he liked his new brother.

Darrell frowned. "I guess he's all right," he said doubtfully, "except he has black ears."

"There's nothing wrong with that," I said, more than a little annoyed at this criticism of our new baby. "He might become that color all over, and that's all right, too. If you go and look in a mirror, you'll see that you're pretty dark yourself."

Darrell's face fell, and I regretted instantly having said it. Strangely enough, that was the last time Darrell mentioned color.

When Darrell reached kindergarten age in 1958, there was no question about where he would go to school. The public schools were not only segregated, they were overcrowded and poorly equipped. We wanted the best possible education for our children, and Christ the King School, a Roman Catholic parochial school for Negroes, provided it.

The school was well staffed and not crowded, and while it put a dent in our small budget, it was more than worth it. The teachers were mostly white Catholic sisters, though there were three Negro lay teachers on the staff as well. All were marvelous people, deeply interested in the children and terribly protective during times of crisis and tension. Knowing that Darrell and, later, Rena were there made educating our children in Jackson bearable. I don't think I could have stood having them in the segregated public schools for long.

Here, again, was the strange conflict with which we were constantly faced. Here were white Catholic sisters and a white priest, Father Gasper, deeply devoted to our children, totally trusted by us to protect them. Yet other white faces meant hatred and perhaps even death.

Aaron Henry, who became president of the State Conference of Branches in 1960, illustrated perfectly this same kind of conflict in a personal story he never tired of telling. He had grown up in Clarksdale, in the Delta. As a youngster, he had been friendly with a white boy his own age. They had done everything together, played and fished and hunted and wrestled, until the age at which both white and Negro parents traditionally put an end to such relationships. Yet, even then, Aaron and his white friend maintained a friendly relationship, calling each other by their first names, greeting each other on the street.

Aaron grew up and went to Dillard University in New Orleans, became a pharmacist, returned to Clarksdale, and opened a drugstore. Over the years the Fourth Street Drugstore became one of the leading Negro businesses in Clarksdale and, as Aaron turned more and more of his attention to civil rights and the NAACP, a center in the Negro community for information on all sorts of programs and drives. Sitting on a stool at Aaron Henry's soda fountain, you were generally surrounded by NAACP membership applications, leaflets on voter registration, injunctions to pay your poll tax, copies of various NAACP publications.

Over those same years, Aaron's white childhood companion also grew up, also went to college. By the early 1950s he had settled in Indianola, Mississippi, where he operated a cotton plantation. In 1954 it was he who started the White Citizens Councils. His name was Robert Patterson, but Aaron always called him by his nickname, "Tut."

It will seem to many a wild, ironic coincidence that these two, one white, one Negro, who played together in youth, should grow up in early manhood to lead the two organizations that confronted each other in Mississippi on the particular subject of race. It is not. Similar stories could be found in every city and town of the South. But the particular story that Aaron could not resist telling came later, after the two men were well established as leaders on opposite sides of the race issue.

When Judge Brady wrote his *Black Monday*, the White Citizens Councils began selling a paper-bound edition of it. Aaron, who had heard about it, thought he ought to read it, the better to denounce it. An advertisement in a local paper directed purchasers to send their money to Patterson.

Aaron wrote his old friend, enclosing his money, asking that a copy be sent to him. When it didn't come, he wrote again. Weeks later, he wrote a third letter, reminding Patterson that he had sent his money and still not received the book. Then, one night just before the drugstore closed, Patterson walked in with a package in his hand.

"Hello, Tut," Aaron said.

"Hi, Aaron. I thought I'd better drive over and bring you this. It's the book you ordered. Sorry it took so long."

Aaron shook his head. "You didn't have to come all the way over here just for that," he said. "Why didn't you just mail it?"

Patterson handed him the book, wrapped in an unmarked envelope. "I thought I'd better give it to you in person," he explained. "I didn't want to get you in any trouble with your people. You know what the book is."

Aaron thanked him for his caution but assured him that it had not been necessary. "We read everything you people put out, just to keep informed," he said.

Patterson smiled. "We keep pretty busy reading your stuff, too," he said.

That, at least, is the way Aaron Henry tells the story, and

there is no reason at all to doubt it. For Mississippi is the state with the split personality, and it bequeaths this psychosis to many of its sons and daughters. Aaron himself is one of the joyous few who has somehow escaped any obvious scars: happy-go-lucky, jovial, friendly, understanding, he is also serious, sincere, and utterly devoted to his family and to civil rights. When white racists attempted to frame him for having allegedly made homosexual advances to a white man, every Negro in Mississippi who knew Aaron knew in his bones they could not have selected a more unlikely target for their plot. Aaron, above all else, is a man.

## ———— XV ————

The change of tide in Mississippi did not begin until 1961. Then, almost imperceptibly, Negroes took the offensive in the struggle for full citizenship.

It began, I think, on March 27, when nine Negro students from Tougaloo Southern Christian College, all members of NAACP youth groups, entered Jackson's white public library, sat down, and began to read. Within minutes the police were there.

Chief of Detectives M. B. Pierce asked for their leader. They said they had none. "All right," he said, "every one of you get up and get out of here."

No one moved.

Another officer spoke. "You will have to move on. The colored library is on Mill Street and you are welcome there." The students continued to read.

Chief Pierce told them they were under arrest, and the students rose as a group and left peacefully. Herded into waiting police cars, they were taken to jail. They remained overnight, charged with a breach of the peace, to be released on bond the next day. It was, all in all, a quiet beginning.

The next day students at Jackson State College held a mass

meeting to protest the arrests. They began a march on the city jail. They were halted ten blocks from the college by tear gas. That night at an NAACP mass meeting, Medgar reported what had happened, denouncing "police state tactics in an effort to intimidate students from the use of peaceful protest against segregation and discrimination in Jackson."

On April 1, Negroes and whites gathered on the sidewalk across from the Municipal Court Building where the trial of the nine students was to be held. The students arrived in cars, and the Negroes cheered them. Jackson police moved in with police dogs, scattered the Negroes to the cheers of the whites. Though the police maintained that no one was bitten, a UPI photograph showed one of the dogs with a grip on a Negro's arm. The nine students were convicted, fined $100 each, and given thirty-day suspended sentences.

Two months later, James Meredith, a sophomore at Jackson State, filed suit in federal court seeking admission to the University of Mississippi. A week later, Roy Wilkins, in Jackson to address a mass meeting of the Jackson branch, said that "Operation Mississippi whose objective is to wipe out segregation in all phases of Mississippi life" had been launched. It had indeed.

By July there were two new anti-segregation cases in the federal courts alongside James Meredith's. One, filed by three Jackson Negro businessmen, challenged state laws segregating transportation facilities. The other, filed by the Department of Justice against voting registrars in Clarke and Forrest counties, charged discrimination in voter registration.

Meanwhile, four students of Jackson State and Campbell College, all members of the intercollegiate chapter of the NAACP, had been arrested for taking seats in the front of a Jackson city bus. Three other young students had conducted a sit-in at the city zoo and were sentenced to a year's probation, a six-month curfew, and an essay of 1000 words on juvenile delinquency.

When the public schools opened in September, they were, of course, still segregated, but there was something in the air that hinted at a new beginning. On October 4, 114 Negro students walked out of Burglund High School in McComb, Mississippi, in protest against the school's refusal to enroll two fellow students convicted in a sit-in. Nine days later, 400 Jackson State students boycotted classes after college president Jacob L. Reddix dissolved the student government and dismissed its president for participating in protests against segregation. The young people had begun to sense their power, and they were using it for the first time.

In December the Reverend Robert L. T. Smith, the Negro grocer, qualified as a candidate for Congress to run in the Democratic primary in June against Representative John Bell Williams, an ardent racist. Four days after Christmas he won a battle for television time and gave an address that must have surprised white Mississippians. Calling for voters "to ignore the shouting of outworn slogans and the screaming epithets of bigotry," he said that Mississippians "should realize that we cannot live in the past. The time is far spent when men of insight and ability can afford to remain silent while unscrupulous politicians get themselves elected by waving the red flag of hatred and bigotry, thus confusing the minds of people who are inherently good."

Of such politicians he said, "They use time-worn slogans of the past to detract the people away from a sensible and workable solution of the many problems that beset us. Mississippi needs a positive approach to its problems. If we do not solve these problems, the blame will, in large part, be due to shortsighted planning by men holding high elective offices in our state government and by cunning men and predatory organizations who peddle hate with the use of our tax money." With the White Citizens Councils openly receiving state money from the official State Sovereignty Commission, there was no question in the minds of Mississippians what was meant by this.

Reverend Smith spoke well; he seemed at ease, and he impressed his Negro viewers with his sincerity and intelligence. But the impact of his televised address is hard to imagine without the knowledge that it was the first time in the memory of anyone that a Negro had been seen on Mississippi television giving a political speech. The blackout of television news on civil rights had gone so far that network news programs originating in New York were systematically interrupted with signs indicating technical difficulties whenever the news turned to race. We had been denied all of the network documentaries on civil rights. We were cut off from news developments within our own state. The only news we received on race relations was the distorted news the local stations decided we should have.

Against this background of suppression, the sight and sound of the Reverend Robert L. T. Smith, the first Mississippi Negro candidate for Congress since Reconstruction, were like the lifting of a giant curtain. No one believed that he could win the Democratic nomination with Negroes largely excluded from voting, but he was a voice, and he was on television, and he was saying things that had never before been said by a Negro to whites in Mississippi.

The pace of events continued to quicken. In January 1962 a suit was filed in federal court to desegregate all of Jackson's public recreational facilities. Jack Greenberg, who had succeeded Thurgood Marshall as director-counsel of the NAACP Legal Defense and Educational Fund when Marshall was appointed to a federal judgeship by President Kennedy, announced that an all-out desegregation attack would be made in Mississippi. "Within the next year or two," he predicted, "Mississippi will cover ground that took decades for the rest of the South."

If Negroes were slowly taking the offensive in the civil rights struggle in Mississippi, it followed that white segregationists would gradually move to the defensive. One of the first indications of this shift was a statement by William J. Simmons, administrator of the White Citizens Councils of Mississippi. The suit to desegregate recreational facilities, he said, "intensified the mortal fight for racial integrity in Mississippi." Insisting that "this attack must and will be defeated as have other attempts in the past," he said, "it points up the seriousness of the long-range war we are in and the resources, both in manpower and in money, that must be mobilized by the Citizens Councils to win the war.

"Another phase of the same war," he added, "is the appearance in Mississippi of the first Negro candidate for Congress since Reconstruction. The white people should be alerted to the true significance of this move. The radicals do not expect to win—but they do expect to build up a Negro bloc vote which will be extremely dangerous if it materializes. The power of Negro mass organizations and white 'moderates' has brought us to this pass. Only the power of organized white people will prevent black supremacy from becoming a reality instead of a nightmarish dream."

In February 1962, fifty-two Negro parents in Leake County filed a petition asking for immediate desegregation of schools. As usual, pressure from whites brought withdrawal of some of the parents, but the petition itself remained. R. Jess Brown, the parents' Negro attorney, said, "We're not assuming there'll be a need for a lawsuit."

Others, however, were, and, as had been the case so frequently in the past, they found a Negro willing to do their work for them. O. S. Jordan, the principal of a Negro school in Carthage, county seat of Leake County, addressed a letter to each of the petitioners. "I call upon you to remove your name from the petition that is now in the superintendent's office," he wrote. "This document, if allowed to be executed, is going to set race relations in Leake County back 50 years."

In a series of questions to the petitioners, he asked: "Do you know that if a suit is filed here, it calls for the automatic closing of all schools? Do you have enough money to pay for a private school? How many jobs can you give to members of your race? Are you educationally prepared to obtain employment in some other area? Are you willing to allow your anger to override your better judgment? Do you believe in the Christian concept of life?"

In a way, Jordan's questions raised the very issues that Medgar and the state NAACP were trying to force Mississippi Negroes to face. It was true that the state legislature had provided for the closing of schools to avoid desegregation, but didn't that prove that a lawsuit was necessary? It was true that few Negro parents could afford private schools for their children, but didn't that indicate clearly that the only hope for decent education lay in desegregated public schools?

It was a fact that few Negroes in the state were in a position to offer jobs to other Negroes, and surely that proved that Negroes were being systematically excluded from all but the lowest rungs of the white business ladder. Many Negroes *were* educationally unprepared to find jobs in other areas, and that in itself was the best proof of all that Mississippi's Negro schools were inferior.

The same month the parents in Leake County filed their petition, U. S. District Court Judge S. C. Mize announced his decision in the Meredith case. The evidence, he said with a straight face, "fails to show that the application of any Negro or Chinaman or anyone of any race had been rejected because of his color or race.

"The proof shows on this trial, and I find it a fact," he added, "that there is no custom or policy now, nor was there any at the time plaintiff's application was rejected, which excluded qualified Negroes from entering the university. The proof shows, and I find as a fact, that the university is not a racially segregated institution." Judge Mize's amazing ruling was appealed to the U. S. Fifth Circuit Court of Appeals.

In June a long seventeen months after his original application, James Meredith won his court battle for admission to the University of Mississippi in the Court of Appeals. The two-to-one majority opinion, written by Judge John Minor Wisdom, responded to Judge Mize's finding that Ole Miss was not a segregated institution in the bluntest possible terms. "This about-face in policy, news of which may startle some people in Mississippi, could have been accomplished only by telepathic communication among the University's administrators, the Board of Trustees of State Institutions of Higher Learning."

On the contrary, according to the opinion, a "full review of the record leads the court inescapably to the conclusion that from the moment the defendants discovered Meredith was a Negro they engaged in a carefully calculated campaign of delay, harassment and masterly inactivity. . . . Reading the 1350 pages in the record as a whole, we find that James Meredith's application for transfer to the University of Mississippi was turned down solely because he was a Negro."

But the university's policy of delaying actions was to be continued, for State Attorney General Joe Patterson immediately announced plans to petition the court for a review. If rejected, he said, the issue would be appealed to the U. S. Supreme Court, which, because it was then in recess until October, might result in another long wait for Meredith.

Within weeks, it could be seen that Mississippi had at least one ally on the Appeals Court bench. Judge Ben Cameron of Mississippi, who had had nothing whatever to do with the Meredith case, three times stayed a court's order that the university accept Meredith as a student. Three times the three judges who had heard the appeal met to set these stays aside. When Judge Cameron issued a fourth stay, Meredith appealed to the U. S. Supreme Court, and Justice Hugo Black set aside the final delay. The way was now open for Meredith to enter Ole Miss in September. Medgar, who had worked closely with him from the beginning, felt almost as though the fight James Meredith had apparently won was the same one he himself had started when he applied for entrance to Ole Miss years before.

In the midst of that summer's activities, Medgar's brother, Charles, came to Jackson for a week. Medgar had agreed to take a week's vacation to coincide with his visit, and Charles was disturbed to find that Medgar's idea of a vacation was to go to the office each day around noon and come home at six. After two days of this, I took Medgar aside and told him he wasn't being fair to Charles. Medgar reluctantly took the next day off.

In a way, Medgar's behavior was strange, for the Evers family had always been close-knit, and Medgar and Charles had always been particularly close. Charles, for his part, had left his wife and children in Chicago, where he owned a tavern and had interests in other businesses, solely to see Medgar. The explanation, of course, was that Mississippi

Negroes were finally on the move, and Medgar, after all the years of frustration, had time for nothing else.

We had seen a lot of Charles and his wife, Nannie Laurie, when we lived in Mound Bayou and they in Philadelphia, Mississippi. Charles had even then been doing well in business, managing a funeral home, broadcasting as a disk jockey over a white-owned radio station, and later running a motel and restaurant as well as Philadelphia's first Negro taxi service. We had visited them often on our way to and from Decatur.

But Charles' successes in business had not blunted his determination to vote and to encourage other Negroes to register, and, in the end, these activities had begun to affect his businesses. First he lost his radio job; then the taxi business began to suffer. Word was spread in the Negro community that powerful whites were out to get Charles, and business at the motel and restaurant fell off.

It was a minor automobile accident that finished everything. Charles said a white woman ran into his car. She claimed he ran into hers, and she sued for damages. The sheriff padlocked Charles' apartment, holding his clothing and furniture against the claim. Charles accepted defeat, and he sold what he could and moved his family to St. Louis. Later they moved to Chicago, where at first Charles taught school. It wasn't long before he was in business again and doing very well.

During his week in Jackson that summer, Charles expressed his annoyance at Medgar's dedication to his work, his inability to stay away from the office, to relax and take a real vacation. "You're just foolish," he told Medgar. "You'll work yourself to death, and people won't even appreciate it. You'll end up just the way you are now, poor and struggling."

Medgar shrugged. "It's what I want to do. I never thought I'd make a fortune at it. Someone has to do it."

Before he went back to Chicago, Charles got Medgar and me together and gave us fifty dollars. "I want you to go someplace for a weekend and enjoy yourselves. Don't spend it on groceries or to pay bills. I want you to spend it on having some fun."

A new Negro motel, Mason's, had just opened in New Orleans, and the next weekend we drove down with the Tates. The first thing Medgar did when we walked into the motel room was pick up the telephone and call the local NAACP office. Fortunately, no one answered. We went back to Jackson refreshed and relaxed, thanks to that and to Charles' generosity. Medgar plunged immediately into his work.

In September, James Meredith's long struggle to enter Ole Miss turned from the courts to the streets in Mississippi's first sharp confrontation with federal power. The showdown began September 13, when Governor Ross Barnett issued a proclamation interposing the sovereignty of Mississippi against recognition of federal authority in the field of education. He defied the mandate of the Fifth Circuit Court of Appeals for Meredith's entrance without interference. He defied the reluctant order of Judge Mize. He defied the order of Supreme Court Justice Hugo Black. He called on "every public official, including myself, to be prepared to make the choice whether he will submit or whether he is willing to go to jail, if necessary, to keep faith with the people who have placed their welfare in his hands."

In the end, it was Governor Barnett himself who made a secret deal with Washington to seem to stand firm while being overwhelmed by federal marshals. Whatever else his play acting accomplished, it did not prevent a bloody riot, a riot that began, ironically, after Meredith had secretly reached his room in Baxter Hall on the Ole Miss campus. Before it was over, there were two dead and scores injured. Ole Miss was never again to be quite the same.

Meanwhile, in Jackson, a petition had been filed with the school board asking for "immediate concrete steps leading to early elimination of segregation in the public schools." It was signed by nine Negro parents, all promptly identified by the Jackson *Daily News*, right down to the jobs of husbands and wives. Medgar's name and mine led the list.

I confess I did not share Medgar's excitement and enthusiasm about the petition and the suit that followed. Being a pioneer is one thing; volunteering your children as pioneers is quite another. I was well aware of the distinction. Darrell was by this time ready for fourth grade. Rena was ready for third. I saw the necessity for the petition and the suit, and I supported it, but I could not remove from my mind the picture of my two oldest children, bearing the controversial name of Evers, being singled out for every kind of mental and physical torture in a newly desegregated school. I knew that as Medgar's wife I had to sign the petition, and I did. But I signed it reluctantly.

Once, months later, a friend asked me if I weren't fearful about the children if the suit were won. I admitted that I was, but I pointed out that, with Medgar in the position he was, it was simply expected that we would be the first to sign such a petition. Medgar overheard my remark and later told me to speak for myself. "My name isn't on that petition because it's expected to be. It's there because I want it there." I hadn't even thought of it in that way, but, as the months wore on, I drew strength from Medgar's enthusiasm about the suit. In the end, I was almost as enthusiastic as he was.

Four days before the agony of Oxford, James Meredith had written and released to the press a statement of his objectives in trying to enter Ole Miss. It ended with the words, "I dream of the day when Negroes in Mississippi can live in decency and respect of the first order and do so without fear of intimidation, bodily harm or of receiving personal embarrassment and with an assurance of equal justice under the law.

"The price of progress is indeed high, but the price of holding it back is much higher."

As Meredith entered on his ordeal by harassment, as the federal government spent more than $4,000,000 to protect him during his first month at Ole Miss, as the charges and countercharges raged over who was responsible for the rioting, more and more Mississippi Negroes began to dream of the kind of Mississippi James Meredith had defined. It was, of course, Medgar's old dream, the dream that had driven him now for years.

For myself, there were times when the dream was all but obliterated by the hostility and hate of the day. The telephone would ring, and I would answer. A woman's voice would shriek at me, "What are you trying to do? That nigger husband of yours is going to get himself killed if he doesn't watch his step!"

Hanging up just meant another call, and usually I put the telephone down and went on with whatever I was doing. Once, during the tension over Meredith's admission to Ole Miss, I couldn't resist. I had to talk back.

"You must be a fool to say things like that," I said. "You're only hurting yourself. Hate like that will build up inside you until it poisons you."

The woman loosed a stream of invective, and in the background I could hear a man's voice prompting her.

Then I heard Medgar's voice on the other telephone. "Hang up, honey," he said calmly to me. "I have it." And then to the hysterical woman, "Hello, this is Medgar Evers. May I help you?"

"Are you the head nigger of that NAACP or whatever you call it?" she asked.

"The head what?" Medgar asked mildly.

"The head nigger!"

"Well, if you want to call me that, yes," he said.

For fifteen minutes she raged drunkenly at him. When he tried to respond, she raved on. When she began cursing him, I lost my temper. "Why don't you go to hell?" I asked.

The next voice I heard was Medgar's. "Get off the phone, and don't ever do that again."

I hung up, but when the conversation went on and on, I picked it up again.

"I bet that nigger woman of yours is sitting up there right now with a baby inside of her!" she screamed. "That's all you niggers do is get babies!" She went on to the morals of Negro women and how cheap they were.

Medgar interrupted. "Do you have a Negro woman working for you?"

She calmed down a little. "Yes, I have one. She comes here every day. And she has three or four illegitimate children, too."

"Do you mean to tell me you let her look after your children?"

"She looks after them."

"Aren't they precious to you?"

"Yes, they're precious to me. I see what you're getting at."

"Are you at home all of the time?"

"Why?"

"Is your husband home sometimes when you aren't?"

By now she was really puzzled. "Yes. Why?"

"Well, how do you know that this woman didn't have an affair with your husband?"

For almost a minute she was speechless. When she finally recovered, she said, "I know my husband would never have anything to do with a black woman."

Medgar laughed out loud. "You don't know that. You're not there to keep watch all the time."

We both heard the husband take the phone from her. He was cursing from the moment he starting talking.

Medgar asked him his name.

"I don't have to tell you my name!" he shouted.

The conversation went on and on. Several times I put the telephone down and went about my work, only to wander back and pick it up again. Medgar was perfectly calm, and the conversation ranged over every conceivable aspect of race. After a while, the man calmed down, and, before the conversation was over, the two of them were talking almost cordially. When Medgar finally said goodbye, he came to me. "Myrlie," he said, "don't ever do what you did. If you can't take it, just put the phone down. But don't curse at them. You can sometimes win them over if you are just patient enough."

Medgar's patience was not his only astonishing quality. He developed a way of living with fear, of recognizing it, of dealing with it, of refusing to allow it to paralyze him, that I could barely understand and never emulate. He never ran from danger; I guess he knew he couldn't and still perform his job. But he never courted it either. He would take every precaution intelligence dictated and then, having done all he could, push his fears into the back of his mind.

Once, after Meredith had started classes at Ole Miss, Medgar and Aaron Henry drove to Oxford to see him and report to the national office on the tensions on the campus. They took our new Oldsmobile, a car Medgar had bought over my protests that we couldn't afford it. We couldn't, of course, but it was one of his intelligent precautions. He needed a new car, he said, to be able to outdistance pursuers.

The two of them were starting back after their visit with Meredith, and, since darkness was approaching, Medgar was driving as fast as the speed limit allowed. Then, just outside of Ruleville, a tough Delta town where there had been some shooting into Negro homes a few months earlier, Medgar heard a loud clunk under the rear of the car.

"We limped into Ruleville," he told me, laughing at his fears, "and we finally found a garage that was open. The man who ran it and the mechanic were both white, and there was something in the way they looked at us, the way they ignored every attempt to be polite and friendly, that told me they knew who we were. They looked the car over, found the trouble in the universal joint, and said it would take until the next day to fix. That meant we were not only identified but trapped in Ruleville for the night.

"It took a while, but we finally found a place to stay with some NAACP members. It was a long night, and every car that drove past woke me. Then, in the morning, we went back to the garage. The car was ready, and I paid for the work, again trying to use my charm to get a friendly response. There was nothing but suspicion and hostility, and I thought I detected something else—I wasn't sure what—in the man's attitude. When we went to the car, which was parked out in front well away from the garage, he watched us as though something was about to happen.

"We got in and I reached for the key before I thought of it. Then, suddenly, I knew what was going to happen. When I turned on the ignition, the car was going to blow up. I told

Aaron what I was thinking, and he looked at the key as though it were a loaded gun, pointing at his head. We glanced back toward the garage, and the man was still standing there, staring at us."

Medgar paused and I swallowed hard. "Well, what could we do?" he asked. "We couldn't get out and look under the hood with the man standing there watching us. We couldn't just sit there until he went away." He paused again.

"So Aaron crossed his fingers, and I reached out for the key. It took everything I had to turn it, and the sound of the engine catching made us both jump. We drove for miles waiting for something to happen, both scared half to death, each unwilling to insist that we stop the car and look under the hood. It was the most exciting ride I ever had, and nothing happened. Nothing at all."

I never achieved Medgar's ability to laugh at past dangers. I was convinced that no one could continue to do what he was doing indefinitely. I knew in my bones that something would happen if he kept it up. I saw the fear in the faces of many of the national office staff when they came to Mississippi to speak or investigate some case. I heard the hesitation in their voices when they asked about precautions taken for them.

Yet it seemed to me that the only times the national office warned Medgar to be careful were times when a member of the New York staff was with him. They would come in, do their work and get out, sometimes within a few hours. I wondered, resentfully, if they really cared about Medgar's life as much as they obviously cared about his work. Medgar, I guess, understood it, because he never complained.

In March 1963, our petition for school desegregation in Jackson having been ignored, Jack Young, one of the four

Negro attorneys in Mississippi, filed suit in federal court. Three days later a similar suit was filed by R. Jess Brown to desegregate the schools in Leake County, Governor Barnett's home county. Federal troops still guarded James Meredith in Oxford.

Meanwhile, a new problem had arisen, a problem that required all of Medgar's patience and tact. For years the NAACP had been the only national group of its kind on the scene. The early battles for equalization of white and Negro teachers' pay had been fought and won by the NAACP. The first school desegregation petitions had been gathered and presented under the leadership of the NAACP. The boycott of the segregated state fair in Jackson was an NAACP-sponsored project.

There were many other battles that would never have been fought without the presence in the state of an increasingly strong and effective NAACP. Not the least of them was the fight to publicize the murders, the brutality, the cruelest aspects of racism that, on several occasions, drew the attention of the nation to the state. And for years, of course, the NAACP alone had provided a haven for Negroes in trouble.

But with the acceleration of activity in 1961, with Negroes slowly taking the offensive, with the beginnings of boycotts and demonstrations and the involvement of young people, two things had inevitably occurred. White racists, as in every other state, had been forced into increasingly defensive positions, and other civil rights organizations had begun to send paid workers into Mississippi.

The Student Non-Violent Coordinating Committee (SNCC) sent Robert Moses, a Harvard graduate and private school teacher, as its field secretary. The Congress of Racial Equality (CORE) sent David Dennis. The Southern Christian Leadership Conference (SCLC), the third national organization that, with the NAACP, eventually combined to form COFO, the Council of Federal Organizations, sent various people over the years.

In general, Medgar's attitude toward these organizations was one of hearty welcome. He knew the volume of work to be done; he knew the need of numbers of dedicated workers. But he was also the national representative of the oldest of all of the organizations, oldest nationally, oldest in Mississippi, and while the main mission of the NAACP had always been to put itself out of business by the final elimination of racial discrimination in the United States, the prestige of the organization in the meantime was a vital consideration.

There were, of course, organizational scuffles. The first had taken place some years before when Martin Luther King first organized the Southern Christian Leadership Conference at a meeting in New Orleans. Medgar had been invited, and he went. Before the meeting was over, he had been elected secretary of the new organization. When the national office of the NAACP indicated its feelings that to hold office in SCLC created a possible conflict of interests, Medgar reluctantly resigned.

Much later, in the spring of 1963, with the enormous build-up of activity and tension in Mississippi, Dr. King expressed an interest in coming to the state. He would not, he said, come without an invitation. Medgar favored extending one. The national office discouraged it without flatly rejecting the idea. In the end, Medgar never had a chance to make a decision. As activities multiplied and there was more than he could possibly do alone in the late spring of 1963, he sent out a plea for help to the national office. Gloster Current was sent from New York and Ruby Hurley from her regional headquarters, now in Atlanta. The legal staff sent Robert Carter, Barbara Morris, and Frank Reeves to help our local lawyers, and several secretaries from the New York office came with them. With his immediate superiors on the scene, Medgar was relieved of both the necessity and the opportunity of making policy decisions.

There had been problems, at first, with both SNCC and CORE. Some of the workers of each organization took to securing NAACP membership lists from local branches and using them as the basis for organizing their own activities. Occasionally, an overzealous worker would downgrade the work and the zeal of the NAACP in an attempt to win supporters away. Some of these efforts succeeded, and Medgar would have to drop what he was doing and go to these towns to rebuild a branch that had been raided for both membership and loyalty.

In the end, Medgar met with Bob Moses and Dave Dennis and explained what was happening. Their efforts, which should complement each other, were being wasted in factional disputes, he said. There was plenty of work for everyone, but it was insane to undo work that had already been done over years when memberships and loyalties had been much harder to win. Both men agreed, and it was not long before the three organizations were working reasonably well together.

But the national office was subjected to different pressures. In New York the competition among civil rights groups for the loyalties of Negroes, for the adoption of techniques and programs that differed somewhat from each other, and for the financial support without which none of them could operate effectively was even more fierce. While none of the national leaders was so blind that he could not see the vital necessity of a united front in public, there were more than

253

casual differences behind the scenes. Occasionally, opponents of civil rights would spot a rift developing among the organizations, and then all of the force of the enemy's propaganda would be directed at widening the split. Medgar, in Mississippi, was sometimes caught in the middle.

Knowing Mississippi and its problems better than any of the others, he felt he wanted the help other organizations could bring. He felt strongly that he could protect the NAACP's reputation and assure it a fair share of publicity about Mississippi projects. But he felt just as strongly the need for help from the national office on a wider publicity front. After all, the NAACP was the oldest, best-established civil rights organization in the country. It had a long record of working through existing institutions to effect lasting change. The newer organizations seemed to him to be garnering the boldest headlines for the smallest of accomplishments, most of them due largely to groundwork laid in the past by the NAACP. Medgar felt the record should be set straight in a booklet listing the organization's accomplishments in Mississippi before the other groups had even appeared on the scene.

But even on the state level there were organizational differences. At first, Medgar did not take kindly to the idea of demonstrations. He had seen them accomplish results in some places, but he felt that the time and place had to be chosen carefully. He was critical of the tactics of the Southern Christian Leadership Conference, tactics that had too often meant the total organization of a community to precipitate a crisis and win concessions and then the collapse of everything as the organization moved to another city, leaving the local Negroes to suffer the inevitable consequences.

But the drive to register Negroes as voters, which at

first took precedence over nearly everything else, was one that Medgar heartily endorsed, and as SNCC, under Bob Moses, and CORE, under Dave Dennis, joined the NAACP in a concerted effort to persuade Negroes to attempt to register, Medgar threw himself with renewed energy into the campaign.

By the end of the summer of 1962, the other civil rights organizations had learned what Medgar had known all along. Negro voter registration was all but impossible in most parts of the state. For all of the courage of the registration workers, for all of the beatings and shootings connected with their work, progress was negligible. As Bob Moses put it that summer with an understatement typical of him, "If you're really going to help the people all over the state and really make a change in this system down here, then there's going to have to be some additional help from the federal government. They're going to have to weigh a little more heavily on the scales."

Two summers later, in 1964, the Mississippi Summer Project, a COFO effort that brought 800 Northern college students into Mississippi, two of them to their deaths, dramatized the need for federal help in such a way that the Civil Rights Act of 1964, with its stringent voting provisions, was one result. That massive project was perhaps the peak of the cooperative effort of the organizations united in the Council of Federated Organizations: the NAACP, SNCC, CORE, and the SCLC. It was a cooperative effort of precisely the sort that Medgar had long favored. It was one of many things he did not live to see.

## XVI

Looking back, I can see that the final build-up of activity
and tension in that spring of 1963 really began in May when
Clarence Mitchell, director of the Washington Bureau of the
NAACP, addressed a mass meeting in Jackson on the an-
niversary of the Supreme Court's 1954 decision. Clarence
came to Mississippi at least twice a year to address meetings,
and he was one of Medgar's and my favorite people. Warm,
understanding, encouraging to Medgar in his work, Clarence
was one regular visitor we always looked forward to having
with us.

Clarence's speeches were always well received, but there
was something special in the air this night. It was nine years
since the Supreme Court had decreed that separate schools
were inherently unequal, eight since the South had been told
to desegregate with all deliberate speed. More important,
James Meredith and the troops of the United States government had shown that even that shining citadel of Mississippi's
white supremacy, Ole Miss, could be stormed and taken.
Mississippi had not changed, but it was changing.

After Clarence spoke, Medgar announced the plan of a
special committee to boycott two products heavily dependent

on Negro patronage, Barq's soft drinks and Hart's bread, as well as a Jackson department store, McRae's, whose customers were mostly Negroes. All three had been chosen for the same reason: they had made large contributions to the White Citizens Councils. The announcement was greeted with a roar of approval by the meeting.

Within a few days, the boycott had been widened to include virtually all of the shops on Capitol Street, the main downtown shopping area. It was a success from the beginning. Inspired by the new sense of unity, college students began talking of sit-ins at the lunch counters in Woolworth's, Walgreen's, and H. L. Green's. Medgar, thinking no doubt of the long list of court cases the NAACP had defended since the beginning of the sit-in movement, had doubts about the wisdom of more of them. But even his doubts could not dampen his excitement when he learned that the students were going ahead.

The afternoon the sit-ins were to take place I picked up the children at school and drove to Medgar's office to find out what had happened. I had the children of two neighbors in my car, and I sent Darrell and Rena in to get Medgar. They were so long in returning I finally got out to go up to the office myself. I met Medgar and the children at the door.

The children were in a state of high excitement, babbling that they had seen the students and that they looked awful. "I thought it was blood," Rena said wildly, "but it was only catsup!" Medgar explained that whites had poured sugar, catsup, relish, and anything else they could find over the heads of the students as they sat at the lunch counters. One student had been pulled from his stool and kicked, but no one had fought back.

Medgar, still neither approving nor disapproving, was

257

clearly excited, and he hurried back to the office. That evening we watched the television news, hoping to see what had happened, but as usual the Jackson stations skirted the story and omitted pictures. By now, however, we had our own communications system, a nightly mass meeting, and that night the young people themselves told their story to the growing enthusiasm of many adults who had only lately begun to catch the spark of their excitement.

The schools were still in session, and when Negro high school principals issued instructions for their students not to participate in mass demonstrations, students at Lanier and Brinkley high schools walked out of class. In minutes both schools were surrounded by armed police and civilian deputies with clubs. More students rebelled, and long lines formed at the telephones as they called their parents to come and get them. Some managed to leave on their own, and one young girl who talked back to a policeman was slapped. The students' answer was a barrage of bricks and bottles.

A mother walking through the police lines to get her child was knocked down and dragged by a policeman. Boys throwing bottles were chased across the school grounds. One boy who took refuge in a classroom was defended by a teacher who refused entrance to the police.

Nothing could have united the Negro youth of Jackson the way that day of violence did. At every mass meeting now there were young people demanding the right to demonstrate. One group approached Medgar privately. He listened to their plans and then urged them to postpone the demonstration until they were better organized and disciplined. A demonstration, to be effective, he said, had to have a purpose. They couldn't wait, and the next day they marched. They were promptly arrested, and the NAACP had more legal cases to defend.

Willie Ludden, the NAACP's youth field secretary, flew to Jackson and began organizing the youth. Now, when they marched on Capitol Street, there was a stated purpose. Now, when they were arrested, there were lawyers ready to defend their right to demonstrate. Now, when they were attacked, they knew how to drop to the ground and protect themselves.

The first really large student demonstration was prepared like a military campaign. Picket signs were painted and assigned. A line of march was worked out. An assembly point was designated. When the students finally left to march to Capitol Street, there was nothing to be seen but an enormous mass of humanity, flooding the street, spilling over the sidewalks. They walked three blocks in the broiling sun before they were surrounded by the police. Packed closely together by the tightening police lines, they were pushed, beaten, cursed, thrown into dirty garbage trucks, and hauled, nauseated by the stench, to the state fair grounds. Willie Ludden, who participated in the march, was brutally beaten to the ground when he refused to give up a small American flag.

The fair grounds, surrounded by a sturdy chain-link fence, had recently been designated by the city of Jackson as an emergency jail, to be used when arrested demonstrators overburdened the facilities of the city jail. It was already known among Negroes and other civil rights workers as Mississippi's concentration camp. There, in the animal stockades, the boys and girls were separated from each other and left presumably to ponder their delinquencies. But their spirits far from dampened, both sections rapidly came to resemble old-fashioned revival meetings, with freedom songs ringing in the air and tears of joy and excitement staining the faces of many. Speeches were made between the songs, pledges given to remain in the outdoor prison and refuse bail, and plans for further demonstrations mapped.

Some of the youngsters remained in the stockades for more than a week. Worried parents, many denied permission to see their children, tried to post bond. Some of the youngsters refused to accept it. If the bond was accepted, the police made careful note of the names, addresses, employment, debts, and activities of parents and child, requiring in addition sworn statements that the youngsters would not demonstrate again. Many of the young people refused to sign such statements, and negotiations to get them out had to begin all over again.

Medgar was caught in the middle, advising parents, reassuring those whose youngsters refused bail, trying to raise bail money from local bail bondsmen. When all of the bondsmen refused his requests, a cash fund of nearly $200,000 was sent in by the national office.

When word finally came from the police that the mass of children were to be released, it spread rapidly through the Negro community. Attendance at the mass meeting that night was greater than the ability of the huge room at the Masonic Temple to accommodate people. We sang the songs of our movement, of encouragement, of a better day ahead, heard reports on progress and upcoming events, sang some more, and waited for the expected release of the students. When the deadline passed and there was no word, someone whispered to me that the police were stalling to keep the young people from appearing at the meeting. I sent a note to Medgar on the platform, and he left to telephone police headquarters.

Moments later he reappeared on the stage to announce that he would have to leave to check on the youngsters' release. There was a rumble of disappointment and anger as he left the crowded room, and for the next three hours we sat there waiting for news.

At the fair grounds Medgar was told that the parents of the young people would have to come individually to claim them. He reminded the police of their promise that they would be released to a representative of the NAACP, but the police were adamant, and Medgar returned to the Masonic Temple for the parents. A caravan of cars drove to the fair grounds, and slowly, laboring through an unbelievable amount of red tape, the parents secured their children's release. They returned to the meeting together, the parents tearful with relief, the young people carrying their pride like a banner. The audience went wild.

When the emotional welcome quieted down, some of the youngsters reported personally on their treatment. The food had been terrible; most had been without a change of clothing for a week; few had had so much as a toothbrush with them. Some, transferred to the city jail, had been harassed, cursed, and threatened with being stripped and whipped. One young girl had been slapped by the police during an interrogation.

But throughout the recital the youngsters themselves insisted it was all a tiny price to pay for freedom. One young boy, describing the lack of facilities for brushing his teeth, ended by crying out, "Look, Mom! Cavities for freedom!" The audience screamed its approval.

In the end, it was these courageous young people, the high school and college students and their leaders, who set the tone for the demonstrations that followed. Parents who had wavered in their support of the drive for civil rights, adults who had remained aloof, teachers who had feared for their names to be associated in any way with the NAACP—all were caught up in admiration and envy of the youth who were showing the way. Medgar, who had had his doubts about demonstrations, who had borne the brunt of the legal repercussions of all of the arrests, who had feared for the students' safety and doubted their ability to discipline themselves, was won over completely. As they had in so many other parts of the South since the original sit-ins in North Carolina, Negro youngsters, with their contagious enthusiasm, brought the masses to the civil rights movement.

But it was not all just heady excitement. The Negro sections of Jackson quickly took on the look of an occupied city after the demonstrations began in earnest. Helmeted police rode four to a car, sometimes with snarling police dogs caged in back. Others roared up and down on motorcycles. Police vans circled the blocks of the Negro business districts day and night. In front of the Masonic Temple Building, where Medgar's office was, there were always two or three squad cars. Officers sat and watched, noting names and descriptions and license numbers on their pads. Arrests of Negroes for minor traffic violations—and for no violation at all—soared. It became rare to see a white person in the Negro areas, even driving through in cars. Those whites who did appear on the streets were carefully watched and often questioned by the police.

Resentment against the police became almost tangible; you could see it in the faces of the oldest grandparent and the youngest child. Everyone knew that these men in uniform who had occupied our streets were not there for our safety and protection. They were there to harass, to intimidate, to arrest—to keep the Negroes off balance and out of the white parts of town.

There were almost daily incidents when this simmering resentment boiled over. A young boy would throw a brick at a policeman and run. A bottle would crash to the sidewalk just inches from where a uniformed officer was standing. Before long, the signs of fatigue and nervousness were evident in the drawn and jumpy faces of the police. White women's clubs in Jackson sent out calls to their members to prepare box lunches, coffee, desserts, and snacks for the police. Distribution points were set up where the haggard officers could pick up these tokens of the white society's appreciation.

I worried more and more about Medgar. He moved through each day with an energy denied by a single glance at his face. He was at the office at seven each morning; all over the city during the day, skipping meals, jumping when the telephone rang. At night he was on the platform of whatever church hosted the mass meeting, reporting the events of that day and the plans for the next. We saw each other in snatches of time, talked several times a day on the telephone, and I wondered each day how long a man could keep it up.

Responsibility rested on his shoulders, and he would not shirk it. Even when he sagged under its weight, there was a new spirit, a new source of energy within him: for the first time, the entire Negro community was behind him; for the first time, volunteers were everywhere.

The office, when I visited it, was a madhouse. Hot, sticky, dusty, uncomfortable, it churned with activity. No one walked; everyone ran. There were telephone calls and telegrams and letters and strategy meetings. Clipping the news stories from the newspapers became a full-time job—and one of the most peaceful.

It was the same at home. Though we had finally applied for an unlisted telephone number soon after James Meredith got into Ole Miss, Medgar had to give it to dozens of people. Somehow it got out and the telephone harassment began again. We couldn't change the number again; too many important calls were coming in. Soon it was as well known as the old, listed number had ever been.

For a while, there was someone to be met at the airport on almost every incoming flight, and that, usually, was my job. The telephone would ring and I would drop my mop or iron or pot holder and run. Inevitably what work didn't get done at the office Medgar brought home. Almost inevitably it was someone he had to talk to, and there were snacks and meals and coffee to prepare. Even the children were caught up by the air of excitement and activity. When the students planned a new demonstration, three-year-old Van asked if he could march on Capitol Street with a small American flag I had bought at his insistence. All three of them knew the times of every television news program, and they would come in from play to see what was happening.

They always called me when the news came on, and they listened carefully for their father's name. The two older ones could report with clarity and precision everything that appeared on the programs, and by this time the television stations could no longer ignore the story. White people now wanted to know.

Rena worried about her father. "He never gets any rest, Mama," she told me, repeating my own despairing remarks. Darrell took enormous pride in what his father was doing. Van, too young really to understand, clung to the words he heard the others speak, memorized the slogans, aped his older brother and sister. And I—I tried somehow to hold within me the palpable fear that almost dominated my thoughts when Medgar was out of my sight. It seemed impossible now that he could survive each day.

Tension, higher now then in the oldest Negro's memory, continued to rise. Jackson was like a pressure cooker without a relief valve. Everywhere you went, there was a sense of impending crisis. On May 12 the state NAACP threw down the gauntlet in a demand that Mayor Allen Thompson of Jackson move to end all segregation and discrimination in the city. Unless a bi-racial committee were appointed to pursue these goals, the statement continued, Jackson faced intensified boycotts and demonstrations.

The mayor responded with a flat rejection. Backed by seventy-five local white businessmen, he categorically refused to deal with *any* bi-racial committee. "The only thing that can come of such an arrangement," he told reporters, "is compliance with the demands of racial agitators from outside. The agitators decide who will represent them on such committees, not local Negroes."

There may actually have been whites who still believed this ancient mythology of outside agitators and innocent, happy local Negroes. I don't know. But it was the old familiar story, the story that had been woven deeply into Southern beliefs about Negroes, that had salved white consciences for generations. The mayor returned to it that night in an appearance on local radio and television, pinning the blame for Jackson's troubles on the NAACP and other "outside" organizations, singling out Medgar as one of the agitators.

Despite terrible trouble in neighboring states, he insisted, "We are going to continue our way of doing things." Turbulent times were ahead, he admitted, but he promised that when all of the agitation was over, "Jackson will be prosperous, people will still be happy, and the races will live side by side in peace and harmony."

It had an Alice in Wonderland quality to it, but it was not funny, for the mayor went on to say that there would be no meetings with the NAACP or any Negro group, that the city would permit no demonstrations. Whites were asked to "continue your efforts to work out all of our problems peacefully and to be tolerant and sincere." Medgar immediately demanded equal time from the television stations for a reply.

While he waited for a response, word drifted in of attempts by the mayor to find Negroes who would publicly take his side. A number of prominent Negroes were quietly approached. On May 16 the front page of the Jackson *Daily News* boasted a letter from Sidney R. Tharp, a Negro attorney, backing Mayor Thompson's position and praising the "tremendous progress" the city and its Negroes had made under his leadership.

The Negro community responded immediately. A public statement by a committee of prominent Negro citizens, business and professional leaders and ministers, cut through the ancient myth like a knife. "We are indeed dissatisfied with the status quo," the committee said, "and we hereby call for an immediate end to segregation and discrimination in our community."

Surprisingly, Medgar received word that equal time to reply to Mayor Thompson had been granted him. He had several days to prepare his speech, and he began at once. Again and again, over the next few days, he read versions to me, stopping to make changes, asking my opinion, going on, and finally retiring to write some more. He had always taken speeches in his stride, usually speaking just from notes, but we both knew this was different. This time he would be speaking not just for the NAACP but for all of the Negroes of Jackson, of Mississippi, and, in a way, everywhere.

Mixed with natural feelings of pride and awe and nervousness as I watched him prepare for the speech, I felt a new surge of fear. This speech would receive widespread advance publicity. Thousands of Mississippi whites who had never seen a picture of him would now be seeing Medgar on television. They would have time to become familiar with his appearance. When it was over, he would be recognized everywhere: at a stop light in the city, on a lonely road in the Delta, in the light from the fuel pump at a gas station.

Announcement of the speech brought immediate threats of violence to the television station chosen to tape it, and secret arrangements were worked out for the taping session. Medgar went to an out-of-the-way studio at an undisclosed time. He taped the speech on May 20 for broadcast that evening.

I suppose the television rating services could tell how many people, white and Negro, watched Medgar that night. I only know that as I sat and watched the tape of the program with Medgar and the children I felt as though the whole world watched with us.

Medgar spoke forcefully and well. He spoke in a calm and reasoned manner. He spoke as a native Mississippian, a veteran of World War II, a product of Mississippi's schools. He refuted claims that the NAACP was an outside group, pointing out that half of its membership was in the South, that a branch had existed in Mississippi since 1918, in Jackson since 1926.

He spoke to the belief that, left alone, Mississippi would solve its racial problems, citing the history of race relations in the South, pointing out that only victories in the United States Supreme Court had brought advances in the right to vote, to attend state-supported schools, to travel without discrimination, to use public facilities without segregation. He cited the laws that made peaceful demonstrations legal, calling particular attention to a Supreme Court decision of that very day in a sit-in case and indicating its applicability to Jackson.

He urged Mayor Thompson to appoint a bi-racial committee and mentioned other Southern cities that had done so. The world, he said, had changed and Negroes even in Mississippi knew about the changes. They, too, watched television and listened to the radio. Asking what the Negro saw in his own home town after noting the great changes in the world, he then reviewed the long list of grievances.

Then, speaking solely to the whites, he asked, "If you suffered these deprivations, were often called by your first name, 'boy,' 'girl,' 'auntie,' and 'uncle,' would you not be discontent?

"The NAACP believes that Jackson can change if it wills to do so. If there should be resistance, how much better to have turbulence to effect improvement, rather than turbulence to maintain a stand-pat policy. We believe there are white Mississippians who want to go forward on the race question. Their religion tells them there is something wrong with the old system. Their sense of justice and fair play sends them the same message.

"But whether Jackson and the state choose change or not, the years of change are upon us. In the racial picture things will never be as they once were. History has reached a turning point, here and over the world. Here in Jackson we can recognize the situation and make an honest effort to bring fresh ideas and new methods to bear, or we can have what Mayor Thompson called 'turbulent times.'"

Within an hour I knew from the telephone calls that poured in that my own impression had been correct. Medgar had delivered a masterful speech. It was a speech of reason, a speech that asked calmly for the white man to put himself in our place, a speech that, in contrast to Mayor Thompson's, avoided racial clichés, emotionalism, and mythology. It was a speech that insisted that, in our place, the white man, too, would insist on change, demanding the rights that belonged to him. But, more than that, it was the speech of an intelligent, thoughtful Negro, a Negro who stood without fear or subservience and spoke with self-assurance as an equal to the white man.

It must have been a revelation to many whites, for the reaction of the white community was noticeable immediately. You could sense it in the smiles of white people on the street, the reports of unusual politeness in the shops and stores, in the sudden, quiet removal of racial signs at the bus depot and the train station. Most impressive of all were the telephone calls, some from callers who admitted they were white, others from people we could guess were white, nearly all commending the speech, congratulating Medgar, urging their good wishes upon us. Most of these calls, like the threatening ones we had received over the years, were anonymous. Few whites dared give their names.

In the Negro community there was a sense of calm, of pride, of achievement in the days that followed the speech. The very next night a meeting called by the NAACP drew up a list of fourteen local Negroes to serve on a committee to negotiate with any white committee that might be appointed by Mayor Thompson. The meeting was open; the names were chosen by ballot. Medgar's was one of them.

Medgar sent a telegram with the names of the committee members to Mayor Thompson, asking for "meaningful negotiations for change in practice and treatment in downtown businesses." The message reaffirmed the right to demonstrate, indicating the Negro community's preparedness to do so if necessary.

The next day, May 22, despite his previous refusals to meet

with any Negro group, Mayor Thompson named a committee of fourteen Negroes with whom he said he would meet. Of the fourteen originally selected by the Negro community, all but four had been eliminated. The ten new names included some of the best-known Negro collaborators with the white power structure: Percy Greene, the newspaper editor; Joseph Albright, a public relations man who worked with the segregationist State Sovereignty Commission; Sidney Tharp, the lawyer whose letter on the front page of the Jackson *Daily News* had infuriated the Negro community a week earlier.

Within twenty-four hours the Negro community had rejected Mayor Thompson's white-oriented committee and the four Negroes of the original group had resigned. In a telegram to the mayor, they gave their reason as "the fact that the majority of the committee named was not democratically selected by the Negro community as their representatives."

Once again, tension began to rise. On May 24, NAACP telegrams rejecting the mayor's committee went out to Jackson businessmen, calling on them to negotiate directly with the democratically selected Negro group or face intensive direct action. The same day, white and Negro ministers meeting for the first time to discuss the city's racial problem agreed to devote their Sunday sermons to the issue. The Mississippi Council on Human Relations, an inter-racial citizens group, called on "the people of Jackson, on those who carry political responsibility, on leaders of business and industry, and on all other thinking people to see that a responsible bi-racial committee is set up now, and to pledge themselves to the changes in our way of living which will bring human dignity and respect to our citizens regardless of race or color."

Finally, on May 28, Mayor Thompson met with an

NAACP committee. Before the meeting ended, he had agreed to accept applications from Negroes for jobs as policemen and school crossing guards; to declare all public facilities open to all citizens on an equal basis; to remove all Jim Crow signs from public buildings; to secure the order of the city commission for removal of Jim Crow signs from gas stations; and to order the use of courtesy titles by all city officials in their contacts with Negroes. On the issues of desegregation of lunch counters and public schools, he maintained he was powerless.

Still, it was a victory of major proportions, and word of it spread like a tidal wave across the city. Minutes later came the cruel shock: Mayor Thompson had almost at once repudiated the agreement, claiming he had been misrepresented. That afternoon, sit-in demonstrations began. Four Negro youths and a white professor from Tougaloo College took seats at the lunch counter in Woolworth's. Police stood by as a mob of 200 whites stormed past them to kick and beat the demonstrators. When the worst of the beatings were over, the police arrested the victims. One of the students went to the hospital. That night Medgar reported the mayor's treachery to more than 2000 Negroes massed at the Pearl Street AME Church. When he asked how many were ready to march, the entire audience rose.

I had stayed home that night with the children, but Medgar called from the office after the meeting to let me know that he would be home after a strategy meeting. There was a terrible weariness in his voice, and as I sat down to wait for him, I wondered for the hundredth time how long he could keep up this killing pace. He had aged ten years in the past two months; the lines in his face had deepened and his facial muscles had lost their elasticity. I knew that he was strong and basically healthy, but I knew, too, that a body could

271

take only so much punishment and neglect before it collapsed.

For weeks now I had heard each ring of the telephone with a sinking suspicion that he had collapsed or had a heart attack. When it didn't ring for two hours or more, I waited in fear of something worse. He was like a man possessed, up by six in the morning, at the office by seven. It was a rare night now that he was home by eleven. When he did come home, he would want something to eat; often he had not eaten since breakfast.

As I warmed up some food for him, I would ask what had happened that day, and, after filling me in briefly, he would stop my next question. "Let's not talk about it, Myrlie. I've been up to my ears in it all day."

When I asked what I could do to help, he'd say, "You're working almost as hard as I am. Just you keep home the way you have it for me." And I would melt in the face of the greatest compliment he could have paid me.

After eating, he would lie down on one of the sofas in the living room, avoiding the one with its back to the front window. I'd put some records on the phonograph and, when the dishes were done, sit down with him and put his head on my lap. We rarely talked as we sat there, but I could feel the tension and bruises of the day slip away from him as I stroked his hair and rubbed his temples. In a few minutes he would drop off to sleep, and I would sit there looking down at him, so tired, so much like a little boy who had pushed himself beyond all endurance. It was all I could do not to cry out in frustration because there was so little I could do to help.

We would stay like that as the minutes slipped by, until, finally, hoping he'd be more comfortable in bed, I'd wake him, usually with a kiss. In bed he would toss and turn, waken and plunge back into a nightmarish continuation of the day. A dog would bark, a car pass the house, and he would freeze in instant alertness. If it was Heidi, our own German shepherd, that barked, he would leap up, snatching in one instinctive motion the rifle he now kept by the bed, and run to the living room to peer out the curtained windows.

One night we had a terrible fright when Medgar, startled from sleep at a noise in the house itself, rose so swiftly it awoke me with a strange sense of foreboding. Seconds later I found him standing at the bedroom door, his rifle in his right hand, his left hand at his forehead. Opposite him, across the hall, I could dimly see Darrell using the bathroom. Medgar turned as I touched him and said in a voice as close to despair as I had ever heard, "My God, what am I doing?"

There was no escape for any of us from the strain of living at the edge of disaster, and that night, as I waited for him to come home from the strategy meeting, I searched my mind for the hundredth time for something I could do to make it easier for Medgar. The children were asleep, and I had finally forced myself to concentrate on the words of a book when a dog barked on the street outside. Automatically I went to the Venetian blinds to look out. As usual, I saw nothing.

I turned out several lights and tried again to read. Cars passed more frequently than usual, it seemed, and at the sound of each, Heidi would raise her head and give a little bark. After a while, I ignored her.

It must have been midnight when I heard another car pass. I had just decided to ignore it when I heard the crash of splintering glass in the carport. My mind had told me it was a brick smashing the car window, when I heard the whoosh of a muffled explosion and saw as I moved from the bedroom to the hall a blaze of fire beyond the living room. Three steps more, and I could see the carport bathed in flames, a huge fire blazing beside the car.

I froze, fear almost choking me, my mind refusing to work. Then I found myself at the telephone, dialing a neighbor, Thomas Young, and waiting in panic as the number rang and rang and rang without an answer. When a sleepy voice did finally answer, I blurted out what had happened, asked if Tom could see anyone outside, my mind visualizing the children and me being cut down by gunfire as we fled the burning house.

For a few moments I waited for him to call back. Then the thought of the fire next to the full tank of gasoline in the car struck me, and I opened the door for a closer look. The giant blaze had dwindled, but a three-foot flame was licking the air near the gas tank, and, dressed only in a slip, I ran past the car to the spigot where the garden hose was attached. Twisting it frantically, I saw water spurt from the middle of the hose, where the fire had burned it through. There was still enough to reach the fire, and I pulled it closer and aimed it at the largest part of the blaze.

As the flames went down, I saw that they came from a rag in the broken neck of a brown half-gallon bottle. I crouched lower, still wondering if there were someone in the darkness waiting to shoot me. When the fire seemed out, I dropped the hose and ran into the house to call Medgar. My hands shook so that I had to force myself to concentrate on dialing his office number. With something close to agony I heard the busy signal.

Back at the door, I saw that the fire had revived, and I ran out into the smell of burning rubber to pour more water on it. I was at the spigot turning off the hose when Tom

Young appeared from across the street. Another neighbor, Jean Wells, who had reached Medgar at the office and assured him we were all right, came out of her house next door, and as I tried to collect myself and tell them what had happened, a squad car with a uniformed policeman and a plain-clothes inspector appeared. Medgar, I learned later, had called the police before leaving the office.

The policemen were calm and businesslike as they walked into the smoky carport, looking around. "You're lucky," the inspector said, his hand on the gas tank of the car. "This thing was hot enough to explode. It's still pretty hot. You'd better back it out of here."

I asked them to move the glass from behind the tires and backed the car out of the carport. The two policemen went on with their inspection. As I turned to Tom and Jean again, there was a screech of tires at the corner, and two cars roared down the block and stopped in front. Medgar leaped from one of them and ran to me. Before he reached me, he was asking questions. "Are you all right? Are the children all right?" Then, looking around, "Did anyone come out here to help you?"

I assured him we were all right, realizing with amazement that the children hadn't even wakened. As for help, I reminded him of the hour. "Everyone was asleep. They came when they knew."

Medgar turned his attention to the policemen, and all at once the reality of what had happened reached me. My body began to shake. In the storage compartment at the rear of the carport, the police inspector had found a gasoline can. Turning to me, he asked, "Is this yours?"

"Yes, that's ours," I said, a hint of what was to come in the back of my mind.

"What do you do with it?" he asked.

"It's gasoline," I said, "for the lawn mower."

Then, with a knowing look, "Have you used it recently?"

I stopped shaking and looked straight at him. "We certainly haven't used it tonight," I said.

"Well," he said, looking away finally, "there's nothing to worry about. It was just some kind of prank."

The uniformed policeman had found a newspaper and was carefully piling the remnants of the brown bottle on it. When he began to wrap it carefully, Medgar asked what he planned to do. "I don't see what we can do," he answered calmly. "It was just some people having some fun probably."

While the police wound up their inspection, the front yard filled with neighbors and NAACP workers who had somehow heard about the incident. I was talking with them when the two policemen brushed by on their way to the squad car. I watched them drive off with a feeling I couldn't describe then and can't now. It was a mixture of fear and hatred and contempt.

We stood around outside for another hour, listening to the worried warnings of our friends and neighbors to be careful. A newspaper reporter showed up and we told him what we could, and then, finally, people drifted off to their homes. As we turned toward the house, I asked Medgar why it had taken him so long to get home. He put his arm around me, looked at me, and then laughed abruptly. I knew exactly what had happened. He had waited an extra minute to call the newspapers and the wire services. He admitted it immediately and, with a grin, he said, "Good public relations, honey. Good public relations." It was by this time a standing joke between us, and for a few moments it broke the tension.

But then we were back in the quiet house, walking on tiptoe from room to room, looking down at the lovely sleeping faces of the children, and the real meaning of the whole experience hit home. Someone had tried to kill us. Sitting on the couch together, I started shaking. This time I couldn't stop. Medgar took me in his arms and held me and rocked me back and forth. "I don't know what I'd do if anything ever happened to you or the children because of what I'm doing," he said softly.

"It's not us," I said, trying to control my shaking. "It's you they're after. And if anything happened to you, I don't think I could live."

He held me closer then, and I could feel the imprint of his arms across my back, the rhythm of his breathing, and yet I was miles away in a world without him, a world in which murderers were permitted to destroy him, a world so barren and without hope of joy that I felt dead inside. It was then that the tears came in a rush.

The next morning we told the two older children what had happened. There was a tiny story in the newspaper and all of the neighbors knew. We felt the children should hear it from us. It would have seemed strange to anyone else, I suppose, that when we had finished, none of them asked why anyone should throw a fire bomb at our house. They didn't have to ask. They knew.

They had asked such questions before, and Medgar had proved much better at answering them than I. He could sit with them and explain without bitterness why some white people hated Negroes. I listened with something approaching awe to the matter-of-fact way he explained the history, the emotion, the ignorance that resulted in hate.

Once Darrell, angered by something he had seen on television, blurted out his pent-up feelings: "I hate white people."

Medgar spoke harshly. "Then you're wrong. You're hurting yourself. You shouldn't hate white people. You shouldn't hate anyone. That's no way to live." And then, seeing Darrell's lips quiver, he softened his voice. "It's not good for a little boy's heart to hate," he said.

That discussion took place at breakfast, the one time of day we were all together. It had become by that time almost a ritual with Medgar and me to make as much as we could of those few moments each day with the children. I would take the telephone off the receiver, and we would laugh and have fun together. Once, Rena had sobered us all for a moment when she turned to Medgar and said, "Daddy, I wish you wouldn't work so hard. You look all tired out."

I told him one morning I wished he would take a whole day off and go fishing where no one could reach him, where he could be alone and relax. It had been a long time since he had done anything like that, and he shook his head slowly. "You know, honey," he said, "I'm going to have to do that. I've never been so tired before in my life."

Little Van, who insisted on sitting next to his father at meals, turned to him then and without warning burst into song: "Come right in, sit right down, let nobody turn you round!" It was one of those moments you never forget, and after a brief pause of surprise we all laughed. Medgar shook his head, reached over, and hugged Van. "That's Daddy's boy," he said. "That's all I needed to make me get right up and go out and do a good job today."

In the weeks that followed, he remembered that moment and talked about it. Telling me about a particularly depressing day, a frustrating defeat, a moment of despair, he would say, "And then I remembered little Van sitting at the breakfast table singing that song, and I laughed all over again and went on with my work. It was like a tonic."

The weekend after the fire bomb, Medgar spent an hour teaching the children how to protect themselves in the event of another attack on the house. We had talked about it together, had wondered if it might make them more fearful, but we had decided, finally, that it could not be helped. Their lives were at stake, and whatever harm such training might do, their lives were the most important consideration. Medgar felt that with all the talk they undoubtedly overheard, with all of the tension of our lives, it might actually be a relief for them to feel that there was something positive they could do to protect themselves.

I had always watched them carefully when they were playing in the front yard, and we had warned them never to go to a car that stopped, even if someone called to them. They had been taught never to talk to strangers, because we knew that someone might well try to punish Medgar by doing something to his children. Most of their playmates played on the street or in the vacant lots. We couldn't let our children do that. There were even places in the house where they couldn't sit; the furniture had to be arranged away from the windows; and where the television set was placed, we couldn't use the chairs to watch at night. We had to sit on the floor or present inviting targets through the front windows.

Now Medgar taught them to fall to the floor at the sound of a strange noise, to train their ears to the sound of Heidi's bark, of passing cars, of anything at all unusual. He taught them how to fall without hurting themselves, how to wait until they were sure it was nothing before they got up. To three-year-old Van, it was all a game, and he dropped to the floor with complete abandon. Darrell, eleven, and Rena, ten, were serious about it; they listened carefully and practiced conscientiously. In the midst of the lesson, Darrell asked what they should do if Van forgot to fall. Medgar told him to pull Van down with him.

There was much discussion of what might be the safest place in the house in the event of shooting, and each of the children had a nomination. The three of them walked through the house with Medgar, discussing the problem almost academically, until they decided unanimously that the bathtub, if they could reach it, would provide the greatest protection for the children.

I listened to all of this with a feeling of horror, the same feeling I suppose any mother would have had. I remembered the outburst of criticism when public schools throughout the country began teaching children what to do in the event of a missile attack, the pictures in national magazines of kindergarteners lining the walls of schoolrooms doubled up on the floor with their backs to the windows. Now it was happening in my own home. And the enemy here was not a foreign power but white American citizens.

The picketing and sit-in protests continued. The day after the attack on our house, nineteen more demonstrators were arrested. That night at the mass meeting, Medgar told what had happened at our house. It was the first many had heard of it. The next day protests were stepped up, and twenty-seven arrests were made, some of them Negroes kneeling in prayer on the steps of the downtown post office. Negro prisoners—trusties—were used by the Jackson police to carry demonstrators to the police wagons. Mayor Thompson issued a statement charging that "the civil disobedience demonstrations of the past two days were planned for the purpose of creating strife, arousing passions and disrupting business."

The young people had thrown themselves into the effort with enthusiasm and ingenuity. When youngsters wearing

NAACP sweatshirts were arrested for parading up and down the sidewalks on Capitol Street, a new tactic was devised. A group appeared on the sidewalk, each with a single word painted on his sweatshirt. At a signal, they arranged themselves in order, spelling out the sentence: DON'T BUY ON CAPITOL STREET. They, too, were quickly arrested.

But the message of the boycott was spreading. One hundred thousand leaflets were distributed, and the daily reports of arrests in the newspapers and on radio and television made it impossible not to know what was afoot. On May 31 state highway patrolmen with carbines and shotguns were called in by the local police, and, before the day was over, more than 500 demonstrators were arrested by riot-trained, heavily armed troopers. Most of those arrested were children.

When the load became too heavy for the police wagons, highway trucks, and finally garbage trucks were used to cart the demonstrators to stockades at the state fair grounds. Roy Wilkins, in Jackson to speak at a mass meeting, compared what was happening to Hitler's tactics. "In Birmingham," he said, "the authorities turned the dogs and fire hoses loose on peaceable demonstrators. Jackson has added another touch to this expression of the Nazi spirit with the setting up of hog-wired concentration camps. This is pure Nazism and Hitlerism. The only thing missing is an oven."

The next day Medgar and Roy went together to Capitol Street to demonstrate their willingness to do what others had been doing. Carrying signs, they attempted to picket. They were promptly arrested. The organization provided bail, and they were released within hours, Medgar to return to the frantic office.

The first days of June were upon us, and with Jackson in the grip of a sweltering heat wave the demonstrations continued. Mayor Thompson claimed the protests were failing for lack of support, but the number of arrests continued to soar. On June 6 the city went into court with another story. Contending that if the demonstrations were allowed to continue it would cause "injuries to or loss of life to policemen . . . and will cause damage to property owned by the city of Jackson," the city asked for an injunction barring further civil rights demonstrations. The court granted the injunction.

NAACP General Counsel Robert Carter appealed to the State Supreme Court, filed suit in the U. S. District Court, and announced that a suit attacking discrimination and segregation in places of public accommodation would also be filed. Meanwhile, despite the injunction, demonstrations continued. Forty-two were arrested carrying anti-segregation placards and small American flags. An attempt was made to integrate Primo's Restaurant, and more arrests followed. The count was now 664. Six persons quietly integrated the city golf course and were allowed to play, but subsequent groups were rejected.

The night of June 7 was hot, and the huge exhaust fans in the auditorium of the Masonic Temple seemed barely to move the air as 3500 people jammed the large room for a giant rally. Police ringed the building and patrolled the halls and doorways inside. The press was out in force, and the words of freedom songs swelled and echoed and burst through the open windows to flood the air for blocks around. It was a night of tears and laughter, of high emotions, of unity and determination and brotherhood.

When the words of "We Shall Overcome" rang from thousands of throats, we *were* overcome, and elderly Negro men wept along with high school girls. Lena Horne had flown to Jackson at her own expense, and she told of her experiences traveling through the South with Negro bands on one-night stands. She admitted to fear as she got off the plane at the Jackson Airport but said she had been met by Medgar, and she told the crowd how he had made her feel safe and secure. She said how good it must feel to all of us to have a leader like Medgar, and my heart nearly burst at the applause. Finally she sang a medley of freedom songs, and she held each of our hearts in the palm of her hand. We were caught up in something larger than any of us, and as she sang and I looked around me, I had an instant flash of certainty that here in this room 3500 people were all feeling the same emotions at the same moment.

Dr. Claude Hudson of Los Angeles spoke of how he had lived and worked for civil rights in Louisiana, how he had been threatened, how he had moved his family to Los Angeles and continued to fight. He was a fiery speaker, and he almost turned the meeting out with his speech. There were others on the program, but the man we all waited to hear was Dick Gregory, who had come to Jackson not long before to picket on Capitol Street. Just before he was to leave with a group to demonstrate, word had come from Chicago that his infant son had died, and he had flown back to be with his wife. Now he was with us again, and when he rose to speak, the applause was deafening. He spoke for nearly an hour; he made us laugh and cry; he stiffened our determination, gave us pride in our unity, and shared our wonder at how far we had come, all with a humor that was irresistible.

Finally Medgar spoke, reporting the events of the day and the plans for tomorrow. After routine announcements, he made the appeal for contributions that was a fixed part of each of the nightly mass meetings.

I had known he was to speak, but I was unprepared for what he said. He began by saying that the price of freedom comes high, and he spoke, then, of the young people jailed in the stockade, of the families that had been intimidated, the people who had been beaten. "It's not enough just to sit here tonight and voice your approval and clap your hands and shed your tears and sing and then go out and do nothing about this struggle. Freedom has never been free. Those who can do nothing else can at least help to raise bail money for those who are still confined. There is something for everybody to do."

And then he told the price he was willing to pay for freedom. I had heard him say it privately; friends had told me of his saying it to them. I knew it had been on his mind particularly since the fire bomb. But I had never heard him say it publicly, and I had never heard him say it quite this way.

"I love my children," he said quietly, "and I love my wife with all my heart. And I would die, and die gladly, if that would make a better life for them."

In the silence that attended these words, I felt a chill at my heart. I was proud; I was happy; I was on the verge of tears; but it was too close to reality, too much like tempting fate. And I knew what perhaps no one else in that vast audience knew for certain: I knew that he meant every word of it with all his heart.

Something had happened in these past few weeks, something I could see happening and could neither stop nor even understand completely. It was as though Medgar had been transformed into something bigger, something more important, something almost beyond reaching. It was nothing he had done, nothing he had sought. It was as though events had cast him into a new role, had forced on him a new and larger loyalty, a responsibility for thousands. He had responded not with fear or withdrawal but with love, with a love that now included not just his family and his friends but every black face in this silent audience and every one beyond it.

It had happened, not suddenly, but gradually, and I had stood and watched it with a heart that ached with pride and loneliness. I had told him a hundred times that I didn't want to be a young widow, that I would rather be deprived of some of the things he was fighting for, that I would rather see the children deprived of the future he wanted for them than to lose him. It was a price I didn't want to pay.

Each time he had responded in the same way, with a smile and a kiss and the words that told me I had not reached him. "Honey, you really don't understand, do you?" I thought I did understand, and I said so, but I guess I never really did. Of all the thousands of people who heard him say what he said that night at the rally, I guess I was the only one who really didn't understand. I loved him too much for that kind of understanding.

## ——— XVII ———

I had left the children with a friend that night, and after the rally I drove a group of NAACP workers to a party for the out-of-town guests. Medgar followed with another group in the other car. It was a lovely party, full of good spirits, just what was needed to taper off from the high emotions of the rally.

The subject of young marriages came up, and someone told the story of one that had ended badly. There was general agreement that youthful marriages were a mistake. Medgar disagreed. With his arm around me, he said, "Here's one that's working."

Close friends laughed and pointed out that he had been twenty-five when he married me. "But I was robbing the cradle," he said, "Myrlie was only eighteen. The idea is to get them young, while they're still green, and then bring them up the way you want them."

This brought more laughter from friends who knew that Medgar would be the last to claim seriously that he had succeeded in shaping me either into what I was or what he wanted me to be. But as we laughed and joked about it, he turned more serious and said that he would not have had it any other way. And for the second time that evening in public he reaffirmed his love for me. It was not a thing he had done often before, and I remember wondering at it.

It was close to two o'clock when we left the party, and because I had to pick up the children I took with me people who lived in my direction. Medgar, in the other car, offered rides to another group. As he helped me into the station wagon, he warned me to be careful. "If you get home before I do, remember to get out the right side of the car."

I nodded and started the engine. Someone asked me what he had meant, and I explained that one day, some weeks ago, Medgar had walked around the neighborhood, surveying our house from every direction. He had found that by standing in a vacant lot across the street and up from us he had a clear view of the left-hand doors of our car parked in the carport. The lot was overgrown and provided excellent concealment, particularly at night, and he had come back to the house with some new rules. We must always turn out the headlights before getting out of the car at night, he said, and we must remember not to leave the light on in the carport when we were out. That would give us the benefit of darkness to get into the house. In addition, we must always get out of the right side of the car, putting the car between us and the vacant lot and avoiding the necessity of walking around the car to get to the door.

The precautions were more for him than for me, I explained, because he was the one who most often came in at night, but we had agreed to remind each other frequently. We had also begun to switch cars often in the hope of confusing the people who were forever following Medgar. More recently, Medgar had taken to making notes as he drove of the make of car, the license number, if possible, and sometimes even descriptions of the drivers of cars that appeared to be following him. He didn't say so, but I knew that his idea was to leave some evidence in the event that he was killed or seriously wounded by one of these pursuers.

There had been some talk in our neighborhood of asking the city to clear the vacant lot in our block and charge the expense to the owner, but someone remembered how many times we had asked the city to replace a burned-out street light on that part of the block, and I don't know if anyone ever did call about the lot. That end of our block led to the street on which whites lived and also to a way of entering the main highway. With the street light out and that end of the block in darkness, Medgar and I had agreed never to approach the house at night from that direction.

I expected to reach home at least fifteen minutes ahead of him that night, but just as I pulled into the carport with the children in the back seat, Medgar drove into the driveway behind me. We got the children into the house, and after we had put them to bed, I asked how he had managed to get home so quickly. "I drove fast," he said. "I didn't want you and the children going into a dark house alone." Then he told me about three white strangers who had been in the audience at the rally that night.

Medgar had first noticed them when someone had pointed them out, seated together in the audience. We had begun recently to pick up a few white people at our mass meetings, though most of them were instantly identifiable as sympathizers, police, or reporters. No one had seen these three men before.

After the meeting began, Medgar had noticed that one of the three was smoking. Since the fire laws prohibited smoking in that room, he had asked from the stage that the man put out his cigarette. The man had complied. After the rally, the three white strangers had appeared in the NAACP office upstairs. When a secretary asked if she could help them, they said, no, they were just looking around. She asked if they were reporters, and they shook their heads, and when she showed signs of asking more questions, they left.

Medgar had pushed the incident to the back of his mind during the party, but he mentioned it to the group of workers he was driving home, and one of them said he thought the same three men had followed them to the party. That meant they could have been watching when we left, and Medgar jammed the accelerator to the floorboard. He dropped the people off in a hurry and raced to get home before I did.

The day after the rally was a Saturday, and Medgar got up early and went to the office. Weekends had long since ceased to have any special meaning. The office was already full of people when he got there, and the telephone rang constantly. Several times during the day he escaped from the confusion to run office errands and drive slowly down Capitol Street to observe the effects of the boycott. Each time he noted with delight that the street seemed almost deserted. There was a meeting of some of the young people who planned to try to go to various white churches the following day, and during the afternoon Medgar called to tell me about that and ask about the children.

He had begun to make it a habit, when he called, to speak to each of the children. This afternoon they weren't in, and I thought I detected a sound of distress, a little extra weariness in his voice, as he said he'd see them later. I asked what was wrong, and he said, "Honey, guess what happened a few minutes ago?

"I've been followed by the police everywhere I've gone today," he continued. "It seems as though that would satisfy them. But when I came back to the office the last time, I parked across the street, just behind the place where the police usually park. They were there when I pulled in, the engine running, just sitting there watching everything."

He sighed, and I could feel the weariness right over the telephone. "I got out, locked the car, and stepped off the curb between the two cars, and they jammed the police car into reverse and tried to back into me. I jumped away just in time."

I couldn't believe it.

"I have witnesses, Myrlie," he said. "Several other people saw it. It was no mistake." He said he was going to call Chief Pierce as soon as he hung up.

I missed the mass meeting that night and was surprised when Medgar got home around eleven o'clock, earlier than usual. He looked completely done in. I tried to avoid asking about his day, babbling about the children and what they had done, and then, almost desperate for another subject, I mentioned how much he needed a new suit.

He looked at me strangely and said, "What do you expect me to do? Go down on Capitol Street and buy one?"

"No, Medgar," I said. "We can go to Vicksburg."

He shook his head. "What do you think we're going to use for money?"

"We'll cut corners and manage some way. After all, you're in the eyes of the public all the time, reporters here from everywhere. I'd like to see you have a new suit. You need one."

He argued at first that he didn't need one, and mostly out of relief at having found a subject we could talk about, I pressed him further.

Finally, almost in desperation, he turned to me and, raising his voice, said, "Myrlie, I wish you'd leave me alone about that suit. I'm not going to need one."

I thought at the time it was a strange way to put it, but I saw that he was distressed and changed the subject.

It was hot that night, and neither of us could sleep. Finally, after what seemed hours of tossing, Medgar reached out and pulled me to him. We lay without speaking, my head on his chest, and after a while I told him how good it was to hear the sound of his heart beating. "I don't think I could make it if anything happened to you."

Medgar squeezed my shoulder. "Nothing's going to happen to me, honey." He sighed. "But I worry about you, depending on me so much. Do you think you *could* make it if something did happen?"

I could feel the worry in his voice, and I tried to reassure him. "Oh, I'd get along somehow. I depend on you because I have you. If I didn't have you, I'd make it somehow for the children's sake."

We were silent again, and I thought of the times we had lain in bed like this and talked of other things. Some months before, we had talked of having another child. Medgar had always said he wanted four children, and I certainly did. Now I asked if he remembered that talk.

He sighed again. "Myrlie, this seems such a hopeless situation. Even though we are making strides, it's going to take a long, long time. I don't know, I guess I really don't want to be responsible for bringing another child into this world."

For what seemed like a long time after he finally fell asleep, those words ran through my mind like an endless recording of despair.

It must have been three in the morning when the telephone rang. It was a radio station in Chicago asking for a telephone interview with Medgar. It had happened before, and I knew he would insist on taking the call, so I handed him the phone. He was drugged with sleep, but he answered every question and then hung up. When I asked him about it next morning, he couldn't even remember the call. It took me a few minutes to convince him he had been interviewed, and then he sounded worried. "What did I say, honey? Did I sound all right?"

We were awakened that Sunday morning by another telephone call. This was a call I could handle myself, and, when it was over, I decided to get up, knowing there would be more calls to answer. When Medgar made a move to get up, I pleaded with him to sleep some more. It took every argument I could think of to convince him that I could take care of the calls we knew would be coming. It was a pathetic scene, my fighting to hold back the tears, urging him to stay in bed, assuring him that all he needed was rest and that everything would be all right. I knew as I said it that it wasn't true, that something would happen, that the police would get him the next time they tried or that he would collapse from sheer exhaustion. He argued feebly, but this time he was so tired it was really no contest, and he buried his face in the pillow as I left the room.

Later I served him breakfast in bed. He had hardly begun eating when the telephone rang. It was one of the office staff calling from downtown, saying that the office was locked, wondering what was keeping him. Medgar explained that he had given the keys to someone else the night before, knowing he might be a little late. And then, very meekly, totally unlike his usual self, he said he would finish his breakfast, dress, and come right down to the office. It was as though he had reached a point of being too tired to care.

I was boiling mad. No one knew his real condition as I did, and it seemed to me that the more he did, the more was expected of him. I insisted that he come into the dining room and finish his breakfast before he took a shower and dressed. He did it with the air of an obedient child. He hadn't finished when the telephone rang again. I answered to find someone else asking where he was and why he wasn't at the office. It was just too much. "He'll be there when he gets there!" I said in an angry voice and slammed down the receiver.

Medgar pushed back his plate, and I followed him to the bedroom. Dazedly, he took off his pajama top, put on a shirt without an undershirt, pulled some slacks over his pajama pants, and left for the office. I was too stunned to say anything. Medgar, who was always so neat in the way he dressed, had never done anything like that since I had known him.

He opened the office, stayed a while, and then came home in time to take a call asking for transportation for some of the young people testing the churches. Out he went to do it himself. When he returned, he collapsed on the sofa. I asked if I could do anything for him. "No," he said, "just love me."

I laughed. "That's not a hard thing to do." I left the room quickly so he would not see me crying. I went straight to the telephone and took it off the hook. I gathered the children and in a whispered conference explained that their daddy was trying to rest, that they should play outside and use the back door if they had to come in. They were perfect conspirators and practically crept from the house.

Later Medgar told me about taking the group of young people to the white Baptist church that Governor Barnett attended. He had parked and sat in the car with a police car just behind him and watched as they were turned away. "It was good to see them walking up those steps to the church door," he said, "even if they didn't get in."

At Sunday dinner that afternoon, it was almost like old

times. We were all together, and the children's joy at having their father with them sparked him to respond in kind. After dinner, Medgar went back to bed. He was still sleeping that evening when I left to play for the church choir. When I got home, he was up and reading the funny papers to the children and in much better spirits.

After I had put the children to bed, I came back to the living room to find him lying on the sofa. I sat across the room on the sofa with its back to the front window, and he asked me about the church services. I told him that several people had asked about him, expressed their concern about his health, and said they were praying for him.

He nodded. "I'm going to need all the prayers I can get." He looked up at me then, stared hard, and then said, "Girl, if you don't get up from there, you're going to get your head blown off!"

I laughed and quoted something he had often said. "My philosophy is that I'm not going until my time comes."

He was not amused. "There's no need courting it."

"Where do you expect me to sit?" I asked. "You've got your big self stretched out all over that sofa."

"It doesn't make any difference where you sit. Just move. If you have to, sit on the floor."

I took it as an invitation and moved to where he was, taking his head in my lap and rubbing his temples. He heaved an enormous sigh, and I could feel him relax.

Then, quietly, he began talking about a life insurance policy he had allowed to lapse when we simply didn't have the money to pay the premiums. "I have a feeling I should borrow some money tomorrow and pay a premium," he said.

I objected. "We're enough in debt as it is. You'll get paid Friday; you can do it then without borrowing."

But he said, "It really needs to be done now. It should

have been done a long time ago." And then, for the first time, he expressed real fear of something happening to him. As we talked about it, he said that if anything should happen to him, I must promise to take good care of the children.

I pretended to take offense and reminded him that I, too, had played some part in their being here, that they were my children, too. And then I noticed tears in his eyes, and I said, "Oh Medgar!" and we both broke down and cried together.

We clung to each other as though it were our only hope, and in my heart I felt that time was running out. There was no anger, no bitterness, not even a sense of having been robbed of what other people took for granted. There was just a bottomless depth of hopelessness, of hurt, of despair. I think I first felt all through me then that we were lost, and wordless tears were the only possible response.

But there was another day to get through on Monday, and after breakfast, the two older children ran off to play next door. Little Van stayed with his daddy, and when Medgar went out in back to look at the plum tree he had been spraying every day or so, Van was at his side, carrying a tiny football. I watched through the kitchen window where I was washing dishes as Medgar threw him a pass and then returned to examine the tree. Finally he turned to the window and called, "Myrlie, I think we're going to have our best year ever for plums."

I went out then and told him that he had worked hard enough on that tree to deserve a good year, and we walked around the back yard together, I chattering away and Medgar examining the shrubbery, deep in thought. He turned to me suddenly and said, "Myrlie, let me be by myself and think a little, will you?"

Van had come up with his football, and I asked, "Without Van?"

He nodded. "Please."

I took a protesting Van next door to play with the other children, and when I got back, Medgar had moved a lawn chair under the plum tree and was sitting there with his head in his hands. I wondered what he was thinking; I ached with wanting to go to him; but something held me back. In half an hour he came in. "I've got to go. I'm late already."

He kissed me, called goodbye to the children, got into the car, and backed out of the driveway. As usual, I watched him go, and for the first time he slowed almost to a stop at the corner and looked back and waved.

Medgar called several times during that day, and each time he asked to speak to the children. When they were all in the house at such times, there was a battle to be the first to talk to him, and on this day, as always, Medgar assured them there was enough of him to go around for all of us. I was beginning to have my doubts.

There was no mass meeting that night, and when he came home around eight-thirty and played with the children and read to them before they went to bed, it was almost as though there had been a temporary truce in the demands that were being made on him. Later, when he went into the children's bedrooms to check on them, as he had every night for years, I noticed that he bent over and kissed each of them, and I felt that the truce was to be a short one.

I dropped off to sleep that night and then woke suddenly to find the light still on and Medgar lying on his back, his eyes open, staring at the ceiling. I asked what was wrong.

He turned to me and said, "Nothing, honey. Nothing. Everything's going to be all right."

And once again, almost compulsively, as though we couldn't leave the subject for more than a few hours at a time, we began talking of our fears of what might happen to him. Finally, in a voice so calm it frightened me, he said, "If I go tonight, if I go next week, if I go next year, I feel I'm ready to go." It was as though he had made up his mind.

I shivered and told him not to talk that way, but he put his arms around me and said, "You shouldn't be afraid of death, honey. I know it's hard not to be, but it's something that comes to everyone someday."

Next morning I was up at five o'clock, creeping silently from the bedroom to iron shirts for Medgar. With the telephone ringing every few minutes all day, I had fallen far behind in my housework and had been ironing a shirt each morning for Medgar to wear that day. Today I was resolved to get ahead, and by the time he woke I had ten freshly ironed shirts neatly hung on hangers, the way he liked them. I took them to the bedroom and found him staring at the ceiling again. He smiled as I came in.

I held out the shirts. "See what I did this morning?"

"You're awfully smart."

"Aren't you going to thank me?"

He smiled and beckoned, and I went over and sat on the bed, and he squeezed me.

"I'm still waiting," I said.

And then he said, "I thank you for ironing all the shirts, but I'm not going to need them."

"Oh, come on," I said, getting up. "It's time to get out of bed."

I didn't know it until later, but Medgar had kept some things from me. Just the day before, Dr. Felix Dunn, president of the Gulfport NAACP, had called to tell him to be careful, to have someone see him home each night, to arrange for guards around the house. A white lawyer, sympathetic to the

NAACP, had told Dr. Dunn an attempt was going to be made on Medgar's life, and while Dr. Dunn couldn't prove it, he wanted Medgar to know and to prepare for it.

After breakfast, Medgar kissed us all and went to the car. As usual I followed him to the door. At the open car door, he stood a moment and looked out across the street at the vacant lot with the high grass and overgrown bushes. Because I didn't want him to know I had seen this, I went back to the children at the table.

He came through the door a moment later, came back to the table, and kissed us all again. I felt a twinge of panic. At the door once more, he turned and looked pleadingly at me, his shoulders slumped, his face a mirror of conflicting emotions. "Myrlie, I don't know what to do. I'm so tired I can't go on, but I can't stop either."

I ran to him and held him, and we stood like that for a moment. Then he kissed me and walked out the door, got into the car and drove off. I prayed that he would somehow get through this one more day.

It was quite a day. As far behind as I was in my housework, I couldn't seem to get started. There were postponed projects wherever I looked, but I couldn't concentrate, and I'd find myself sitting somewhere, thinking, worrying, trying to see some way out. Medgar called three times that afternoon, once right after the televised "schoolhouse door" confrontation on the campus of the University of Alabama between Governor George Wallace of Alabama and Deputy U. S. Attorney General Nicholas Katzenbach. He was happy about Governor Wallace's surrender and the subsequent admission to the university of its first two Negro students since Autherine Lucy: Vivian Malone and James Hood.

The first two times he called he talked to the children. The third time I jokingly accused him of loafing. He asked what I meant. "Well, you've called three times today. I didn't think you'd have the time."

"I'll take the time," he said, "to check on my family."

I told him I was tired and was thinking of missing the mass meeting that night. I asked him if he needed me.

"No," he said, "you stay home and rest. You need the sleep."

I told him I'd rest and then fix him something to eat when he got home. I could hear someone enter his office then, and Medgar laughed at something that was said. "I've got to go, honey. See you tonight. I love you."

"All right," I said. "Take care." Those were our last words to each other.

Medgar had told me that President Kennedy was speaking on civil rights that night, and I made a mental note of the time. We ate alone, the children and I. It had become a habit now to set only four places for supper. Medgar's chair stared at us, and the children, who had heard about the President's address to the nation, planned to watch it with me. There was something on later that they all wanted to see, and they begged to be allowed to wait up for Medgar to return home. School was out, and I knew that Van would fall asleep anyway, so I agreed.

We moved the television set into my bedroom, and I stretched out on the bed, the children clustered on the floor out of range of the window. When President Kennedy appeared, all three children fell silent, knowing despite their youth that he was going to be talking about them.

He spoke of the events at the University of Alabama that afternoon, congratulated the students who had kept the peace by acting responsibly. He spoke of the ideals of the founding fathers; that all men were created equal and said that the rights of all men were diminished when the rights of one were threatened.

"Today," he said, "we are committed to a world-wide struggle to promote and protect the rights of all who wish to be free. And when Americans are sent to Vietnam or West Berlin, we do not ask for whites only. It ought to be possible, therefore, for American students of any color to attend any public institution they select without having to be backed up by troops.

"It ought to be possible for American consumers of any color to receive equal service in places of public accommodation, such as hotels and restaurants and theaters and retail stores, without being forced to resort to demonstrations in the street, and it ought to be possible for American citizens of any color to register and to vote in a free election without interference or fear of reprisal."

I felt that he was talking directly about our Capitol Street boycott, our voter registration drives, and suddenly I felt very close to the President of the United States. The children listened intently.

"We are confronted primarily with a moral issue," he said. "It is as old as the Scriptures and as clear as the American Constitution.

"The heart of the question is whether all Americans are to be afforded equal rights and equal opportunities, whether we are going to treat our fellow Americans as we want to be treated. If an American, because his skin is dark, cannot eat lunch in a restaurant open to the public, if he cannot send his children to the best public school available, if he cannot vote for the public officials who represent him, if, in short, he cannot enjoy the full and free life which all of us want, then who among us would be content to have the color of his skin changed and stand in his place? Who among us would then be content with the counsels of patience and delay?"

I thought of Medgar, watching the address somewhere, and my heart filled with the joy I knew he would be feeling at these words. Medgar had said something very like this in his television speech three weeks earlier.

"We face, then, a moral crisis as a country and as a people," President Kennedy said. "It cannot be met by repressive police action. It cannot be left to increased demonstrations in the streets. It cannot be quieted by token moves or talk. It is a time to act in the Congress, in your state and local legislative body, and, above all, in all of our daily lives."

He outlined the program of legislation that was to become the Civil Rights bill of 1964, asking Congress for a law to open places of public accommodation to all, a law to accelerate the pace of school desegregation, a law to protect the right to vote.

"This is one country," he said. "It has become one country because all of us and all the people who came here had an equal chance to develop their talents.

"We cannot say to ten per cent of the population that you can't have that right; that your children can't have the chance to develop whatever talents they have; that the only way that they are going to get their rights is to go into the streets and demonstrate. I think we owe them and we owe ourselves a better country than that. . . ."

It was a moving speech, the most direct and urgent appeal for racial justice any President of the United States had ever made. It moved me and gave me hope and made what Medgar was doing seem more important than ever before. I remember wondering what the white people of Mississippi were thinking as I lay back on the bed and the children switched the set to another channel. I must have drifted off into a light sleep, because I woke, later, to settle an argument over which program was to be watched next. Then, still buoyed up by the President's words, I relaxed, to watch with the children. Darrell heard the car first.

"Here comes Daddy."

We listened to the familiar sound of the car. I roused myself as the tires reached the gravel driveway, stretched, and then heard the car door close. I wondered what Medgar would have to say about the speech, and I sat up on the bed.

A shot rang out, loud and menacing. The children, true to their training, sprawled on the floor. I knew in my heart what it must mean.

I flew to the door, praying to be wrong. I switched on the light. Medgar lay face down at the doorway drenched with blood.

I screamed, went to him, calling his name.

There was another shot, much closer, and I dropped to my knees. Medgar didn't move.

The children were around me now, pleading with him. "Please, Daddy, please get up!"

Behind Medgar on the floor of the carport were the papers he had dropped and some sweatshirts. Crazily, across the front of one, I read the words, "Jim Crow Must Go." In his hand, stretched out toward the door, was the door key. There was blood everywhere.

I left the children and ran to the telephone. I dialed "O" and tried to breathe and screamed at the operator for the police and gave her the address and ran back outside.

The Youngs were there and the Wellses and more people were coming and someone had turned Medgar over and he was breathing heavily, in short spurts, and his eyes were open, but they were set and unmoving.

I called and called to him, but if he heard me he showed no sign.

I heard the children being led away, screaming and crying for their father, and I remember some men carrying the mattress from Rena's bed from the house, putting Medgar on it and carrying him to Houston Wells' station wagon. I followed and tried to get in beside him, still calling to him, but they held me back, and as the car pulled off, I fell trying to reach him, and someone picked me up and I ran back into the house. There had been a police car in front of the Wells' car as it tore away through the night, but I had not yet seen a policeman.

I ran to the living room and fell to my knees and prayed. I prayed for Medgar and I fought for breath and I prayed that God's will be done and I sobbed and I prayed that whatever happened I would be able to accept it.

Someone found me there, and I got up and ran to the telephone and called Attorney Young's house where Gloster Current was staying. "They've killed my husband!" I screamed. "They've killed my husband!"

A woman took the telephone from me, and I wandered off to the bedroom, dazed with grief. One of the women followed and found me packing Medgar's toothbrush and some pajamas for the hospital and asking out loud how many pairs he would need.

Jean Wells took my arm and said that Dr. Britton had called from Ole Miss Hospital. Medgar had regained consciousness. I searched the room for my clothes and began to dress.

Then Hattie Tate came in the door and looked at me and I knew.

"Is he gone?"

She couldn't speak. She tried but she couldn't speak. She turned and ran from the room, and I slumped like a marionette whose strings had been cut.

I called Aunt Myrlie in Vicksburg. "Medgar has been shot. He's dead." She screamed and dropped the telephone.

I called Charles in Chicago and spoke to his wife, Nan. She said, "Oh no!"

And then everything became a blur.

There were people in the house and all over the yard when Mrs. Young led me across the street to her house to see if I could quiet the children. We walked through crowds of men and women crying, and they parted silently to let us pass. I was mute, numb, beyond tears. The children stood together looking bewildered and lost, and I went to them and put my arms around all three at once and pulled them close and said, "Everything's going to be all right." They didn't speak.

I asked them to go to bed and said I would see them in the morning, and I left and walked back through the shocked, silent crowd.

There were policemen standing in my yard, stooping down over the blood in the carport, everywhere, and I saw them and recognized them as the men who had followed Medgar everywhere for months, the men who had tried to run him down a few days before, the men who had asked me if I had used the gasoline can recently, and they looked at me and I screamed at them, "Get off my property!"

I clenched my fists and wanted a machine gun to mow them down, knowing and not caring that I, too, would be cut down as Medgar had been. For the first time in my life

I felt a hatred so deep and malignant I could have killed every one of them.

To the police who were examining the place where Medgar fell, I screamed, "Is a Negro's blood any different? Do you have to look at it? Do you think that by killing him you can put an end to what he's been doing? You'll have to kill me and a lot of other Negroes first."

Someone led me into the house, but there were detectives and policemen everywhere. They asked me questions, and I answered some of them. I found myself going back to the door again and again to look at the pool of blood that was all that was left of my husband. Once I stepped out and touched it. When I came inside with the blood on my hand, I saw a detective at the window beginning to measure off the path of the bullet and I said, "You won't do anything anyway. His blood is on all of your hands."

I was half out of my mind, but I saw Dr. Britton come through the door, and I ran to him. He took me in his arms and cried, and I felt very close to him.

"I was there all the time, Myrlie," he said in a choked voice. "I couldn't treat him, you know, because it's a white hospital, but I saw that they did everything they could. It was no use."

He had been our friend and our doctor and he had delivered Van, and he had gone to the hospital with Medgar and he had never left his side until it was over. When the white doctors moved too slowly for him, he had asked if they knew who this man was. "This man is Medgar Evers," he told them, "field secretary of the NAACP."

One of the white doctors looked up and said, "Oh my God."

"There was no way of saving him, Myrlie," Dr. Britton said.

"Did he regain consciousness?" I asked.

"I don't know. I called to him once, and he turned his head toward me. I asked if he knew who did this to him, and he took a deep breath and a big clot of blood jumped from the wound in his chest and he sighed and that was the end."

Later, Dr. Britton and Hattie Tate and Jean Wells tried to get me to take a sedative, but I refused. I didn't want to sleep. I wanted to stay up and fill my being with hate to relieve the awful aching pain. I wanted to watch the police that swarmed over the place now that Medgar was dead and hate them for not being there when he needed them. And then I remembered Medgar telling Darrell that hate was not good for a little boy's heart, and I cried again.

It was three in the morning before I finally took a sedative and let Dr. Britton give me an injection. I fell into a drugged sleep that lasted just two hours. I was awake at five and, looking out the window, saw the crowds were still there. I walked to the door and Medgar's blood was still on the floor of the carport, and I turned back toward the kitchen to get a bucket and some rags.

They stopped me when they saw what I was doing and took me back to the bedroom and turned on the television set. I saw Lena Horne and Roy Wilkins on the "Today" show but I had no idea what they were saying. People kept coming back to check on me, but I just wanted them all to go and leave me alone. I knew what had happened with a part of my mind. I knew, but I didn't want to believe it, and the presence of so many people made it true.

When I left the bedroom again and walked to the front of the house, I saw that a large piece of wall had been torn out.

"What happened?" I asked in wonderment. No one answered. Suddenly I was angry. "What happened?" I shouted.

Someone took me to the living room and showed me a large hole in the screen and window. "This is where the bullet entered the house, and here," pointing to the damaged wall, "it went through the wall, and here," taking me to the kitchen and showing me a broken tile, "is where it hit the tile wall." There was a deep dent in the refrigerator, where the bullet had hit and ricocheted, and the coffee pot on the counter was shattered. They had found the bullet on the opposite counter beside a watermelon I had bought that day. Even then I wondered what the white policemen had said to each other when they saw the watermelon.

I walked from the kitchen to the living room, tracing the bullet's path backward, and suddenly I remembered Medgar's voice saying, "Girl, if you don't get up from there, you're going to get your head blown off!" I saw that if I had been sitting in that spot that is exactly what would have happened. I looked out of the window in the early morning light, looked through the hole the bullet had made, and saw the vacant lot that Medgar had stared at the morning before. I wandered back to the kitchen and touched the broken tile and stood by the sink where I was often washing dishes when he came home late at night and knew that I would have been in the line of fire if I had been standing there and that we would both have been killed by the same bullet. And suddenly, with all my bruised and aching heart, I wished that we had.

I felt that my life was gone, over, without reason or meaning. Then I remembered the children that were all I had left of Medgar, and I walked out of the house straight into the lens of a television camera.

Mrs. Young was in tears when I got to her house. She had not been able to talk to the children. I went to them, took them off into a room by ourselves, and told them their father wouldn't be coming home any more.

"Is he dead, Mommy?" Rena asked. And I died a little as I told her that he was.

I took them home and packed their things to get them out of the neighborhood with a friend. Darrell and Rena watched in a daze, eyes dry, lost. Van didn't want to leave. He kept running to me everywhere I went, asking, "Daddy's gone? Daddy's gone?" It tore me apart. When the time came for them to leave, he said, "Mommy's going, too!" I took him in my arms and said I'd be here when he got back.

The rest of that day was like a dream. Someone told me that thirteen Negro ministers had been arrested when they left the Pearl Street Baptist Church and walked silently, two by two, toward City Hall. Later, 200 Negro youngsters marched out of the Masonic Temple Building straight into the arms of 100 city policemen, Hinds County deputy sheriffs, and state highway patrolmen armed with riot guns and automatic rifles. One hundred forty-five were arrested, a young girl was struck in the face with a club, deputies wrestled a middle-aged woman spectator to the sidewalk, and other Negroes were pushed around. One of the young demonstrators wore an NAACP T-shirt with lettering that read: "White Man, You May Kill the Body But Not the Soul."

Governor Ross Barnett said: "Apparently, it was a dastardly act and, as governor of the state of Mississippi, I shall cooperate in every way to apprehend the guilty party." But he felt it necessary to add, "Too many such incidents are happening throughout the country, including the race riot last night in Cambridge, Maryland."

Mayor Thompson flew back to Jackson from a Florida resort and announced a $5000 reward by the city. "Along with all of the citizens of Jackson," he said, "the commissioners and I are dreadfully shocked, humiliated, and sick at heart that such a terrible tragedy should happen in our city. We will not stop working night or day until we find the person or persons who are responsible for such a cowardly act, and we urge the cooperation of everyone in this search."

A city policeman said of the assassin, "He destroyed in one minute everything we've been trying to do here. We're just scared to death. That's the truth."

But Jimmy Ward, the editor of the Jackson *Daily News*, took the prize for hypocrisy that day with his front-page column. "Despite numerous, most earnest appeals for law and order at all times and especially during the current racial friction in Jackson," he wrote, "some conscienceless individual has stooped to violence and has greatly harmed the good relations that have existed in Jackson. All Mississippians and especially this shocked community are saddened by the dastardly act of inhuman behavior last night."

A white man in a beer joint at the edge of town was quoted in a Northern newspaper. He said what the others undoubtedly thought: "Maybe this will slow the niggers down." All of this I read later in the newspaper clippings poeple saved for me. Someone told me about this time that the shot I had heard as I stood by Medgar's body was Houston Wells firing into the air to frighten the killer and summon help.

My aunt Myrlie came that morning. And once, unaccountably, there were cameramen in the house. Friends kept trying to get me to bed, and I kept getting up, walking, pacing, talking about Medgar, remembering things he had said and done, touching chairs he had sat in, trying to push back the knowledge that I would never see him again. I talked and talked and talked. I don't know what I said.

Once I asked if there were a mass meeting that night, and someone said there was. I said I wanted to go, and everyone opposed it. I said I'd walk, if necessary. I couldn't explain then, and I can't now, but I knew I had to go. When the time came, Ruby Hurley and several other people came and drove me to the Pearl Street Baptist Church where there were hundreds and hundreds of people and Reverend Smith was talking.

I remembered in a flash how Medgar had spoken and laughed and exhorted the people here, and I could almost see him standing in the pulpit. Then Reverend Smith said something about me and I was standing before a hushed crowd with television cameras in their midst and lights in my eyes, and I knew they were all there, but I didn't really see anything. I just spoke.

"I come to you tonight with a broken heart. I have lost my husband. No one really knew how hard he worked, how much he sacrificed over the years to help his people. No one but me. I knew. I know.

"I am left without my husband and my children without a father, but I am left with the strong determination to try to take up where he left off. And I come to make a plea that all of you here and those who are not here will, by his death, be able to draw some of his strength, some of his courage, and some of his determination to finish this fight.

"Nothing can bring Medgar back, but the cause can live on. It was his wish that this movement be one of the most successful that this nation has ever known. We cannot let his death be in vain."

When I finished speaking, I turned and walked to the

door. People wept as I went by, and outside, as we walked to the car, I heard them start to sing and I don't know what they sang because I had no heart to listen any more and I closed my ears and my mind and my thoughts.

## XVIII

I remember walking and talking and finding myself in a room or at a drawer or by a window and not knowing what I had come there to do. I remember waking in the morning and, with my eyes still closed, reaching out to the other side of the bed and finding nothing. I remember going to the closet and seeing the shirts I had ironed and smelling them and feeling reassured. And then remembering what Medgar had said: "I thank you for ironing all the shirts, but I'm not going to need them."

A hundred times a day I found myself wondering what time he would be home or what he was doing at the office or when he would call and then catching myself and forcing myself to know again what had happened. I found I couldn't hear things, and I went to the doctor, and he said that I had screamed so long it had temporarily affected my hearing.

I was questioned and questioned and questioned by detectives. Did I know anyone who would want to kill Medgar? I laughed bitterly and stared at the white face of the man who asked. Did I know any Negro who might want to kill him? I shook my head and said, "No Negro. No." Had he had an affair with another woman? I exploded, and the detective said he'd come back later.

The police found the murder weapon, a 30.06-caliber rifle with a telescopic sight, near a cleared space in some honeysuckle bushes in the vacant lot that had worried us. He had knelt there waiting, the murderer, the scent of honeysuckle in his nostrils, until Medgar came home, drove in the driveway, parked behind my car and got out, for some reason, perhaps because he was so tired, on the left side of the car. The killer had found the white shirt in the crosshairs of the telescopic sight, held it there, and squeezed the trigger, watching as the bullet tore through the flesh, as Medgar staggered toward the doorway, thirty feet away. Then he had run, hiding the rifle in a thicket on the way.

The children came back to me, and I stood one morning looking out the bedroom window at Darrell playing baseball with some boys. He hit the ball as it was pitched to him, and a boy ran to catch it, and Darrell stood there a moment and then threw the bat on the ground. His whole body shook and he broke into sobs and he ran from the street around the house to the back yard and the plum tree. I ran to meet him, and he cried as though his heart would break standing there under the tree that Medgar had planted. It was the first time he had cried.

Rena had cried, and Van had cried and looked puzzled at the swarms of people and asked if his daddy would come back until I could answer no more. But Darrell hadn't cried until that morning.

Medgar's sisters had arrived and Charles had come from Chicago. Dr. Britton was taking care of the funeral arrangements, so I had nothing to do but wander through the house and talk to people. There were people there constantly.

There were press conferences and interviews, and sometimes I was involved, though I didn't want to be. Everyone was always white—the cameramen, the interviewers, everyone—and a white skin had come to have a meaning I didn't want to explore.

The day after Medgar died, ninety Negroes were arrested for demonstrating. Jackson police charged the porch of a Negro home and clubbed a group of youngsters and adults into submission after they had chanted and jeered at them. The next day, Flag Day, thirty-seven youngsters were arrested on Capitol Street for walking singly and in twos and threes down the sidewalk, some of them carrying tiny American flags.

Charles kept after me to choose the clothes Medgar would be dressed in for the funeral. I didn't want to—it was too final—and I put it off, but eventually I did. A *Life* photographer appeared from nowhere and was there constantly, in the house, outside, and he followed me when I took Darrell and Rena to the funeral home. I hated it and didn't know who had given him permission, but I could never remember to ask anyone.

Medgar had been dressed in the clothes I had selected for him. I asked the funeral director to have the others leave so the children and I could be alone. Everyone left but the *Life* photographer, who went on snapping pictures. I had thought about bringing the children to see their father dead, and I had thought and thought and thought. My natural impulse was not to do it, but I remembered the way they had last seen him, his broken body stretched out in a pool of blood, the terror and ugliness and hatred of that night, and I decided that Darrell and Rena should see him once again, peaceful and at rest.

I had said I wanted the casket closed at the funeral, and

this was the last opportunity, so I brought them with me, and he did look peaceful, and I think it helped. The children left after a moment. I stayed. The tired lines were gone from his face, and I had a terrible urge to hold his head and stroke his temples and say that everything would be all right. And then I sensed that I was not alone. I turned and the *Life* photographer was there. His eyes were filled with tears. For the first time since Medgar's death the hatred I had felt for all whites was gone. It never returned.

Telegrams and letters and telephone calls poured in, and I read the messages without knowing what I was reading, spoke to people without hearing what they said. Relatives and friends ran the house, cooked our meals, kept track of the mail, and maintained a guest register so that someone would know who had come to the house.

Medgar had been shot just after midnight on Wednesday morning. The funeral was held on Saturday at the Masonic Temple. Leaving someone else's funeral once, Medgar had told me the kind of funeral he wanted. It should be short, he said, no longer than a half hour, and it should be soon. He wanted to be buried as soon as possible after he died. "And I don't want any long eulogies either," he said. "They might not be true, and the people that give them usually don't mean them anyway. But most important, I don't want an expensive funeral. When I'm gone, I'm gone, and I won't know anything about it."

I had told all this to Ruby Hurley, and I was particularly worried about the expense. Medgar had had no insurance, and we had bills that had to be paid. Everyone told me not to worry, but I couldn't help it. Then Ruby and others asked me what I would wear to the funeral, and I showed them a black dress Medgar had bought me. They said it wouldn't do, and I asked why not. He had liked it and it was the best he could afford. I must have said it in an aggressive way, because Ruby apologized and said she had meant no harm, but that she would like to see me in something different. Again I wondered about the money, but she said not to worry. The office staff in New York bought dresses for me and for Rena to wear.

Saturday was the third straight day with temperatures over 100. Van stayed home, but the other children and I were driven to the Masonic Temple in a line of cars. The crowds were immense, both outside and after we got in, and it took a while to make our way through all the people to the rows of folding chairs up front reserved for the family and close friends. Both of my grandmothers were there, and my aunt from Chicago, and I learned later that neither of my grandmothers had been able to reach the family section because of the crowds.

There were 4000 people in that huge stifling hot room and there were television cameras and lights and still photographers and reporters. The casket was open. I felt resentment boil up inside me. I wanted to get up and announce that there would be no funeral and that everyone could leave. Medgar had lived and walked in dignity all his life, and I wanted him to be buried that way, but it was all too big; there was nothing I could do about it. I had shared my husband's life with the rest of the world, and I was going to have to share his death as well.

Dr. Howard had decided he should make some remarks, and there were others who spoke. It was not at all what I wanted. I wondered how many of the people had come to pay a final tribute to Medgar and how many out of curiosity or simply to be seen.

I had neglected my children in the days since Medgar's death, and though the older two sat beside me, I remembered them now only occasionally. Rena had cried off and on ever since that night, but Darrell, who sat beside me, had cried only that one time under the plum tree. He would disappear into his room and sit there alone, not speaking, not playing, and it was hard for me to imagine what was going on in his mind. Now, sitting beside me at the funeral, I saw him stare at the open casket, and I felt what he must be thinking. There would be no more telephone calls from his father, no more basketball and football with him, no riding bicycles with him in front of the house, no fishing. The promise, so often deferred, to take Darrell hunting would now never be fulfilled. The nights when Medgar came home with boxes of Cracker Jack for each child—they, too, were over. Darrell sat there and stared at the casket, shoulders straight, one hand in the other, his head slightly bowed, and then suddenly he sobbed and sobbed until I guess no more tears would come.

I found it hard to cry. I was not pleased with the way the service had been arranged. I looked at Darrell and Rena and knew that I had to try to be strong for their sakes. I thought of what Medgar had said so many times on so many different occasions. "Don't be weak, Myrlie; stand up and be a woman." And I knew that if there was ever a time to stand up and be a woman it was now.

I came close to breaking down as the procession started out of the temple and I saw the casket being carried out in front of me. I told Charles I didn't think I could make it, and he said, "Don't break down now, Sis."

I turned to him. "Do you realize this is the last time Medgar will ever be in this building?" And I thought of the days and weeks and months he had spent in that building—in his office and at mass meetings—and somehow that got me outside to where the cars waited for us.

The cars proceeded slowly down Lynch Street in the broiling sun. I looked behind and saw a multitude of people, and I remembered Diane Bevels asking me a day or so earlier if the young people could march after the funeral. I had thought about it and finally said I had no objection if it were done in a way that would have made Medgar proud. She reassured me, and I forgot about it, and now I turned to Aaron Henry in the car beside me and asked what all those people were doing. He said they were going to march the twenty-odd blocks to the Collins Funeral Home.

I forgot about them then, but ten blocks later as we reached the bottom of a long sloping hill, Aaron said, "Look behind you."

I turned and saw a mass of people behind us. The driver stopped, and I stared at the unending parade of black faces, filling the street from one curb to the other, and I suddenly felt good inside. I found myself asking why, why could they do it today when they weren't allowed to do it while Medgar was alive and could have seen it.

We started moving again with the police escort ahead of us and police all along the route, and I noticed that when the casket, covered by an American flag, passed by, some of the police took off their new blue riot helmets. Maybe it was prejudice on my part, but it seemed they were doing it against their will. I thought they might be afraid that the Negroes would run wild.

On Farish Street I saw a few white people standing in the doorways of buildings watching us. Someone told me later that a jukebox was blaring from the door of a white restaurant. When the marchers behind us reached it, several young Negroes went in, unplugged it, and told the astonished whites to keep it off until everyone had passed. None of the whites said a word.

When we reached the funeral home, I asked to be taken home with the children. I was tired and felt suddenly old. Someone took the children, and I went into my bedroom and stayed there, alone.

Downtown, the marchers gathered in front of the funeral home. They stretched for blocks, silent, many weeping, a solid phalanx of mourners. Someone started "We Shall Overcome!" and the words were taken up by the entire crowd. A friend told me she saw elderly Negroes who had walked that whole mile and a half under a blistering sun stand with their heads bare and sing as though their hearts would break. There were teachers, too, who had avoided the NAACP out of fear of losing their jobs, who sang with tears of relief streaming down their faces, the tension of indecision over, committed now to the goals they had always really favored.

The song ended and a new one began. The words rang out from hundreds of throats: "Before I'd be a slave, I'd be buried in my grave, and go home to my Lord and be free!" Then someone shouted, "Capitol Street!" and several hundred youngsters broke and ran toward the street that symbolized our frustrations. The police were caught off guard and retreated before what must have seemed a flood of black faces surging toward them. Negroes poured out of the doors of stores and shops and taverns along the route, and the crowd became a mob, and sorrow turned to anger, and four motorcycle patrolmen let them through one intersection and into the next block.

Two hundred and fifty policemen, sheriff's deputies, and state highway patrolmen moved to cordon off the crowd of nearly 1000. Deputy Police Chief A. L. Ray met the surging Negro mob as it reached the end of the block. His voice, amplified by a bullhorn, carried for blocks: "Your leaders said you wanted to have a private, mournful march, and we agreed under those circumstances." Then he ordered the crowd to disperse.

There was a ripple of movement as some in the crowd armed themselves with rocks, bricks, and bottles. "We want the killer!" someone shouted. "We want equality!" screamed another. "We want freedom!" cried a third. A group of youngsters stamped their feet and shouted in cadence, "Freedom! Freedom! Freedom!" The police moved in with police dogs on short leashes.

Fifty white newsmen and a group of Negroes were forced back, and, one after another, Negroes were plucked from the crowd and hustled into waiting police vans. The police had drawn their pistols, riot guns came out, four fire department pumper trucks rolled into view.

Of the next few minutes, Claude Sitton wrote in the New York *Times*: "With newsmen out of the way, the police went to work in earnest to clear the area. A television cameraman caught in a doorway said a Negro man who did not move fast enough was struck in the face with a shotgun butt by a deputy sheriff. Another deputy cut a soundman's microphone cable.

"The cameraman said a Negro woman was clubbed by a policeman. She fled to a car, but was dragged out and clubbed again.

"Two men in one camera crew said the police had threatened to turn a police dog on them if they did not move out of the area quickly.

"By this time, most of the Negroes had been sealed off in a one-block area. They began throwing bricks, bottles and other missiles at the police. Most fell short of the mark.

"One group taunted the officers with cries of 'Shoot! Shoot! Shoot!'

"Although some of the policemen had drawn their pistols, none used them. Steel-helmeted highway patrolmen backed up the police, holding automatic rifles and shotguns at the ready.

"Deputy Chief Ray called over the bullhorn to the rioters: 'You came here to honor a dead man and you have brought dishonor. You have brought dishonor, dishonor.'

"The crowd, many of whose members were in their 20's and 30's, screamed at him. The growling and barking of the police dogs, the crash of bottles on the pavement and the cursing of the policemen added to the uproar.

"One policeman pointed to a man who was throwing bottles from atop a building. 'That nigger up there has got a gun or something,' he shouted. A deputy sheriff went after the man.

"Other officers raced along the streets, pounding their nightsticks on the hoods and tops of automobiles and yelling, 'Get on out of here!'"

Suddenly, dodging bricks and bottles, a white man wearing a white shirt and a dark tie stepped from the crowd into the no-man's land of broken glass and stones. "You're not going to win anything with bottles and bricks!" he shouted to the Negroes.

The crowd continued to roar and move toward him. "Hold it!" he shouted. "Is there someone here who can speak for you people?" A Negro youth came out of the crowd and stood beside him. "This man is right," he shouted.

The white man faced the Negroes and shouted once more. "My name is John Doar—D-O-A-R. I'm from the Justice Department, and anyone around here knows I stand for what is right." He repeated the statement again and again.

321

Other Negroes joined the youth in trying to calm the crowd. "Come on," Doar called to them all. "Let's disperse now. Go on home. Let's not have a riot here." There were many there who believe that without John Doar's efforts a full-scale riot would have occurred. Today John Doar is Assistant U. S. Attorney General for Civil Rights.

Medgar and I had bought a burial plot in a Negro cemetery in Jackson. It was just ten minutes from the house, and when I had finally accepted Medgar's death, I told everyone who asked that he would be buried there. Medgar had recently been elected to the national board of the American Veterans Committee, and they suggested that his body be buried at the National Cemetery in Arlington, Virginia. I said no. Ruby Hurley asked me to think about it, pointing out that many more people could visit the grave if it were near Washington and that it would be a tribute to Medgar.

I did think about it in the days before the funeral, and more and more I realized how selfish I was being to want his grave near our home. I had shared Medgar with others all of our marriage, and, much as I had regretted it, I had known for years that he did not belong to me alone. When I mentioned the expense of the trip to Washington, I was told not to worry about it. Eventually I gave my reluctant consent.

Medgar's body was sent by railroad from the Collins Funeral Home. It was met at the station in Washington by a large group representing the NAACP, CORE, SNCC, and other Negro organizations. A thousand mourners marched behind the hearse to a Washington funeral home. Later the casket was opened and the remains viewed at the John Wesley A.M.E. Church, where Medgar a year or so earlier had spoken to a group of 200 people. Now, in death, 25,000 people passed by his casket.

Aunt Myrlie and Aunt Francis volunteered to stay with Van in Jackson, though both were afraid to stay in the house. I assured them that no one would dare return, that they had accomplished their goal when Medgar died, and arrangements were made for the house to be guarded day and night.

The older children and I left Jackson on Tuesday, three days after the funeral. Charles and Ruby Hurley and the funeral director, Mrs. Harvey, took the plane with us. Darrell and Rena had pleaded with Medgar for a plane ride, and he had solemnly promised them one someday. What he hadn't been able to give them in life, he gave them in death.

David Nevin of *Life* interviewed me throughout the trip. Charles had suggested cooperating with the magazine in its desire for a picture and text story, and I had agreed. I was promised an opportunity to approve the text the following morning.

At the airport in Washington we were met by a large and solemn delegation of the Washington branch of the NAACP. Flashbulbs popped and television cameras rolled as I was presented with a huge bouquet of roses. Secretary of the Interior Stewart Udall had sent his chauffeur and private car for our use during our stay in Washington, and we were driven to the Mayflower Hotel. The suite reserved for us was filled with flowers and fruit and nuts, a gift of the manager. There were plain-clothes policemen in the halls for our protection. Seeing them, my perverse mind flew back to the nights that Medgar had sped down the dark highways of the Delta with a car behind him, "shaking the car's tail" at pursuers, with only the protection of his wits and his driving skill between him and death. Now he was dead, and we were all protected.

Wednesday morning I saw and approved the *Life* article. We were driven to the church, and I was asked if I wanted to view Medgar's body for the last time. I was restless and eager to get the burial behind me, remembering Medgar's feelings about wanting to be buried quickly, and I said no. The church was surrounded by people and cars; I later heard a Negro taxi company had sent its entire fleet to drive people to Arlington without fare.

After what seemed a long time, the procession of cars started for the cemetery, and it was on that ride that I decided I had been right to agree to have him buried in Washington. Along both sides of the route, block after block, there were people standing, many with heads bowed, many making the sign of the cross as we passed by. Most of them were white.

The procession drove past the Lincoln Memorial, and our car stopped for just a moment before driving on, and suddenly I felt almost happy. My pride in Medgar had never been so great, for somehow this whole experience was the final evidence that the man I had loved and married, the man whose three children I had borne, was truly a great American being put to rest in a place with many other American heroes.

At the cemetery there were hundreds upon hundreds of people. More, of course, followed us there. When the car stopped, Charles was unable to move. He sat in the car after the children and I got out and trembled, overcome with grief. I pleaded with him to get out, and he sat there and sobbed. Eventually he got control of himself and stepped out. We were taken into tiny Fort Myer Chapel, just a few of us, and it was cool and silent and serene. I remember how thankful I was that Medgar had this quiet simple service before being laid to rest.

Bishop Stephen Gill Spottswood of the African Methodist Episcopal Church, chairman of the Board of Directors of the NAACP, spoke quietly. "He is not dead, the soldier fallen here. His spirit walks throughout the world today.

"I hope Medgar Evers will be the last black American to give his life in the struggle to make the Constitution come alive. He laid down his life for Negroes that they might be free from segregation and discrimination, that we might share in the full fruits of democracy. Now, he rests from his labors."

Leaving the lovely chapel, we passed between an honor guard of soldiers, entered the car, and drove to the graveside. It was a beautiful spot on a gentle slope under tall oaks. It reminded me instantly of the place in Vicksburg National Park that Medgar and I had called "our place," where we had gone whenever we could to sit under the trees, look down the long hill, and dream.

We were seated at the graveside, and the final service began. Rifles cracked three times, and I jumped, though I had been warned. I heard them as the sound that had killed my husband, and I told myself to control my emotions, that there were cameras everywhere waiting to catch me if I cried out. A bugle sounded taps, the saddest sound there is, and i saw Rena sob. Darrell sat there, hands together in his lap, the saddest little boy in the world.

Mickey Levine of the American Veterans Committee said, "No soldier in this field has fought more courageously, more heroically than Medgar Evers. We pledge that this fight is not ended. We shall go to the Congress; we shall go to the people; he shall not have died in vain."

The smoke from the rifle volley hung over the plain gray casket. The air was acrid with gunpowder. Roy Wilkins spoke the final tribute: "Medgar Evers believed in his country; it now remains to be seen whether his country believes in him."

Clarence Mitchell, Jr., began the song, and as the rest picked it up and the words, "We shall overcome," rang out over the graves of so many who had given their lives for their country, I steeled myself and held my head high and looked up at the trees with the sun sifting through the leaves and was thankful that Medgar was buried here, near the nation's Capitol. For the first time in my life, I had a sense of pride in being a real American and not merely a second-class citizen.

Finally, it was over. I took a last look at the casket, murmured a goodbye to Medgar, and, holding the triangular-folded American flag the soldiers had given me, took the children to the car.

The next morning we were taken to the White House to meet the President. Rena saw him first, striding toward the building, and she squealed, "Momma, here comes President Kennedy!" He had a charming smile, and the children were almost overcome with excitement. When his secretary, Mrs. Lincoln, introduced us, he took my hand and shook it and held it.

He began to say something and stopped. "How are you doing?" he asked finally.

"Fine, thank you, Mr. President," I said. But I wanted to say that I was dead inside, that my life had been snatched from me, that I wished he could do something about it personally. I wanted to say that my husband had fought for his country and come back home to find he was still not free and had died for his belief that all Americans were entitled to first-class citizenship. I wanted to say that I knew that nothing would be done about it. But I just said, "Fine, thank you, Mr. President."

He said, "You're a brave woman."

And I said, "Thank you, Mr. President."

He turned to the children and talked to them. He showed them the secret door in his desk and the coconut souvenir of his experience in the Pacific, and I thought, he's different from what I expected. His hair is lighter and he looks older. And I remembered how Medgar had aged so rapidly and thought to myself, the same thing is happening to this man.

He told the children they should be very proud of their father and of their heritage, and he took two slim boxes and gave one to each of them. Rena's gift was a Kennedy pin and a charm bracelet with a PT-boat medallion; Darrell's was a pen and a PT-boat tie clip. The children thanked him politely.

He turned to Charles and talked with him and then called in a photographer. We had our pictures taken with the President. He said he would autograph them and send them to us, and he autographed a copy of the Civil Rights bill and gave it to me. Before we left, he arranged for us to tour the White House, including a private tour of the living quarters upstairs. Rena sat on the bed in which Queen Elizabeth had slept, and when we were taken to the Lincoln Room, I had a special feeling of pride in being a Negro. The man who guided us called us to the window, and we saw a helicopter land on the lawn. President Kennedy walked to it and got in, and John-John stood on the lawn and waved to him. I looked at Darrell, watching through the window, and thought that he would never again wave goodbye to his father, and I almost broke down.

Back at the hotel, friends who were terribly excited over

our meeting the President asked if I weren't thrilled at the privilege. I was pleased at the warmth and gentleness and what seemed the genuineness of President Kennedy's reception of us, but I could not consider meeting him a privilege. I had paid too great a price for that. Most of all, I was happy that the children would have something more to remember of their trip to Washington than the burial of their father.

We left Washington the next day and arrived in Jackson to find that the new airport, which had been built with the double restrooms of segregation, had been opened as a completely integrated building. Medgar had fought for the integration of the old airport. When he and others had succeeded in integrating the restaurant, the management had taken the seats out and put the chairs and tables in a room for which one had to have reservations. Only white people got reservations.

But now the city had taken federal funds to build the new building, and that meant that it had to be integrated, and it was. I remember thinking that Medgar had fought for this, too, and had not lived to see it. It seemed wildly unfair.

At home, I looked at the things that had been returned to me after Medgar's death at the hospital. It was obvious that Dr. Britton had tried, not too successfully, to wipe the blood from them. There was a tie clasp in the form of the scales of justice, and I decided that someday it would be Darrell's. There was his wristwatch and the key ring with the house key on it that he had held in his hand, outstretched toward the door as he lay on the floor of the carport. Even in death, he had held it, and they had had to pry it out of his hand. There was his wallet, and, inside it, pictures of the children, of his younger sister who had died, and one of me, taken at Alcorn. He always said it was the best picture ever taken of me.

And there was a five-dollar bill. On the bill was Lincoln's face, and on Lincoln's face was Medgar's blood. I stood there staring at it, my hand trembling, my heart bruised and aching, and I thought about these two men who had lived a hundred years apart. One had freed the Negroes from slavery, but they had not been really free. The other had worked to finish the job. Both were assassinated.

# ─── XIX ───

We returned from Washington to find we were a tourist attraction. The house was full of friends; people came and went, bringing food and gifts, taking the children for a day. And then, strangers—at first mostly Negroes—began to appear.

They would drive slowly by the house, pointing and looking. On weekends the traffic was almost bumper to bumper. At the vacant lot where the murderer had hidden, some would park their cars, get out, explore the honeysuckle thicket. Others, with cameras, would stop in front and take pictures of the house and the carport.

When the children were outside, there was extra excitement. The people would point and argue over which were my children, snapping pictures just in case. I kept my children in the back yard as much as I could.

Some of these strangers actually came up the driveway to inspect the broken window, to point to the spot where Medgar had fallen. One man rang the doorbell to ask if he could put his finger in the hole where the bullet had passed. Others asked me to pose by the window for a picture, and, when I refused, many of them went away angry.

Two Japanese reporters came to the door and asked for an interview. I refused politely. They asked if they could photograph the house, and I told them to go ahead. Minutes later I looked out the window and saw they had found the children and were posing them in the carport. Angrily I sent them away.

After a week or so, whites began driving by. One afternoon when the children were in front, three Negro men got out of a car, asked which were the Evers children, and began asking questions. As I reached the door, I heard one ask Darrell to stand and point to the place where his father had fallen so he could take a picture.

I stormed out of the house. "What's the meaning of this? What are you doing here?"

The man said he had meant no harm, that he was interested in the case. Before I knew it he was asking me questions.

"You look like an intelligent man," I said angrily. "How could you ask a child to do such a thing? We've been through enough. They saw their father dying and so did I. We're not curiosities; we're human beings. We have feelings. And we'd like to be left alone. This isn't a circus, and the best thing for you to do is take your camera and get off my property."

As they left, apologizing, a neighbor walked over. "I think I'll put up a fence," I said, close to tears. "As long as people are as cold and cruel as they are, maybe I should be the same. Why not charge admission for them to walk inside, with an extra charge for putting their fingers in the hole in the window, an extra charge for coming into the house and viewing the wall where the bullet went through, an extra charge for holding the piece of broken tile and an extra charge for touching the dent in the refrigerator."

There was never any question of people finding their way to our house. The Jackson *Daily News* had published not only the address but a map with directions for reaching us.

Medgar's death left the job of Mississippi field secretary vacant, and during the days before the funeral in Jackson the press had hounded Ruby Hurley for the name of a successor. Again and again, she said no one had been selected. In fact, no one had had time to think of it, no one, that is, except Charles. Charles had told Ruby of a pact he and Medgar had, an agreement that one of them would stay in Mississippi and work for civil rights. If anything happened to him, they had agreed, the other would take over.

Ruby, in the frantic press of those incredible days after the murder, found herself asked about Medgar's job at a televised press conference. She mentioned Charles' story about the pact and said he would replace Medgar. Charles agreed.

I heard all this with great surprise on a radio news broadcast. I knew of no pact. Medgar and I had once discussed who would replace him, and he jokingly looked at me and said, "What about you?" I said that it would be a challenge but that I wouldn't take a million dollars to work with the Negroes of Mississippi and against the whites. It was such a thankless job. Medgar knew what I meant. There were so many who refused to help out of fear.

Charles sought the job, I think, with only one thing in mind. He wanted vengeance. He said he was taking the job to make sure neither the whites nor the Negroes forgot what happened to his brother. As long as he was there, the name Evers would be there, and they would remember. He wanted to show them you couldn't get rid of an Evers that easily, and he had in mind particularly the middle-class Negroes who had often refused to contribute or help.

He said that Medgar had worked long and hard in dangerous circumstances and had not been appreciated until his death. He spoke of how the Negro teachers' association met in Jackson each year and how Alcorn classmates of Medgar's had each year avoided him lest they lose their jobs. He talked angrily of the story he had heard of a strategy meeting during the height of the tension after the fire bomb had been thrown at our home. James Wells had reportedly stood up and pleaded for the national office or the citizens in general to provide protection for Medgar. A high-ranking official of the national office was reported to have said that this was no time to discuss securing guards for Medgar, that there were more important things to discuss.

I don't know if it actually happened that way. It might have. Charles was convinced of it. He felt providing guards for Medgar was the least the association could have done, and in his hurt and anger he was determined to make everyone pay; white Mississippi, Negro Mississippi, and the NAACP. It was the driving force behind everything he did for a long time.

With me and with the children, he was kind and gentle. For a long time, seeing the children upset him terribly. But he called often to see how we were, came by occasionally to take the children out, brought them gifts, and made sure we understood we should turn to him immediately if we needed anything.

Two days after we returned from Washington, on June 23, the FBI made an arrest. Jess Brown called that night to tell me. I couldn't believe it. I had been sure no one would ever be arrested. I had been sure the investigation was make-believe. I had even suspected that the local and state police helped plan the murder. Now I dropped the telephone and ran to the television set.

I heard his name that night: Byron de la Beckwith. He was a fertilizer salesman, lived in Greenwood, worked in Greenville, both in the Delta. He was a known racist, a member of the White Citizens Councils, and the gun and the sight had been traced to him. He was a former Marine, a gun collector, and a frequent writer of letters-to-the-editor on the subject of segregation. He was five feet seven inches tall, weighed 160 pounds. He was forty-two years old and had attended Mississippi State for a single semester. He was a member of the Sons of the American Revolution, of the Protestant Episcopal Church, and his mother had come from a well-known Greenwood family that traced its roots back to Old South plantation life and a friendship with Jefferson Davis. He was married, once divorced, had remarried the same woman, and was now separated from her. He had a teenage son. He had been born in California but had returned with his mother to Mississippi at the age of five when his father died. He had lived in Greenwood ever since. The Jackson *Clarion-Ledger* gave the story a five-column front-page headline the next day. With typical white Mississippi schizophrenia it proclaimed: "CALIFORNIAN IS CHARGED WITH MURDER OF MEDGAR EVERS."

Alongside the story were pictures of Beckwith, and within an hour I had received calls from people who identified him as one of the three white men at the mass meeting the Friday night before Medgar was killed. Medgar's secretary, Lillian Louie, swore he was one of the three who had come up to the office after the meeting and left only when she began asking questions. Ruby Hurley also recognized him.

The telephone calls poured in. I was asked for a statement

by reporters. I said I had none, that I would wait to see what form justice might take. I had begun almost to believe that this was the man, but I still felt sure nothing would be done about it.

Each new development surprised me: when a grand jury actually indicted him, when he was jailed and held without bail, when he was sent to the state mental hospital at Whitfield for psychiatric observation, when he was returned to jail as fit to stand trial, when the trial date was actually set. I finally believed he was the man who had murdered Medgar when I saw on television the pictures of his transfer to the mental hospital. He was all smiles, bowing and gracious to the crowd, and the police smiled at him, patted him on the back, and treated him with respect. He was being accorded the status of a savior of white Mississippi, and that, I felt, meant he must be the man.

About the time that Beckwith was arrested, a letter by an English professor at Ole Miss, Evans Harrington, appeared in the Jackson *Clarion-Ledger*. Somehow it summarized my own bitterness. "Mississippians from the governor down have expressed shock, shame, and dismay at the murder of Medgar Evers," it read, "and certainly I share these emotions. But in the interests of the psychic well-being of the state I feel that a word of caution is in order. Medgar Evers is, of course, by no means the first Negro to be murdered in our state, even within recent years. Nor, barring something approaching a miracle, will he be even close to the last.

"Let us face it clearly: Our way of life is based on keeping the Negro downtrodden—under-paid, unrepresented in government, and excluded from our own society. Now only an ignorant or a supine and powerless people will allow themselves to be so downtrodden. And, manifestly, Negroes in our state are no longer any of these things. Leaders like Medgar Evers are informing them, bolstering their courage and initiative, and welding them into a powerful force. Naturally, therefore, it will continue to be necessary to kill Negro leaders; and, as the people themselves become more enlightened, it will be necessary to kill many of them, more and more as time goes on.

"This is where the psychic damage to our state appears. If we are to feel shock, shame, and dismay every time our way of life brings on an assassination, every time our politicians and newspapermen and other spokesmen trade on and inflame ignorance and race hatred to the point of murder, will we not eventually be overwhelmed with shock, shame, and dismay? Will we not finally be forced to take the logical last step in the long series of withdrawal symptoms which we have already manifested? How much shock, shame, and dismay can a people endure without turning their state into a psychiatric ward?

"The solution to this problem is obvious. If we are to continue in our present objectives, we must accept murder as an integral, even a normal, part of our way of life. We must school ourselves not to feel genuine shock or shame at the assassination of our opponents. Naturally, we should continue to profess shock and shame, at least as long as we are forced by economic and military deficiencies to maintain relationships with democratic countries like the United States. But privately we should learn from other strong and successful peoples who have championed racial superiority and state sovereignty. Consider, for instance, how far Hitler and his Nazis would have gotten in building their master race and state supremacy if they had felt shock, shame, and dismay at the murdering of Jews and other enemies.

"There may, however, be a few among us not quite ready to slough off the decadent democratic timidity concerning murder. There may be some with quaint consciences who cannot escape shock, shame, and even a modicum of grief at the mindless slaughter of good, brave, men. To these recidivists I offer this last desperate consolation: Mississippi, after all, did produce Medgar Evers, a man who (oh rare!) would not learn to be 'practical' or 'shrewd,' would not learn a definition of his 'place' laid down by someone else (the kind of someone who would skulk in a thicket and shoot him in the back for disagreeing). Here was a man who knew precisely how much he was risking and why, and who had the courage and ultimate intelligence to do so; and I, witnessing his conduct, even from the distance of newspaper stories and television programs, have felt myself grow a dimension in aspiration and resolution, an emotion I have not experienced in watching many white Mississippians in recent times.

"Even more hopefully, Evers was not unique in these respects among his people in our state. Mississippi has a number of Negroes (concern for THEIR lives forbids naming them) whose courage, intelligence, and integrity fill many with awe and inspiration. As long as we continue to produce our Everses, even to be murdered by our way of life, we are not completely hopeless. And maybe, in some unforeseeable future, they will even teach us their courage and idealism."

Shortly after Beckwith's arrest, I received the first of many requests to address various groups. Most came from NAACP branches around the country. I talked with Ruby Hurley and Gloster Current about it, and they urged me to wait until the NAACP's national convention in Chicago, early in July. I was to receive the Spingarn Medal, an annual award, in memory of Medgar, and they hoped my acceptance speech would be my first public appearance.

My feelings about speaking were strangely mixed. I had never done it, except for that time at the Pearl Street Baptist Church that I could now barely remember. I had no idea how well I would do, but I knew Medgar would have been proud to have me try. In a way I felt I had to try. No one was better qualified to talk about Medgar and his work, and I had a strong desire not to have him forgotten in a month or two the way so many others had been.

In July I persuaded Aunt Myrlie to come with me and the children to the NAACP convention. Ruby Hurley made all the arrangements. I had worked on my speech in Jackson without success. I had an idea what I wanted to say, but the discipline of getting it down on paper was difficult. I finally wrote most of it in Chicago at the very last minute.

The presentation of the Spingarn Medal was scheduled for an outdoor mass meeting after a march from the hotel. It was a beautiful day, hot, with a slight breeze, and the sky was cloudless as far as the eye could see. There were speeches by a number of people—Roy Wilkins, the Rev. Fred Shuttlesworth—and then Bishop Spottswood presented the award. First I, then the two older children, and finally Charles came forward, and a reverent hush fell over the crowd. Bishop Spottswood put the gold medallion suspended from a satin ribbon around my neck, and the photographers snapped pictures.

Charles and the children took their seats, and I was left standing very much alone, a great crowd of people before me. I had a strange feeling of being there and yet being far removed from it all. I remember looking up at the pure blue of the sky with a sense that perhaps Medgar was somehow aware of this day. I felt I was drawing strength from him and at the same time that I had better do a good job.

I began speaking slowly, and I heard with surprise that my voice was clear and firm. I spoke for ten minutes, and at the end there was silence and then a wild burst of applause. I turned and saw Aunt Myrlie wiping tears from her eyes. There were others on the platform similarly overcome. I was dry-eyed and calm.

For weeks after Medgar's death, I was watched closely by my friends. I had said so many times that I didn't think life without Medgar was worth living that people apparently feared for my safety. Dr. Britton gave me sleeping pills only a few at a time, and if I stayed alone in a room for any length of time, people would knock and ask if I were all right.

Then, after my speech in Chicago, invitations for speaking engagements began pouring in. Two weeks later I began leaving Jackson, mostly on weekends, to fly to various parts of the country to talk about Medgar and the work in Mississippi. The first time I really escaped the watchful eyes of friends at home was the night I returned from Detroit after my first speaking engagement.

Aunt Myrlie had taken the children to Vicksburg, and I arrived in Jackson to find no one at the airport to meet me. The plane was hours late, and I knew there was a dance that night to which all of my friends would have gone. The terminal was empty, and it would take forever for a taxi to come if I called one. I felt lost and terribly alone.

Outside the airport building, two young Negroes were getting into a car. I decided to take a chance and asked if they were driving into Jackson. They said they were. When I introduced myself, they became almost protective. They drove me to my door, carried my luggage inside, made sure there was nothing else they could do. It was after midnight as they drove away, and the sudden quiet of the house was like a trigger on my emotions. I broke down. I cried for hours, questioning God in a way I had never done before, questioning His justice in taking Medgar away, reminding Him of how sincerely I had prayed for Medgar's safety.

I woke the next morning lying fully dressed on the bed, my suitcase still unpacked. For a whole day I hid from the world. I answered neither the door nor the telephone. I didn't eat. I walked through the quiet house, stood by the piano where we had had so much fun as a family, and stared at the hole in the wall. I went to the kitchen, picked up the broken piece of tile, and put my hand in the dent in the refrigerator, fingering the past. I walked; I remembered; and I cried.

In our room I opened the closet door and embraced Medgar's newly ironed shirts, burying my face in the memory of his smell in a fresh, clean shirt. I stood there for what seemed hours, clinging to the past, my mind almost a blank.

Later I went through everything I could find of Medgar's. I had saved every letter and postcard he had ever written me, and he and I had read them together and laughed at them just two weeks before he died. Now, I re-read them, feeling his presence beside me. That night I tried to pray, but there was no prayer in me. I got up from my knees and got into bed.

One of the first speaking engagements I had accepted among the many that came in was to address the National Convention of the Negro Elks in Boston in August. It was a family invitation. Each of the children was to receive a $2000 scholarship for college.

By the time August arrived, it was apparent that my previous commitment to appear at the convention was going to conflict with the March on Washington. When the national office of the NAACP asked me to represent the Negro women of the country in Washington, I felt committed and had to refuse. Arrangements were discussed for me to leave Boston for just a few hours to fly to Washington and back to take part in the march, but the Elks didn't want me to go, and I felt obligated to abide by their decision. They arranged a march in Boston with me as a speaker, and since they scheduled it to coincide with the program in Washington, it seemed I would miss even seeing the Washington March on television.

As it happened, I left the Boston program as soon as I could and rushed back to the hotel room to find that the children and Aunt Myrlie were watching the Washington March on television. Darrell looked up as I burst into the room. "You're not supposed to be here, Momma," he said. "You're supposed to be in Washington. They're calling your name right now."

I listened and heard it myself, and I felt sick at heart. There was applause and cheering, and I felt a great emptiness that I was not there where I should have been.

I was away a lot after that. Every other weekend after school began in September I would leave the children with Ethyl Sadberry, a dear friend, and Houston Wells or Nolan Tate would drive me to the airport. The national office set up the schedule and sent me the tickets. My expenses were paid for. Otherwise, I was on my own.

I was almost never able to get my speeches prepared in time for the press. Usually I spoke from notes scribbled on long legal pads on planes. I knew what people wanted to hear. They wanted to know about the Mississippi story, what had happened, what was happening now, what was going to happen in the future.

I had worried about money from the moment that I had accepted the fact of Medgar's death, but, one by one, my financial problems had been solved. The first thing that happened did not even concern me personally. The day of Medgar's death, Dr. Martin Luther King announced a Medgar Evers Memorial Fund to continue the fight against segregation. The NAACP's national office reacted immediately. Dr. John Morsell, Roy Wilkins' assistant, called and told me about it, suggesting that it was more appropriate for the NAACP to control funds raised in Medgar's name than the Southern Christian Leadership Conference, Dr. King's organization. I agreed.

There had been announcements, also, of fund-raising drives for the children and me, and Dr. Morsell felt we would be better protected if the NAACP coordinated these as well. He issued a statement in my name asking for contributions to go to the Medgar Evers Scholarship Fund to assure the education of the children. The association set $30,000 as a goal. Eventually the scholarship fund reached almost $60,000 with contributions from every conceivable source: movie stars, schoolchildren, churches, Jewish organizations, civic groups, people of every color and every state.

When the association agreed to continue Medgar's salary and made available the proceeds of a small life insurance policy they had taken out for him, I knew that, with what I received from social security and a Veterans Administration pension for the children, I had enough to live on. Then the American Veterans Committee set up a trust fund for the children's expenses for seven years, and that gave us an additional $100 a month.

In September 1963 some well-meaning but impractical souls began a chain letter asking people to send one dollar to Governor Ross Barnett, as trustee, for the Medgar Evers family. The letters stated clearly that the motive was to embarrass the governor of Mississippi while at the same time helping Medgar's family. I first heard of this in November when a friendly reporter telephoned to say that Governor Barnett had begun receiving a flood of dollar bills.

The Jackson *Daily News* ran a picture of a secretary in the governor's office with a pile of 5000 letters. Governor Barnett was said to be refusing to accept the letters. Those with return addresses were being returned; the rest were eventually turned over to a bank in Jackson after the governor asked a court to relieve him of responsibility. A representative of the bank was interviewed, and he said they were not going to give a damned penny to the Evers family or anyone else. They would hold onto the money and eventually give a report of it.

The bank's report came in September 1964, just a year after the chain letter began. The total fund had by that time reached $17,428. Governor Barnett denied embarrassment and claimed the state's economy had been helped. I don't know about that, but I was told later that the bank's fiscal health was improved to the tune of $7428, the amount it kept as its fee for handling the fund. The remaining $10,000 sat for two years in an account, from which no one could withdraw it. Eventually an attorney was able to secure it for me.

My trips to speak at various NAACP branches were enormously helpful to me. I felt I was doing something useful, something that would certainly have pleased Medgar. Forced to put my emotions aside, I found myself working to keep his name alive in people's memories. I think that I was also proving to myself that I could make this kind of contribution. But beyond what these appearances did for me personally, I knew they helped a good deal in fund-raising and membership for the NAACP. Far from resenting that I was a drawing card, I delighted in the feeling that I was involving new people in the struggle.

Above all, it kept me busy at a time that I might easily have retired into a shell to feel sorry for myself. I felt the pull of that desire each time I returned home. Outwardly calm throughout each trip, I found it harder and harder to come home on Sundays. It began, really, as the plane approached Jackson; a sense of emptiness, of bitterness, of resentment would grow in me until I was almost physically sick. Walking into the house past the spot where Medgar had fallen became almost physical torture. Suddenly I would be Medgar, my back exposed to the unseen rifle, and the whole scene would spring to life again. I would reach the door, enter, and walk into a house filled with memories. Immediately I sank into despair.

When I had unpacked my suitcase at home and could no longer put it off, I would go to get the children, masking my feelings as well as I could. The rest of the week I merely went through the motions of living. I had long since ceased to keep what my friends had always called a spotless house. I had no interest in preparing meals. Until the children asked why I had stopped baking cookies, I didn't realize I had. It all seemed so useless.

At times like that, my heart would go out to the children and I would try to make it up to them. But I had little patience with their demands, and I felt guilty about being away on weekends and even guiltier about not really wanting to spend much time with them. There was no question of my love for them; I adored each one of them. It was just that it was painful having them around. The way they looked, the way they talked was too sharp a reminder of Medgar. And then, when I looked in on them at night, I would be filled with remorse and a desire to take each one in my arms and apologize for not being more patient, more loving, as much fun as before.

Still, if I found it hard to help the children, they helped me. Rena would often be overcome and would slip quietly off to her room to cry alone. She didn't want to worry me. She developed a fear of her room at night, whether because her mattress, since replaced by a new one, had been used to carry her father to the hospital or because she hated being alone I didn't know. I let her sleep with me occasionally.

Sometimes we would be together, Rena and I, and without a word our eyes would meet and we'd reach out for each other and she would sob as though her heart would break. She talked little about her father, because she knew how much it disturbed Darrell. She went out of her way to try to help him, offering to play a game with him, presenting him with little gifts. With Van, she was a little mother, though you could tell at times she would rather be alone.

As time went by, we all found ourselves talking a good deal about Medgar. We searched our memories for every detail of time we had spent together as a family. I had to be careful not to let the bitterness I felt creep into my words.

Darrell was deeply affected. He would sit for hours on the steps to the carport and stare at the place where his father had fallen. He never spoke of it, and if I asked what he was thinking, he'd say, "Nothing." When he cried, he tried to keep it from us. I think he remembered Medgar's

345

admonitions when he left on trips that Darrell was the man of the house in his absence. For a long time, Darrell slept with a toy rifle at his side in a frightening imitation of Medgar. In the morning he would put the rifle away, just as Medgar had.

He groaned and mumbled in his sleep, and often he had nightmares. He became quite withdrawn, and he went through a period of blaming the NAACP for Medgar's being away from home so much before he died. You could tell how he felt in his rejection of various people from the national office.

Things seemed to get worse when he knew I was getting ready for another trip. His appetite disappeared, and sometimes after a meal he would go to the bathroom and be ill. Dr. Britton could find nothing physically wrong. His only release was playing football with the other boys in the street in front of the house. There he would let himself go for at least a few minutes, but always there came the time when he would quietly drop out of the game and walk to the back yard to sit alone with Heidi.

When he knew I was leaving for a weekend, he became hostile and rebelled against everything I asked him to do. "You going again?" he would ask. "When are you going to stay home? You're doing the same thing Daddy used to do. You're going away all the time."

Once, as I got ready to leave, he said plaintively, "The same thing that happened to Daddy might happen to you." I sat with him and reassured him, told him that my talks were out of the state where many people felt differently. It didn't seem to make much difference.

I tried a dozen times to explain to Rena and Darrell the reasons for my trips, the importance of keeping their father's name and work alive. It didn't satisfy them. If I missed one of their performances in a school play or program, it was awful; yet there were a few I did miss because I felt I couldn't cancel engagements made much earlier. When I did go to see one of them perform, it tore me apart to be there alone without Medgar, to see our children growing up, developing their talents without his sharing it with me.

The whole first year without Medgar was a living nightmare. I searched my memory for every tiny detail, every precious moment we had shared. I lived in the past; the present was nothing; the future didn't exist. For the first few months I remembered Medgar as being almost perfect. It was only later, slowly, that I could bring myself to recall moments that had not been so pleasant, that I could return to the reality that both he and I had had faults and that our marriage had not been without problems.

And then, that fall, I went through the whole thing again in a way I could never have anticipated. It was a Friday in late November, and Rena was home from school with a cold. I was leaving for Chicago and New York the next day, and I had an appointment to have my hair styled. I left Van at the Wells' house and told them Rena was home alone. I drove Darrell to school and then went on to my hairdresser's. Her name was Alleyne French—we called her "Skeet"—and she was a good friend, active in the NAACP. Before she started with my hair, I called Rena to make sure she was all right. She was watching television, and the set was tuned so loud I asked her to turn it down. I gave her my number and told her to call if she needed me.

I had a copy of *Look* in my hand, on the cover a picture of President Kennedy and John-John. "Isn't he a lovely child?" Skeet asked.

I was telling her about the scene at the White House, with

John-John waving to his father in the helicopter when the telephone rang. "I'll bet that's Rena," I said.

She answered and gasped and then said, "Oh no!"

"What is it?" I asked, alarmed.

She moved to the radio and snapped it on. "The President has been shot!"

I couldn't speak. I had the identical feeling I had had when I heard the shot that killed Medgar. I knew, without knowing, what would happen. I looked down at the magazine in my hand and burst into tears.

The radio came to life in the middle of a sentence. A reporter was saying that the President had been shot, that his condition was not known, that details would follow.

Skeet cradled me in her arms and said, "I know what you're thinking about. Don't cry so hard. You'll make yourself sick."

I thought of Rena watching television and I forced myself to calm down and call her. When she picked up the telephone, she didn't speak. "Rena?" I said.

"Mommie?" And then she cried out.

"Rena," I said, trying desperately to hold onto myself, "turn off the television and get into bed. I'll come right home."

I called the Wells and asked them to check on her. Then, as the radio announcer said that President Kennedy might have been wounded fatally, I left.

In the car with the radio on, I struggled for control. My knees were like water and I could hardly see through my tears. I thought of Mrs. Kennedy and the children, and I wanted to do something to help.

Rena was in bed, sobbing. I wondered briefly about Darrell, but I knew the nuns at the school would call if he was upset. So Rena and I sat by the television set, my arms

348

around her, and watched and listened. Finally, Walter Cronkite, unable to control his emotions, announced that the President was dead. Rena cried out and I felt a depth of despair for the world that encompassed everything.

The telephone rang and I heard Charles' voice. "Sis?" It was all he could say. Finally, he said he had seen President Kennedy just a few days earlier at the Tomb of the Unknowns in Arlington, that the President had shaken his hand and asked how we were. Then he could say no more.

The telephone continued to ring. Everyone was concerned about me, but few could talk coherently. Finally people began to gather at the house, and we sat, stunned by the news, unable to say much to each other. I remembered saying that if Medgar's murder went unpunished, the next victim of an assassin's bullet might be a white man, and the details as they came over television struck me with their similarity. President Kennedy had been shot in the back. The weapon was a high-powered rifle with a telescopic sight.

A friend picked up Darrell after school. He entered the house expressionlessly and went straight to his room. I followed and asked if he knew. He said they had heard about it in school. He stayed in his room with the door shut, and I checked on him frequently. He was just sitting there, not crying, not doing anything. He couldn't eat supper that night.

I was up all night that night. I couldn't sleep. I packed for my trip to Chicago and watched television and hated to leave the children and knew that I had to. The speech to the Chicago branch of the NAACP might have been canceled, but I felt obligated to attend a dinner of Freedom House in New York to receive a posthumous award for Medgar.

I was sure that President Kennedy had been killed by a

349

racist, and somehow that made it worse. In Chicago it was all people were talking about. When someone said that Mrs. Kennedy didn't have to worry, she had plenty of money, I couldn't contain myself. "Everyone is always so quick to think of material things," I said angrily. "People said the same thing about me, that the NAACP would take care of us. How heartless can you be? She's lost her husband and the father of her children, and you talk about money!" I turned and left the room.

## —— XX ——

The Beckwith trial was eventually set for January 27, 1964. I had no faith that it would be anything but a show staged for the press, and when Charles and I were summoned to the district attorney's office, I insisted we take Jack Young, a Negro attorney, along with us. I felt by this time that Beckwith had undoubtedly murdered Medgar, but I was sure that he had not been alone in the plot. Others must have been involved, and in my mind at that time the most plausible accomplices were Governor Barnett, Mayor Thompson, and William Simmons, the head of the White Citizens Councils.

William Waller, the district attorney, was a big man, six feet tall, with shaggy hair and a boyish look. He didn't, as I anticipated, have a separate waiting room for Negroes. He did have a white face, and I trusted no Mississippi official with a white face. That, of course, meant all of them.

He invited the three of us into his office, greeted Jack Young with familiarity, and asked us to sit down. He told us about his job: to prosecute Beckwith. He was, he said, a fourth-generation Mississippian, and he didn't agree with what Medgar had been doing. He believed in his job, however, and he intended to carry it out to the best of his ability. I wanted to call him a liar, but I said nothing.

He asked Charles and me if we had information we had not yet volunteered. We said we hadn't. He told Charles of rumors that he was giving information to the Justice Department, information withheld from the Jackson police. He said he was just as interested and would do just as much as the FBI would. Charles said he had withheld nothing.

Waller said we must trust his office to see that justice was done, and he asked me how I felt about what they had done so far. "Mr. Waller," I said, "I have no faith or trust in the police, in your office, or in justice being done in Mississippi. I believe you will do just enough to satisfy the press."

He nodded coldly and said he wasn't surprised. But he said he was going to do his job whether we cooperated or not. Then he warned us not to leave town and said he would want to see us both again. We left.

Some weeks later, Waller asked me to come in again. Once more, I took Jack Young with me. Waller greeted me coldly and said once more that he was going to do his job. He said he was not interested in the NAACP except for information that would help him in the case. He said he wanted to instruct me how to behave as a witness. It was the first time I knew definitely that I would be required to testify at the trial.

He said my testimony would deal with the events of that night, and we went over them together. Satisfied, he read to me from a pamphlet on court procedure and then gave it to me to read. He told me I should behave with courtesy and dignity in court, that I should dress in good taste without flashiness. I should not chew gum, he said, or cross my legs so as to call attention to them. Then, looking at me, he said, "I guess I don't have to tell you how to dress. You seem to know."

I should address the judge as "Your Honor," he said, and say "Yes, sir" and "No, sir," and act with humility. "Don't show the attitude you have shown here," he warned.

When he was through, I asked what courtesies would be shown to me in court. He lowered his head and smiled quickly, but when he looked up, his face was serious. "What do you mean?"

"I think you know what I mean, Mr. Waller," I said. "How will I be addressed in court?"

He swung his chair completely around so that his back was to us, and he put his head back. Then he swung around to face us again. "You were born here, raised here, you know what the customs are," he said flatly. "When in Rome, you do as the Romans do."

"If that means sitting in the witness chair and being called by my first name, I can't accept that."

"Just what do you propose doing?"

I looked straight at him. "If I am called 'Myrlie' by anyone in court, I will protest it on the spot. I am called 'Myrlie' only by my friends. Others are treated with courtesy in court, and I expect the same treatment."

He literally threw up his hands. "Don't you realize what you can do to this case?" he asked in a loud voice. "You can go into that courtroom and be a help or you can be an enormous hindrance. I may be able to persuade some of the people on the jury to have some sympathy for you, but if you get up there and complain about not being called 'Mrs.' all that will be down the drain."

This time he swung all the way around in his chair, and when he faced us again he stopped and asked, "Which is more important to you, for me to win this case or for you to be called 'Mrs.'?"

I paused, searching for the right words. "It may seem of little importance to you, Mr. Waller. But this is one of the things my husband lived and fought for. If it is a question of winning the case or my being called 'Mrs. Evers,' well, I have lost a husband for these principles, and I refuse to lose my dignity and pride as well."

His face reflected his shock at my answer, and he quickly dismissed us, saying we would talk about it later. I think he began to respect me then, because after that we had no difficulty communicating. We understood each other.

It took four days to select a jury for the trial. In the end, none of the six Negroes on the panel of 106 jurors was selected, and, when it was over, there were twelve white men in the jury box. During a recess, Beckwith walked over to the jury, smiled, and began talking. A bailiff pulled him away. Once, to his apparent surprise, his wife appeared in the courtroom. He walked to the railing, as the jurors watched, and kissed her. She took a seat beside him.

There were strange stories circulating about Beckwith. In the Rankin County jail, where he had been held after release from the mental hospital, he had been treated like a hero. When he left in November to return to the Hinds County jail, newspapers revealed that he had had his private gun collection and television set in jail with him. The Hinds County sheriff refused to let him bring them along, though Beckwith complained that he might need the guns "mighty bad when I get out."

The stories about his family's old Southern heritage had an odd ring alongside descriptions of the rambling, three-story family home, once supposedly a showplace furnished with valuable antiques. Now, according to newspaper stories,

354

the house where Beckwith lived alone was dilapidated and weather-beaten, unpainted for years. The yard was described as barren, the interior dismal, with wallpaper sagging from the ceilings.

Beckwith himself was described alternately as a man of Southern charm, tasteful dress, and lively gait and as trigger-tempered, hateful of Negroes, and extremely nervous. When the National Council of the Protestant Episcopal Church had announced a policy of non-discrimination, he was said to have printed and distributed handbills bitterly attacking the church. One story had him attending church with a revolver in his pocket in case a Negro tried to enter.

Beckwith was defended by three lawyers: Hardy Lott, Greenwood's city attorney and a prominent member of the White Citizens Councils; Stanny Sanders, a former district attorney and Lott's law partner; and Hugh Cunningham, a partner in Governor Barnett's law firm. His expenses were met by a newly formed White Citizens Legal Fund, with four-teen leading business and professional men on its board of directors. With their plea for contributions they issued a statement: "When you consider the awesome spectacle of one man standing alone against the preponderous power, authority, wealth and ingenuity of the Federal Government, including civil rights investigators, special agents of the F.B.I., Federal Marshals, the Jackson Police Department and all other police authority of the State of Mississippi, not to mention $27,000 reward money, it staggers the imagination."

The federal government, of course, had dropped its charges; the trial was a state trial; and to me it seemed quite different. The combined weight of white, racist Mississippi was arrayed on the side of the accused assassin. All he had against him was a district attorney who, whatever his desires to win the case, was still a segregationist.

355

I testified on the first day of testimony. The night before, I paced the floor long after the children were asleep, fearful of my reaction when I saw Beckwith face to face for the first time. I was by this time convinced that he was in fact the man who had lurked in the darkness of that vacant lot and shot my husband in the back. What I felt for him, I thought, was contempt rather than hate. But I could not be sure.

At the court house the assistant district attorney, John Fox, and Police Chief Pierce emphasized at length how important it was for me to go along if anyone called me by my first name. In the process, each of them called me "Mrs. Evers" at least a dozen times. When they were through, I said that I would not be called by my first name without a protest. Just then, Mr. Waller walked in. "Well," he said with a smile, "what about it? Have you changed your mind?"

I said I had not.

"You might be making a big mistake, Mrs. Evers."

"If so," I said, "it will be worth it. And it probably won't be my last mistake either."

I was the second witness to testify, right after a police captain who told of receiving the call reporting the shooting. A bailiff escorted me to the door of the courtroom. My stomach felt cold and empty as I walked to the witness stand breathing a prayer for help. I looked for Beckwith, but there was too little time. Then, on the stand, sworn in and seated, I caught a glimpse of him. I had no reaction at all. I felt that he was just an instrument used for a job other twisted minds had planned.

District Attorney Waller asked me my name.

"Mrs. Medgar Evers."

"Your first name, please?"

"Myrlie—M-Y-R-L-I-E."

356

And I waited for him to start his next question with that name. Instead he asked, "You are the widow of Medgar Evers, late of Hinds County. Is that correct?" And throughout the rest of my testimony—even on cross-examination—no one addressed me by my first name. Neither Mr. Waller nor Mr. Lott, who cross-examined me, used my name at all.

Mr. Waller led me through the story of that night. Mr. Lott tried to drag in a lot of other things. He asked if I hadn't accused someone at the scene of shooting Medgar. I said I hadn't. He asked if Medgar hadn't been the first to attempt to integrate the University of Mississippi, but, before I could answer proudly that he had, Mr. Waller objected and the judge sustained the objection.

Mr. Lott brought up the suit to integrate the public schools. I said that Medgar and I were both plaintiffs in that suit, along with others. He then asked about Darrell's middle name, Kenyatta, and for whom he was named. The judge sustained Mr. Waller's objection.

Almost before I knew it, I was through. In a way, I regretted being told to step down. I felt I had withstood Mr. Lott's questioning well, and I was eager to test wits with him further. I went home somewhat less skeptical of Mr. Waller than I had been. I learned later that day that he had used the word "nigger" in his opening statement to the jury. It didn't surprise me.

I was eager to hear about the rest of the trial, and as a witness I could not, of course, attend. Friends volunteered to fill me in, and then I got a telephone call from Ted Poston, a reporter for the New York *Post*, who was covering the trial. I had never met him, but he knew Medgar and we had talked on the telephone many times over the years. He was widely known as the first Negro reporter on a large metropolitan daily newspaper. Ted Poston promised to tell me about each day of the trial, and he did. Later Mr. Waller gave me a complete transcript.

I was most interested in Beckwith's reactions and from time to time people would tell me about him. He seemed to be enjoying it all, the publicity and the attention in particular. He smiled a lot and waved to the newspapermen in the balcony.

Over a period of three days, District Attorney Waller presented the state's case against Beckwith. Through witnesses he established the time of the shooting and the direction from which the shot had been fired, tracing the bullet's path to the clump of honeysuckle in the vacant lot. Broken branches and evidence of trampling in a hollow area within the thicket pointed to the recent presence of someone, and a hole prepared in the branches was shown to give a direct view of the spot where Medgar had been struck by the bullet.

Houston Wells testified he had fired a shot into the air with his pistol about two minutes after the shot that killed Medgar. He said his brother, James, had fired a shotgun into the air five minutes later, just as Houston was leaving for the hospital with Medgar. Mr. Waller, questioning Houston, called him by his first name.

Two white people who had been walking near by testified they had heard all three shots. After the first they had heard someone running toward the parking lot of a near-by drive-in restaurant. A pathologist established that Medgar had been killed by the bullet found in our kitchen. Policemen testified to finding a 30.06 Enfield rifle equipped with a telescopic sight in a clump of bushes between the vacant lot and the parking lot. The bullet was a thirty-caliber bullet that matched the empty shell, recently fired, found inside the rifle.

The rifle itself was traced to a farmer who lived near Greenwood. He had bought it by mail four years earlier. He had fired the gun, and shell casings from his firing corresponded exactly with the empty casing found inside the rifle, proving it was the same rifle. Eleven months after he bought it, he had traded the rifle, without its wooden stock, to Bryon de la Beckwith.

A man from Grenada, Mississippi, thirty miles from Greenwood, testified he had traded an identical telescopic sight to Beckwith just a month before the murder. Police testified they had found a fingerprint on the sight—a print estimated as less than twelve hours old, about ten hours after the murder. An FBI agent and a Jackson policeman testified that the print was Beckwith's.

Two Jackson taxicab drivers told of Beckwith's approaching them in Jackson the Saturday before the murder to ask directions to Medgar Evers' home. Beckwith's employer identified the company car in Beckwith's possession: a white 1961 Valiant with a tall, two-way radio aerial and a heavy truck hitch on the back. Witnesses placed the car in the drive-in parking lot the night of the crime. Both the car and a man resembling Beckwith had been seen in the area previously.

FBI agents testified Beckwith had had a semi-circular scar above his right eye when arrested, a scar similar to one inflicted by the recoil of a rifle when a telescopic sight is held too close to the eye. A doctor who examined Beckwith in jail said the scar could have been made by the sight of the rifle identified as Beckwith's. He estimated the age of the wound as ten to thirty days, a period that included the night of the murder.

Beckwith's defense included witnesses who said they had seen this wound before the night of the murder. Several witnesses testified there was no white Valiant parked in the drive-in parking lot that night, but one admitted on cross-examination that he could have missed seeing it. Another saw the car but maintained it was a Dodge, not a Valiant.

A former Alabama police investigator testified that it was impossible to tell how old a fingerprint was. A former Louisiana police investigator agreed. The testimony of both was shaken somewhat by District Attorney Waller's cross-examination.

An auxiliary Greenwood policeman testified he saw Beckwith in his car in Greenwood at 11:45 on the night of the murder. Two regular Greenwood policemen said they saw him at a Greenwood service station at 1:05 the next morning. Since Greenwood is more than ninety miles from Jackson, this would have made it impossible for Beckwith to be the murderer. But all three witnesses admitted on cross-examination that they had not notified anyone connected with the investigation of the case—the Jackson police, the FBI, or the district attorney's office—even after Beckwith was arrested. Yet all three were police officers, fully familiar with the laws regarding withholding evidence.

Finally, Beckwith himself took the witness stand. Under questioning by his attorney, Hardy Lott, Beckwith confirmed that he was a gun collector, denied he was a hunter, and said he often carried as many as thirty or forty guns in his car. He denied shooting Medgar, denied speaking to the two taxicab drivers, denied ever being in the drive-in parking lot, and said he had not been in Jackson the night Medgar was killed. He did not say where he had been.

He said he had owned an Enfield rifle similar to the one found near the scene of the crime, admitted trading for a telescopic sight similar to the one attached to the rifle, and told of having the sight attached to the rifle. He claimed to have received the scar above his right eye shooting the rifle at a target range in Greenwood the Sunday before the murder. The rifle, he said, had disappeared the following day, either from his car or his house, both of which were unlocked.

Under cross-examination by Mr. Waller, Beckwith admitted writing letters upholding segregation to various newspapers, bragging that many of them had been published. "And," he added boastfully, "I don't write under a pen name."

Waller read from a clipping: "'I believe in segregation just like I believe in God. I shall oppose any person, place, or thing that opposes segregation.' Did you write that?"

Beckwith: I sure did write that. You are reading it just like it is written.

Waller (reading): "I shall combat the evils of integration and shall bend every effort to rid the USA of the integrationists." Did you write that?

Beckwith: I sure did write that, sir.

Waller: Do you still feel that way?

Beckwith: As it is written, you read it.

Waller: Do you still feel that way?

Beckwith: Of course, I feel that way, sir.

Waller: And you mean any force, when you say any force you mean. . . .

Beckwith: Within reason, you understand, reason. And moderation. I won't say moderation. I say within reason, civilized reason. Reason within civilized and organized society.

Waller (reading): "And further when I die I will be buried in a segregrated cemetery. When you get to heaven you will find me in the part that has a sign saying 'For White Only,' and if I go to Hades I am going to raise

hell all over Hades until I get to the white section." Did
you say that?

Beckwith didn't answer.

Waller: Anyway, Mr. Beckwith, that's your letter and
written by yourself and mailed to the editor?

Beckwith: Mr. Waller, I want you to understand and where
there is humor intended I want you to laugh and smile
and where it is serious I want you to be serious and so
you have read the letter about like I intended for it to go
into the press.

The letter was offered into evidence. Next Waller read
portions of a letter Beckwith had written six months before
the murder to the National Rifle Association: " 'Gentlemen:
For the next fifteen years we here in Mississippi are going
to have to do a lot of shooting to protect our wives, children, and ourselves from bad negroes.' Did you write that?"
he asked.

Beckwith: I don't know. Let's look at it and see. I probably
did if you say so. That looks like it is on Mississippi Society
of the Sons of the American Revolution stationery. Looks
like I am a Sergeant-at-Arms at the Mississippi Society of
the Sons of the American Revolution and this looks like
my hand. It is possible that I wrote that, sir.

Waller: All right, sir. It is dated January, 1963, the 26th
day. Is that your recollection of the date?

Beckwith: Mr. Waller, I have written so many letters,
they are not supposed to be perfect and please everybody.
But, now this looks like it is in my hand and a lot of
times I would like for my letters to be personal.

Waller: Yes, sir.

Beckwith: Yes, sir. And not for everybody to read, especially folks that are not members of the National Rifle
Association.

Waller: After you talk about killing bad Negroes, I ask you whether or not you asked for advice on setting up a shooting range at Greenwood where white folks could train to shoot weapons?

Beckwith: Mr. Waller, I have been interested in years setting up a shooting range for white folks to use, a rifle and pistol range and run an arsenal range along with it as a way to make a living because I am interested in those things and I think the people should know how to use—have arms and use them.

Waller: In the first paragraph you talk about shooting bad Negroes and then in the three remaining paragraphs you talk about setting up a rifle range . . .

Beckwith: A rifle range . . .

Waller: . . . to train white people . . .

Beckwith: . . . a rifle range for commercial purposes.

Waller: Right.

Beckwith: Commercial purposes. You know, to make a living out of it. Like you make a living practicing law. Because I like guns and I like people that like guns.

Mr. Waller introduced another Beckwith letter into evidence, this one written from jail to the editor of *Outdoor Life* magazine two days before the trial began. He read a portion of it to Beckwith. " 'I have just finished an article on garfish hunting at night'—which you underscored—'which is sure to be of interest to the reader along with several ideas I have on shooting at night in the summertime for varmints.' Those are your words on January the 22nd."

Beckwith: Do you know what a varmint is?

Waller: No, sir, I thought maybe you did.

Beckwith: I do.

Waller: What is it?

Beckwith: A varmint is game, disagreeable game, game

that does no good, for instance, a crow or a hawk. Well, a hawk may do some good, but—well, you might even call a squirrel a varmint, but we don't refer to squirrels as varmints, but down in the Natchez area you might call an armadillo a varmint, or it's wildlife that contributes nothing to the welfare of other animals and it's a—it's a great sport to varmint hunt.

Waller: Are you talking about—would you say an integration leader is a varmint?

Beckwith: Oh, that's a human being, but we're talking about varmints. . . .

Mr. Waller established that Beckwith had written 150 letters in his four months in the Rankin County jail. He then asked, "Now, in four months time and a hundred and fifty letters, I'll ask you whether or not you have referred frequently to the fact that you are making sacrifices for the cause?"

Beckwith: This is a cause, yes sir.

Waller brought out the fact that Beckwith was writing a book about his experiences, which had been offered to publishers. He asked about the book's title. "Is it *My Ass, Your Goat and the Republic?*" Beckwith did not answer. Waller asked him to explain the title.

Beckwith evaded, but reporters who had grown familiar with his twisted humor felt sure they knew what he meant: "They're after my ass, getting your goat, and destroying the Republic."

Asked by Waller if he would do anything he thought necessary to stop an integrationist, Beckwith replied, "Mr. Waller, I am a conservative, an ultra-conservative."

Waller insisted on an answer to his question. "No, sir," Beckwith answered finally, "I am not going to go that far. I won't go that far."

When Waller asked if he was an accurate shot at 200 feet with a 30.06 Enfield rifle with a six-power scope, Beckwith could not resist bragging. "I should do better than that," he said. "I ought to hit something at a range better than 200 feet, sir."

The great gun collector who carried thirty to forty guns in his car at times was found to have only three guns in his possession at the time of his arrest. He claimed to be selling them off to keep alive.

Waller: You were short on money and you just invested sixty-five dollars in a scope on May 12th . . .

Beckwith: No, sir. I traded a forty-five automatic pistol for a high-priced scope—the man told me was a high-priced scope.

Waller: Yes, sir.

Beckwith: I thought it was a good trade, so I traded.

Waller: Now you were over there trading—right?

Beckwith: Yes, sir.

Waller: Now, can you tell me what a man that is short on money, short on weapons, would want with a six-power Golden Hawk scope. It could only be used for one thing, and, namely deer, in the month of June 1963?

Beckwith: If you are a gun trader you know that trades know no seasons. In other words, if you see a man that wants a scope, well, he is ready for a scope right then. He's not going to wait until deer season to get it.

Stanny Sanders, summing up for the defense, told the jury, "I do not believe you will return a verdict of guilty against Mr. Beckwith to satisfy the Attorney General of the United States and the liberal national press." He said the defense had proved Beckwith innocent through the testimony of the three Greenwood police officers who had said they saw him in Greenwood the night of the crime. He suggested that someone who knew Beckwith's views on race could easily have gone into his house while he was at work, stolen the rifle with the telescopic sight, and shot Medgar.

"Every day all of us in this country say we are dedicated to fighting Communism," he said. "That does not mean I am going to take a high-powered rifle out and shoot a Communist." He attacked the "foolish, ridiculous thing" of the taxicab drivers' testimony, urging the jurors to listen to the "witness of common sense." He asked, "Gentlemen, if you were coming down here to commit an ambush shooting, would you come down here in your own car? Now think that one over!"

Hardy Lott told the jury, "If you convict him, you've got to convict him because you think he did it." He, too, mentioned the three Greenwood policemen and their testimony. "Not a single witness has placed Beckwith in Jackson on the night of the killing," he said. "Not a single witness that can place him in Jackson. Now, gentlemen, you talk about a reasonable doubt!"

In his summation for the state, Waller told the jurors that Beckwith had "gotten a real big kick out of being a martyr. Mr. Beckwith has written his true confessions, and he is going to try to sell it." In an obvious allusion to the *Look* magazine confessions of the killers of Emmett Till, he went on, "What worries me is that two or three months from now I will pick a *Saturday Evening Post* and read 'My True Story.' He's already written it."

Waller said that the trial had "more evidence than I've ever seen in a felony case—and the most ridiculous defense." He ridiculed the three defense witnesses who said Beckwith was in Greenwood the night of the murder and yet remained silent for seven months until the defense produced them at the trial. They and Beckwith, he said, were lying.

Waller pictured Beckwith as a fanatic so obsessed by the race issue that he had committed "the most cold-blooded killing I have heard about" to advance the cause of segregation. "He did not come to Jackson just to kill Medgar Evers," Waller said. "He came to kill evil (in his mind) and get the number one man."

John Fox, Waller's assistant, told the jury that Beckwith's conduct during his two hours and forty-five minutes on the witness stand was evidence of his guilt. "Does this man come in and say humbly, 'I'm innocent'? Does he have an air of innocence? He sat upon his throne of glory and reveled in it and his attitude was almost beyond comprehension. He is a fanatic, pure and simple." He reminded the jury of Beckwith's brag that he was a better shot than it had taken to kill Medgar. "This we cannot have, because when I go home, and when you go home, none of us want to stand in our carport with the hair rising on the back of our necks for fear of one-third of 180 grams of lead slamming into our backs." And he added, "When you retire, you take with you the conscience of the people of Mississippi."

Judge Hendrick instructed the jury to return one of four verdicts: guilty as charged, which would bring an automatic death penalty; guilty as charged with a mandatory recommendation of life imprisonment; guilty with jury unable to agree on punishment, which would also bring life imprisonment; or not guilty. The jury retired at one o'clock in the afternoon, on Thursday, February 6, ten days after the trial had begun. Few expected them to take much time acquitting Beckwith.

Then Governor Barnett made his appearance. Entering

the courtroom, he strode straight to Beckwith, greeting him warmly and shaking his hand. If there had ever been a question of where the governor of Mississippi stood, it did not survive that scene.

Nearly six hours later, the twelve jurors went to dinner. They were back by 6:50 to continue their deliberations. At 9:20, Judge Hendrick called them from their room and said, "Gentlemen, I assume you have not reached a verdict. I want you to get a night's rest and breakfast and start considering this case again tomorrow morning." Most of Jackson was stunned.

Next morning the jurors began their deliberations anew. General Edwin A. Walker, who since his controversial retirement from the army had identified himself with various racist causes, showed up to shake hands with Beckwith. Four hours later, Judge Hendrick called the jury out. "We have taken numerous ballots and have not made progress," a juror told the judge. "We have decided if we stayed there a week, we would not have reached a verdict." Judge Hendrick declared a mistrial, and within minutes reporters had discovered that the last ballot had been 7 to 5 for acquittal. Five white Mississippians had actually held out to the end for a conviction.

I found it hard to believe. Nor was I alone in my surprise. A group of Beckwith's friends had rented a restaurant in Greenwood for a "welcome home" party. They had to cancel it. Beckwith remained in jail.

When Beckwith was retried in April, he took it more seriously. There were rumors that he and his lawyers were quarreling over the money raised for his defense. The lawyers virtually ignored him throughout the trial.

The Ku Klux Klan burned crosses in Jackson as the second trial began, presumably as a warning to the jurors. The

Klan and the White Citizens Councils attempted to pack the courtroom to prevent Negroes from attending.

The jury, too, differed from the first trial; seven of them were college graduates, two originally from the North. The testimony went over the same ground as in the first trial, and, as before, the jury was out overnight. Sometime during the second day of deliberation, the jury reported it could not reach a verdict. Beckwith was released on $10,000 bond before nightfall.

Beckwith's trip from Jackson to Greenwood was covered later on television. Smuggled out of town hiding on the floor of an unmarked car, the drive turned into a triumphant "welcome home" as he neared Greenwood. Crowds stood along the highway, some with large welcome signs, cheering and calling to him as the car went past. Beckwith told reporters it brought tears to his eyes. The party that had been postponed earlier was held that night. Beckwith, still under indictment for murder and obviously under restraints imposed by his lawyers, made only a brief appearance at the restaurant.

No one can say for sure what will happen to Beckwith. As this is written, he remains under indictment for murder, free on bond. Tried twice without being convicted, he is unlikely to be tried again unless there is new evidence of his guilt. How long he may remain under indictment is an open question, but from what I have heard, it has not tempered his enthusiasm for racist causes. With like-minded whites, he has harassed white patrons of a desegregated movie theater in Greenwood, among other activities. Nor has he lost the arrogance he displayed at his trials. In February, 1967, he announced his candidacy for the Democratic nomination for Lieutenant Governor of Mississippi, saying he felt the campaign "will provide me with the opportunity to repay the many kindnesses which I have received from my fellow Mississippians by offering myself as a candidate whose political position has already been clearly established." He may, I suppose, remain at large to follow his hate where it leads him for the rest of his life. He would not be the first in Mississippi —nor will he, unhappily, be the last, I am afraid.

In May I was in court again, this time for a hearing on the suit to desegregate the Jackson schools. Judge Sidney Mize sat on the bench in the federal courtroom backed by a huge mural depicting the "Southern Way of Life." Dominating the mural were a large white plantation house and a blonde, blue-eyed Southern belle in a hoop skirt, a tall, handsome Southern gentleman at her side. At one side, Negroes picked cotton in a field of fluffy white while pickaninnies with plaits and ribboned hair played around a Sambo with a banjo. At the river a riverboat pulled up to a dock stacked high with bales of cotton. I thought I knew what kind of justice we would get in that court.

When the case first came to court, Judge Mize had dismissed it. Overruled by the Fifth Circuit Court of Appeals, he had ordered the three school systems involved—Jackson, Biloxi, and Leake County—to submit grade-a-year desegregation plans by July 15, 1964. The present hearing was on an NAACP motion to make his temporary injunction permanent.

On the day I testified as a plaintiff I sat through the entire session in court. My eyes were drawn to a man who stared at me with pure hatred. It was William Simmons, the plump, mustached head of the White Citizens Councils. Irritated, I stared back, and for a long time our eyes were locked in an attempt to outstare each other. I took a small childish pleasure out of the fact that he looked away first.

Jackson School Superintendent Kirby Walker acknowledged on the stand that Jackson's schools were segregated by race. The reason, he said, was that Negroes lagged behind whites in learning ability. When the day's session was over, he came to me and shook my hand. "I've heard a lot about you," he said, "and I'm happy to meet you in person. I deeply regret what happened to your husband."

I was taken by surprise, but I thanked him warmly. It had taken more than a little courage to do this in front of so many people and I appreciated that, too.

In the end, the Jackson schools were ordered to desegregate one grade at a time, beginning with the first grade in September. That meant that Darrell and Rena, even if they had left the private Catholic school they attended, would never go to integrated schools in Jackson. Integration would never catch up to them. But it also meant that some Negro children would have an opportunity to go to decent schools, that no matter how long it took to complete it, segregation was finally broken in Mississippi's public schools.

Medgar was dead, and suddenly there were victories on every side. The Jackson police department hired Negro policemen. Some schools were desegregated. The airport was integrated. And that summer the Civil Rights Act of 1964 was passed by Congress. Federal registrars were sent to several counties in Mississippi to register Negro voters. Negroes were admitted to theaters, restaurants, motels, hotels, and parks.

Medgar had fought for all of these things, had given eight and a half years of his life to lead the fight. There were those who said that his death and the outrage that attended it throughout the country had been the final straw that broke the back of the opposition. Others said it made possible the

Mississippi Summer Project that summer of 1964 by mobilizing the college youths who came South to help. Two of them, Andrew Goodman and Michael Schwerner, died before the same kind of hate that killed my husband.

The casualty list is long, and it may not yet be complete. The fight my husband led in Mississippi is not over. Negroes still starve in the Delta. Many cannot vote. More live in fear of violence and intimidation. On the night of January 10, 1966, Vernon Dahmer, formerly president of the Forrest County NAACP and active in voter registration in Hattiesburg, woke to the blast of a fire bomb exploding against his house. He rushed through the flames to fire his shotgun at the fleeing car. He died of burns.

Six months later, James Meredith, back in Mississippi long after his graduation from Ole Miss, was shot in the back as he walked down a highway, demonstrating, he said, that Mississippi Negroes had nothing to fear. Nothing to fear. . . .

Meanwhile, Charles has purged himself of his original desire for revenge and has helped turn Fayette, Mississippi, into a more decent place for Negroes to live—or at least a city with that promise. He has led the Negroes of Natchez in a partly successful struggle for jobs and decent treatment and simple recognition as human beings. Yet, even here, progress has been opposed by violence. In August 1965, George Metcalf, president of the Natchez branch of the NAACP, was critically injured by a bomb planted in his automobile. Eighteen months later, in February 1967, Wharlest Jackson, a former treasurer of the Natchez branch, was killed by a similar bomb.

Mississippi has changed—a little. But it was the rest of the country that forced that change. It was not done willingly.

And it was the Negroes of Mississippi, a few at first, then more and more, that forced the rest of the country to care. Many have died in that effort. I am not the only woman who lost her husband. There may be still more to come.

One thing I know: it is not over, the struggle of Negroes in Mississippi and everywhere to be free, to be equal, to exercise their God-given rights as human beings. It took me years to learn what Medgar felt instinctively: that freedom has to be won, that it is worth fighting for. It was the lesson of his life. It was the lesson, if there was one, in his death.

## —— XXI ——

I left Mississippi in July 1964. I moved with my children to Claremont, California, entered Pomona College, and put the children in school.

Slowly, with many detours—with relapses into a numbing emptiness—my life has begun to begin again. Whole days sometimes go by when I am so caught up in what I am doing that I do not think of that hideous night of hate and fear and death. And then sometimes at night when the house is quiet and the children are in bed, I think about the man who murdered my husband, and I know that he, too, was a victim.

In Mississippi we were all victims. The disease was hate, fed by fear, nurtured by ignorance, fostered by guilt. We were all, black and white, its victims.

Medgar died from it. His assassin lives with it infecting his very soul. I was wounded by it, but I hope not crippled. My children? Who knows? Who will ever know exactly what it does to children or by what age they still have a chance to escape?

But the disease is worse than that. It kills and infects and wounds and cripples individuals. But it can also kill initiative, infect political systems, wound legal institutions, cripple the conscience of a nation. I had no sooner moved to California than Californians voted an amendment to their constitution to prevent forever laws prohibiting discrimination in housing. It has since been declared unconstitutional.

I wonder sometimes at the people who deplore racism in Mississippi and call it by some other name in Illinois, who urge their congressmen to abolish the poll tax in the South and urge their state legislators to oppose fair housing in New Jersey. I am puzzled by those who weep when a Michael Schwerner is slain, yet who snicker when an anti-Jewish joke is told. I am disturbed by the distinction between a Negro lynched in Poplarville and a Negro denied a job in Pleasantville. Is it possible to be just slightly infected by racism?

I think I know more about the man who murdered my husband than he will ever know of me. I think I know what drove him to that awful act and where he got the insane notion that by killing a man he could kill an idea. I think there is in our lives, in Medgar's and mine, a mirrored reflection of his, a reversed image, twisted by the hate that hung over Mississippi, that still, in large measure, hangs there.

And yet, like Medgar, I love Mississippi. I miss it. I miss my friends, white and black, the people who are changing Mississippi, making it better, burning off the hate of generations with love and devotion and determination and sheer courage. For if this book has led the reader to believe that Medgar was alone in those qualities, if it has given the impression that he was the only Negro consumed by a desire to sweep away the legacies of a dead and cruel past, I have misled you. Medgar, like every human being, was unique. But he was not alone. And for every one like him in Mississippi ten years ago, there are today ten, twenty, fifty. They may not have his job, but they fight his fight.

It is they who by destroying the disease that killed Medgar will inoculate the Beckwiths, the Barnetts, the Pattersons, and the Simmonses of the future. It is they who will make of Mississippi the place that Medgar dreamed it could be. It is they who are the surgeons excising a cancer, the physicians vaccinating against a plague.

We used to speak of the Negro problem. Not long ago someone said, "The Negro is no longer a problem; he is part of the solution." That is the way I think of Medgar. That is the way I hope he will be remembered.

# IN MEMORIAM

These Americans, too, were murdered in recent years in pursuit of the cause of civil rights.

*Rev. George E. Lee*—May 7, 1955—NAACP leader killed by a shotgun blast from a car carrying several whites. Belzoni, Mississippi.

*Lamar Smith*—August 17, 1955—Shot down on the lawn of the county court house in broad daylight after encouraging Negroes to vote by absentee ballot. Brookhaven, Mississippi.

*Dr. Thomas H. Brewer*—February 18, 1956—NAACP leader shot by a white man. Columbus, Georgia.

*Herbert Lee*—September 25, 1961—Civil rights worker shot by a white state legislator. Liberty, Mississippi.

*William L. Moore*—April 23, 1963—Mailman from Baltimore, Maryland, slain by bullet while on one-man protest march across Alabama. Atalla, Alabama.

*Louis Allen*—February 1, 1964—Civil rights worker slain after testifying against a white man charged with killing another Negro. Liberty, Mississippi.

*James E. Chaney*  —June 21, 1964—Three civil rights
*Andrew Goodman*  workers slain after their release from
*Michael H. Schwerner* jail. Philadelphia, Mississippi.

*Rev. James Reeb*—March 12, 1965—white civil rights sympathizer bludgeoned to death by whites. Selma, Alabama.

*Mrs. Viola Gregg Liuzzo*—March 25, 1965—Detroit housewife serving as volunteer in civil rights march shot on highway between Selma and Montgomery, Alabama.

*Jonathon M. Daniels*—August 20, 1965—Episcopal seminarian slain after release from jail for civil rights demonstration. Hayneville, Alabama.

*Vernon Dahmer*—January 10, 1966—NAACP leader burned to death in the fire-bombing of his home. Hattiesburg, Mississippi.

*Wharlest Jackson*—February 27, 1967—NAACP leader killed by explosion of bomb planted in his car. Natchez, Mississippi.